HAROLD K. MAWELA

SUCCESS STRATEGIES FOR THE CREATIVE & FEARLESS PEOPLE

HOW SUCCESSFUL PEOPLE BECOME MORE SUCCESSFUL

ISBN: 9781797917436

This ebook was created with StreetLib Write
 http://write.streetlib.com

Table of contents

Acknowledgments	3
Introduction	5
WHO AM I?	11
THE ULTIMATE VISION	71
BUILDING GOALS	105
THE POWER OF HABITS	207
MAXIMIZE YOUR POTENTIAL	365
About the Author	421

Copyright © 2019 by (HAROLD K. MAWELA)

All rights reserved. No part of this book may be reproduced or transmitted any form or by any means without written permission from the author.

harold.mawela@gmail.com

https://www.facebook.com/haroldleadership/

http://haroldkmawela.over-blog.com/

https://mobile.twitter.com/haroldmawela?p=s

ACKNOWLEDGMENTS

A book is never the result of just one person. I'd like to thank God.." Thanks to My father / Mentor / Spiritual father Apostle SM Mawela for reminding me of my purpose my mother MM Mawela she is a pillar indeed and to the entire Mawela family you are a great nation. AFM Word of faith, AFM Akasia family and AFM GNN Region thank you for helping me to discover my gifts it is an honor to serve you. And last but perhaps most important, thanks to my family, my wife Zanele my Kids Maatla, Seetsa and Botlalo who did without me while I spent countless hours at the computer, in the library, and in my "study" digesting and merging biblical verse and manage-ment wisdom. You provide my inspiration and purpose.

INTRODUCTION

If you fail to lead yourself you will fail to lead others.

I have decided to write this book to make it more helpful and faster acting for people living in more uncertain economic times. This book is for ambitious people who want to get ahead. If this is the way you think and feel, you are the person for whom this book is written. The ideas contained in the pages ahead will save you years of hard work in achieving the goals that are most important to you. After countless talks on various themes, if I was given only five minutes to speak to you and I could convey only one thought that would help you to be more successful, I would tell you this: "Write down your goals, make plans to achieve them, and work on your plans every single day. Your time and life are precious. The biggest waste of time and life is to spend years accomplishing something that you could have achieved in only a few months. By following the proven processes of goal setting and goal achieving laid out in this book, you will accomplish vastly more in a shorter period than you ever imagined before. The speed at which you move upward will amaze you and all the people around you.

Follow the Leaders, Not the Followers

By following these simple and easy-to-apply methods and techniques, you can move quickly from rags to riches in the months and years ahead. You can transform your experience from one of poverty and frustration to one of affluence and satisfaction. You can go far beyond your friends and family and achieve more in life than most other people you know. I have found, over and over, that a person of average intelligence with clear goals will run circles around a genius who is not sure what he or she really wants.

This book contains the distilled essence of all that I have learned in the areas of success, achievement, and goal attainment. By following the steps explained in the pages ahead, you will move to the front of the line in life. This book will help you become a more successful businessperson, partner, coach, parent, colleague, student or friend. It will help you enjoy life more too. It's about what the research says successful people really do, not what they might tell you they do to be successful. Even if their personal insights were accurate, what they do may not work for you.

This book gives us a much more objective and reliable picture of how humans succeed than an autobiography or a magazine article profiling one person. This book provides us with new insights and ideas we can use every waking moment. It confirms that some of what we've been told about such things as motivation, achieving goals and coping with stress checks out. But the book also shows that we've been fed myths and exaggerations about human behaviour. Where it's relevant, I've added some observations and experience of my own and my friends. Here's a necessary question before we start: What do we mean by successful people? Let's acknowledge that public recognition and wealth are narrow definitions of success. Many highly successful people aspire to neither, but become the most valued members of their organisations and communities. For others, their success may be largely confined to the family. They make inspirational parents, form close and enduring relationships with their partners and take pleasure in helping others succeed. Some of the principles may make sense straight away. Others may be counter-intuitive. Certainly, in a world of law suits, public enquiries and management consultancies, you could be forgiven for thinking that knowing why a problem exists is important. This information is important if you want to study the problem or intellectual or historical reasons. This information is important if the problem is mechanical or procedural in nature and you want to prevent the exact same problem from arising in the future. There were no civilian plane crashes in 2017 because the airline industry works tirelessly to identify and prevent the causes of accidents.

However, no two problems involving human beings can ever be the same, because people will evolve and change and will have different experiences to draw upon in each situation. Next time, everything will be different. There are three important points here that you can bear in mind as you are reading. The first is that this is a practical book – there is no theory here, only practice. These tools work, not because of any clever trick or script but because they change the way that people think. The tools here only work when you use them. Just thinking about using them won't make any difference to your problems. The second point is that this approach to get unstuck is creative. Creativity has a special meaning here – it means that you are invited to abandon the way you used to approach problems of getting stuck. Those old ways don't work – that's why you need to find new ways. You may have heard before that if what you're doing isn't working, do something different. The difficulty is finding new ways to think – and this book can help you. Creativity means to detach from a solution, a right answer or a perfect outcome. To be looking for a right answer means that you already know how the answer should be, and that is part of the problem because it's part of the way you're thinking about the problem. Creative problem solvers don't look for solutions, they generate lots of ideas. If one of those ideas becomes a solution then that's a bonus, but it cannot be your objective.

Humans, as a species, are successful because we have innate creative abilities. We can create solutions to problems that are different to a simple linear extension of the problem. We can create solutions that are unique, innovative, or that use existing materials and resources in a new way. When you're at your intellectual peak, you have access to these capabilities. When stuck inside a problem, people often revert to linear thinking that generates solutions like "try harder" or "work faster". The basic creative solution that you will generate with the help of this book is "do something different". There's nothing wrong with being stuck – we all get stuck when our thinking is constrained by a problem. When our minds are caged in this way, it doesn't matter how hard and long you think, because your intellectual capacity is limited by the problem itself. What you need at this point is something to help you break outside of those boundaries. Finally, this book is a guide, not a set of rules. Take what you can learn here, add it to your own experience and create new ideas, new tools and new solutions to old problems. Most of all, enjoy the results you will get. Stop taking being stuck so seriously and treat it for what it is. Just temporary hurdles that stand between you and the life you deserve. Getting stuck is a part of daily life. Many people and organisations seem afraid to use the word these days, instead talking about "issues" or "challenges". This halfhearted attempt to reframe problems as opportunities does not convince most people who still need practical help in solving those daily blocks and dilemmas.

The great news for problem solvers everywhere is that much bigger problems than yours have been solved during the course of human history. The size of a problem is mostly down to perception and being closer to it certainly does make it seem bigger. If a problem is on top of you, you cannot see clearly around or over it. Many people concentrate their effort on getting stuck, possibly thinking that familiarity with it will generate a solution. This is almost never the case. Concentrating your attention on the being stuck will only make it bigger, because you get more of what you focus on. The first priority in being stuck is to attend to the desired outcome. It's no use worrying about what you haven't got – it's what you want that is important. Here's a demonstration for you. Call a local decorator and ask him to paint your bedroom "not blue". Then get into a long and painful discussion that centres around every colour he suggests being wrong. Then finally settle on a colour that he calls "blue" and that you call "turquoise" or "lilac". Perhaps this sounds like a familiar routine for some of the problems you have had in the past? Certainly, using vague language like "blue" or "professional" or "truth" gives rise to many unnecessary problems. It does seem that we are divided by a common language.

WHO AM I?

Chapter 1

Vienna, Europe, the period leading up to WW2. Three Jewish psychiatrists, two learned masters in the field, one the young apprentice. The first master is a man named Sigmund Freud. He has spent years studying people, striving to understand what makes us tick. He's reached the conclusion that the most basic drive in human beings is the drive for pleasure. It's our need for pleasure that explains why we do what we do, how we live. The second master is Alfred Adler. He too has spent years studying human behaviour. His studies have led him to disagree with Sigmund Freud. Adler is convinced the bottom line explanation for human behaviour is power. All of us grow up feeling inferior and powerless. Life is a drive to gain control, to feel we are important.

The third man is a young up-and-coming psychiatrist by the name of Victor Frankl. He hopes to follow in the footsteps of his mentors. But before his career gains any momentum WW2 starts. The Nazis invade and its dangerous for Jews. Freud and Adler are world renowned scholars and so manage to escape before Hitler invades. Frankl is not so lucky. He is arrested and thrown into a Nazi concentration camp for four long years. After the war is over Frankl is released from the concentration camp and resumes his career. He reflects upon his time as a prisoner. He noticed something quite strange – the people who survived were not always the ones you'd expect. Many who were physically strong wasted away and died while others who were much more weak physically grew strong and survived. Why? What was it that enabled them to hang on through a living hell?

Frankl reflected on the theories of his mentors. Freud's pleasure principle couldn't explain it. For four desperate and terrible years the men in that camp knew only pain, suffering and degradation. Pleasure was not a word in their vocabulary. It wasn't pleasure that kept them going. What then of Adler's theory about power being the basic human need? That didn't fare well either. Frankl and his fellow Jews were completely powerless during their time in the concentration camps. Each day they stared down the barrel of a loaded gun, were treated like animals, felt jackboots on their faces. They had no power and no prospect of power.

Victor Frankl came up with his own theory. The difference between those who survived and those who perished was hope. Those who survived never gave up their belief that their lives had meaning, that despite everything going on around them it would one day end and they would live meaningful, purposeful lives. What is the basic human drive? The one thing that gives life value? The ability to live with a sense of meaning and identity. Not pleasure. Not power. Meaning and Identity.

Always remember what you are, really going after the world won't. Make it your quality. At that point it can never be your shortcoming. Defend yourself in it, and it will never be used to hurt you.

Do you now and then ponder who you truly are?

Do you sometimes wonder who you really are?

Do you feel that you are constantly adapting yourself to suit the needs of others?

Do you have multiple, conflicting roles in life that leave you feeling confused or compromised?

Do you feel that you are not relating to others as effectively as you would like?

We live in a complicated world that seems to expect us to be lots of different things all at the same time. Very rarely are we called on just to be ourselves – yet strangely when we see that in others we applaud it and call it things like "individuality", "charisma" and "inspiring leadership". So why is it that true individuality in others seems inspiring and yet individuality for ourselves can seem impossible –

or at least impractical? And if we do "find ourselves", how do we then relate to others in new ways? In this chapter we will explore how we become the people that we are, how and why we "lose ourselves" – and what we can do about it. It then goes on to set out how we can relate to others more effectively and develop high levels of inter-personal skills, enabling us to be our true selves – and create the space for others around us to do that too.

What Inspires Us

Different things motivate different people. In this chapter we will explore what can motivate us as individuals and we will start by examining the priorities of different life stages which heavily can influence each of us.

Inspiration at various life stages

Expectation

Our life in the outside world starts, of course, when we are born – a rude awakening from the warmth, comfort and security of the womb to the harsh clinical realities of a hospital room. Babies are utterly helpless and need to be looked after, needing food, comfort, warmth and all the other things we have already covered at the lower end of needs. The baby depends upon mother and father for everything and – at least in a loving and caring family – all those needs are met, food, warmth and love. At some stage however the baby, perhaps around 18 months, when he or she begins to become aware that they are separate individuals from their parents, begins to realise that they need the care of these adults and without them they cannot survive. There is a battle between wanting to develop their independence whilst also being anxious not to jeopardise the relationship as they need to ensure their safety continues. The original unconditional love for the baby begins to have conditions attached around their behaviour.

Desire

The priorities as a child are to learn and explore and to develop increasing independence, testing it out whilst always ensuring that the parents are still there and supportive. Some of the things that the child learns are how to behave, what to believe and what makes mum and dad happy and unhappy. The natural instincts slowly start to become modified to fit the acceptable parameters. The desire to please, to become accepted by others, by modifying instinctive behaviour becomes set down in early life and dominates motivation for some time to come. In childhood years this may be about pleasing parents by being a "good boy" or "good girl", working hard in school and sticking to the rules. Emerging as teenagers, there is a huge change physically and emotionally and an increasing need to feel independent and a desire to find an identity. The need for acceptance becomes more about acceptance by peers and friends, rather than parents. Yet there is a tension between acceptance by the group on the one hand and finding a separate identity on the other. It is striking what teenagers choose to wear and what music they listen to, there is some individuality in taste, but also a great deal of conformity. So clothes are usually jeans and a t-shirt with whatever variation the fashion industry is driving at the time and music taste is popular music rather than classical, jazz or anything else that is not mainstream.

Foundation

At the end of formal education, the 20s and 30s are dominated by establishing ourselves as independent from our parents and acquiring all that we need for adult life. This includes moving out of the family home if that's affordable, finding a way of earning a living, finding a partner to share life with, maybe locating to a new area and finding new friends. Having children is also a priority, although increasingly this is deferred so that people can establish themselves in their careers. This involves ensuring that the employee is accepted now by colleagues and bosses, rather than just parents and friends. A new set of expectations arrive and a new level of conditioning is acquired, as the employee progresses at work, getting promotions and new jobs along the way. In our hectic pressurised society, the work part of our lives can dominate all others. There comes a point where all the lower levels of Maslow's hierarchy are basically sorted. Consider the family with two young children, where both parents work, living in their own home with cars, holidays and all that goes with an affluent middle class lifestyle.

Widening

The next stage is when all these initial goals and needs have been fulfilled – the career, the house, the spouse, the kids – all acquired. At some point in mid-life there may be a change in outlook, perhaps triggered by a significant birthday, a questioning about the job or career, a relationship breakdown or redundancy for example. All of these could trigger deep reflection, a broadening of outlook and a desire for more meaning or maybe a new direction. It is what is often described as a "mid-life crisis", although it does not need to be a crisis or a single event.

Reflection

The next life stage is older age, probably linked to retirement. The priorities of life may change again and usually work plays less of a part, a new purpose and meaning may be needed. Our motivations and priorities change as we go through different life stages, but the one constant thing is change and an impetus for personal development. Two key things remain constant, the need to relate to others and the desire for meaning and individuation. But when this purpose has been attained and more than attained shall the earning of money, the extension of conquests, and the expansion of life go steadily on beyond the bounds of all reason and sense? Whoever carries over into the afternoon the law of the morning, or the natural aim, must pay for it with damage to his soul, just as surely as a growing youth who tries to carry over his childish egoism into adult life must pay for this mistake with social failure."

The Phases of Life

Nature versus sustain

It is perhaps worth exploring here the perennial question about what shapes us as individuals – is it our nature that we are born with that dominates our future path, or is it nurture – the way that we are brought up and the influences on and around us during that time? Of course the truth is that it is a blend of both. A natural talent and creative flair for music, if not developed, does not automatically lead to a musical genius like Mozart. He is regarded as a child prodigy, a naturally gifted musician. A natural born genius. Well, yes and no. He wrote incredible pieces of music at an astonishingly young age, so it is reasonable to assume it was in his nature somehow. The reality is though that he lived and breathed music under the immense pressure from his father and wrote very many pieces of music so that by the time some of it was pretty good he was still young. From the outside it looks as though he is a genius, if you saw the reality you may conclude it was sheer hard work and dedication. What is true though, is that without the "encouragement" (or pressure) from his father he would not have accomplished the things that he did. In this example the nature and nurture were clearly working together to produce music of extraordinary quality at a young age. Most nurturing is not however done in such a concentrated, focussed and consistent way. Most nurturing

– or conditioning as we might call it is much more subtle as we will now discover.

The craving for acknowledgment

As we have already seen, the main thing that motivates the vast majority, if not all of us, is to be loved and accepted and to know that we are good enough. This desire for acceptance creates in us a sort of rule-book of beliefs and values, a sense of right and wrong, what is acceptable and what is not. They could be helpful beliefs or unhelpful beliefs, true of false. They have been inherited from parents, family, friends, colleagues and society at large. Indeed much of it is neither deliberately, or even consciously taught to us, but is received by osmosis. Long held beliefs and 'common sense' approaches are talked about in an unquestioned way and adopted as fact by the individual growing up. Even as adults we are bombarded with messages and our desire to be individual conflicts with our desire to be accepted. Usually the desire for acceptance wins. The simple reason for this is that the only way that society can operate, i.e. with lots of individuals living together in peace, is if everyone plays to a set of rules. This means sacrificing some individuality in order to gain the security that comes with living together in community. So stealing is outlawed even if you are very hungry and are standing next to some fruit on display at a shop. The immediate desire to eat needs to be controlled until food can be obtained in a way that fits the rules of society – for example buying the apple first rather than just picking it up and eating it.

Or deferring gratification until you can get home to the fridge. This example is a simple one as stealing is prohibited explicitly by law. However most social rules are not in law, instead they are contained in an unwritten social code which needs to be discovered throughout life.

An example of this would be that parents and society expects people in their twenties to be getting a job and establishing themselves in a career. For the individual, the desire to get a well-paid job may outweigh the desire to express their individuality and so a career that does not really fit the individual is chosen. This may be one that is socially acceptable to friends and/or to meet parental expectations. This is the sort of point at which we can start to lose ourselves and set the nagging feeling going that "this isn't really me". Decisions such as this can have long-lasting effects for the individual. There are a myriad of things that you may have adopted as a world view, beliefs about what is good and acceptable. However these fit other people's ideas of what is right and appropriate – and not necessarily yours. You have to test these for yourself and decide whether they are relevant to your life today. Inevitably some of the rules that your parents learnt came from their parents – if those attitudes have not been updated to suit the needs of today's world then you're operating with an out of date manual of how things should be. The powerful desire for acceptance, established from the day we were born, leads us to adapt ourselves – our true selves – in order to be accepted by those around us. Understanding this is key for the journey back to finding yourself and understanding yourself.

Reacting to change

Life in today's society is very different from life even a few decades ago. The pace of global change is remarkable – the growth of populations, the development of technology, the global nature of trade and commerce. Attitudes and outlooks from one generation need to be tested by the next rather than unthinkingly being assimilated. I am sure you can call to mind examples where someone older has made assumptions about the way the world is which are no longer true, maybe because technology has changed or society's attitudes have changed with the next generation. At different stages in our life we are motivated by different things – what pre-occupies us in the morning of life fades away in the afternoon. Without nurture our natural talents may lie dormant. Without an internal sense of acceptance we can continue to compromise ourselves to please others and not be true to ourselves. The world is constantly changing and without understanding yourself you may struggle to thrive – or even survive – in the changing environment. Finding and understanding ourselves enables us to let go of outdated notions and respond to the changing world as it really is – but this is very difficult to do if these beliefs form an integral part of our identity.

Who we think we are

Our roles

We all have roles to play in our lives and these change as we move through it. We all start as a son or daughter, maybe then add to that the role of sister or brother, then friend, pupil, team-mate, student, girlfriend or boyfriend, candidate, employee, colleague, partner, husband or wife, manager, father or mother, aunt or uncle, godparent, grandparent...the list goes on! Just reading that list may have conjured up some images in your mind of what each of those means to you. You will have some kind of perception of each of them, how to behave or not to behave in that role. Relaxing with old school friends over a few drinks will suggest a different way to behave than if you were with your boss or your young niece or nephew. A role, according to the dictionary, is what you are expected to do, or your function. As the Shakespeare quote above suggests, all the players have their assigned role with prescribed directions which are set out in a script. The actions they take are the ones that the other players expect them to take, they have to stay in role in order to relate to the other players who are also in role. And over time each person will have many roles or parts to play. Consider a typical week of a father who works. He wakes up as the husband next to his wife, he gets up and wakes up his children in the role of father. He has breakfast as father and husband and then walks to the station or his car and performs the role of commuter. An hour later, he is performing the role of employee, or manager, or engineer, or accountant, or whatever. In the evening he again practises his role as a commuter and during the journey gets out of his role as employee, just in time to return home as father and husband. The weekend will usually be much more father and husband and less employee. Meeting up with the wider family for Sunday lunch for example will put him into a different set of roles, perhaps uncle or nephew – or son once again. Playing roles is necessary in order for society to operate smoothly – everyone has "their exits and their entrances". The role is about one's function in that relationship and having it defined within a broad area of agreement provides some security for each person entering into that relationship. A feeling of certainty as to what to expect. An unspoken but yet agreed way of operating which enables the interaction between the parties to be more efficient and skip many of the steps otherwise needed to build up a relationship.

Role conflict

One of the challenges with having multiple roles is that there is no reason why these should all be compatible. Indeed it is unlikely that they will all be. For example to succeed in the role of mother you need to spend quality time with your children. Yet to succeed in the role of employee you need to be at work, showing commitment to that role too. It is possible that a tension can arise between doing both to the level that the individual may wish. It can leave a parent feeling guilty for not being there for their children or maybe to a rushed and stressful time at work so that they can go and collect the children on time. There are many combinations of roles that may result in conflicting demands that are difficult to meet. If we are constantly playing roles, we are always doing what we are expected to do – whether that is what others expect of us, or what we expect of ourselves, according to the label on the role that we are playing at that time. By definition these roles cannot be the true us. So if you were to spend your life playing roles, as most of us do, when do we get the opportunity to be ourselves? When does the actor get to put aside the script, take off all the grease paint and be themselves?

Our identity

It is very easy when juggling multiple roles, or intensely living one role for a time, for these roles to become our identity. We identify with a role so much that it feels like it is us. If the actor never gets to take of the grease paint then he will inevitably lose touch with himself and identify more and more with the role. Roles require us to be only a part of ourselves and they may require us to be something that we are not. The more we do things, the more they become a habit and the more that we think in the same way, the more these patterns of thought and behaviour become our identity. The roles that we play can give us strength and self-confidence. For example if you play a technical or professional role at work, you may find that you derive a great deal of satisfaction from that role. People come to you for advice and guidance, they listen to what you say, you're the expert, you are needed. Your feelings about yourself, your self-confidence can come from that role and not from yourself. When our identity is derived from these external roles, our true identity gets forgotten and we believe the lie that we are our roles. If we get used to wearing a mask of one type or another, interacting in a safe, predictable way with others, we can feel secure and more certain about our life. The more that we depend on the masks and the safer that we feel as a result of wearing them, the greater the risk and uncertainty we feel of taking off our mask and interacting openly, honestly and authentically.

Feeling lost

When we identify with an external role, our identity is taken out of our hands. Our identity exists only as long as the role exists. So if it is a job role for example, an unexpected redundancy comes as a huge shock. It is not just the practical difficulty of finding a new job, it is a loss of a sense of self, a loss of a range of comforting feelings such as self-confidence, purpose and status This sense of feeling lost can occur with the end of a variety of roles – when children leave home, a relationship break-up or divorce, a redundancy or retirement. All of these can feel like a loss of identity when the roles made up such a large part of life and of our identity.

Personality and ego

What we describe as our personality is probably taken as a given by most of us, it is what – or who – we think we are. Psychologists have described it as the Ego (meaning

"I") – it is our sense of self. However the more one tries to examine what personality really is, the more it seems to elude us. For example you can hear the confusion in people's language – "she has a nice personality" – which must mean that she and the personality are different. However if the personality is our sense of identity, but is not us, then who are we? Our personality is partly nature and partly nurture, it is partly a given from our DNA and partly developed from our experience of the world, which starts as early as the fourth month of our existence whilst still in the womb. The part of our personality that evolves during our life does so because it is of use to us. The brain comes with little or no hard-wired templates about how things should be and so it has to learn through experience, through relationships with those around us and from the feedback we receive. Our personality can then become a given or continue to evolve. It seems reasonable to assume that once we have been in contact with most of the situations that we will experience in life, that we have got a reliable rule-book to follow. It worked last time and so it should work this time. For example I related successfully to my parents – my early authority figures – in this way and so I will relate to all authority figures in this way. However the authority figures, such as an employer or policeman may not respond like the parents did – there is no reason why they should – and so the rulebook either needs to be updated or life become stressful, puzzling and potentially self-destructive. Our personality is like a piece of armour which is at the same time our greatest shield and also potentially our greatest prison. It enables us to deal with the outside world, but it can also insulate us from it – and from other people. The process of increasing our personal awareness helps us to see our personality for what it is and to enable us to choose to update the rule book.

Internal identity

Practically speaking we have to play roles to operate effectively in society, but these can dominate our sense of identity and we can end up feeling lost when they end. The solution is to find a way of playing the roles without them becoming our identity. We need to find an internal source for our identity, not an external one. When we have found an internal source for our identity we can pick up roles and play them with confidence, knowing that they are not us, just a role we play and that when we step out of role we come home back to ourselves, we do not feel lost. Getting back in touch with who and what you really are – finding yourself – opens up the possibility to play roles and move in and out of them with freedom when you like. We all perform roles in life, yet we are not our roles and if we identify too closely with them we may feel safe – but only temporarily. We are also not our personality, which has in large part been forged as a result of the experiences of surviving and protecting ourselves in the real world.

Getting back in touch with who you really are is about becoming aware of the rules in the rule book that you have acquired during your life – and identifying the ones that do not fit the real you. This journey has to start with self-awareness, which we will look at in the next topic.

Who we really are

When we explored the concept of personality we could see that it started off with our innate programming from our DNA and was then modified mainly over a couple of decades by various outside influences to create what we regard as our personality. This is in many ways a "false self", a self which is created to please others, to fit in with their agenda, to enable relationship with those around us. With the best will in the world it is unlikely that you will turn out as an adult with no unhelpful of unintended modifications – or what we call "conditioning". The authentic self is the real you beneath all the conditioning that you have acquired during your lifetime. The true you is the one that finds life fulfilling in a deep sense rather than theoretically good on a purely intellectual level. For example on an intellectual level life is good because you have the career, the partner, the house and the car – but inside you feel lost. It is the real you that feels lost, whilst it is the learned you, the ego, the intellectual evaluation that is satisfied that the "shoulds" have been fulfilled. Your authentic self is the one that longs to be able to express itself – and critically – is the one with the untapped potential, the uniqueness that other people will recognise as charisma and authenticity. It is the you that can transform your life and the lives of those around you, by being in touch with that which you truly are.

Self-awareness

Self awareness is often cited as being a key to personal development – and potentially it is, depending upon your definition! The personality is not you, you have a personality, so if you want your "self" to be aware of itself, you will have a long wait! The self, as the personality, cannot be self aware. However, you, as an independent observer of your own internal processes, can become aware of what your personality is up to, how it is behaving and the impact on yourself and others. A state of pure awareness enables you to step outside yourself as it were, and to look at yourself from the outside, as an independent observer – much like a coach does in a coaching relationship. In a coaching relationship the coach gives an external perspective on you, in a supportive way and invites you to take that external perspective on yourself as well. When you are outside the system of your self, then you can be objective about it. When you are wrapped up in the self – the either/or dilemmas of what you should do and what you should not do, of what you must do and you must not do dominate your internal processes – the self shuttles between the extremes, it is in the system, not able to observer itself – indeed it is the system. Personal awareness is gained by this shift in perspective – of observing your actions, thoughts and feelings, observing the world around you, the people and the relationships and giving yourself a break from your self. It is only from observing what is really going on that you can hope to change and adapt to the circumstances you find yourself in.

Feedback

Feedback is also a well-used term in coaching and management. Managers are often exhorted to give their team feedback, not just criticism. Managers are sometimes taught to give a "feedback sandwich" – find two positive things to say to someone and use those as the bread of the sandwich and then deliver your killer blow – the criticism – as the meat in the sandwich. Almost inevitably it becomes clear in the delivery that the real intention is to give criticism. It is not difficult to detect the difference between a lukewarm complement and a heartfelt criticism! Feedback is essential for any of us to get to the truth – to hear what it is like to see ourselves from the outside. Otherwise we live in a fantasy world of our own making – although we may be quite attached to our own familiar, comforting stories about ourselves. The most useful form of feedback is the one that is most readily accepted. The one that is most readily accepted is objective and not value laden – i.e. it is factual feedback, not charged with emotion and delivered with the intent to raise awareness. Another aspect is that it is delivered between two individuals of equal standing in the relationship, rather than from one expert or person in authority talking down to the receiver of the feedback. Inevitably the feedback has more weight if it comes from someone whose approval is sought (remember the way of relating to our parents in the past in order to seek approval may spill over into the here and now) and so the way feedback is delivered can have greater impact than intended. It also does little to build the relationship as it reinforces the superiority of one person over the other. In a coaching relationship this more equal relationship can be achieved by entering into the feedback as a joint process of enquiry, in which each party is exploring in a non-judgemental way. This logically leads to the realisation that the best bit of feedback, the one that we most readily accept, is the one we realise for ourselves. As Fritz Perls said "Truth can be tolerated only if you discover it yourself because then, the pride of discovery makes the truth palatable."

So how to apply this in a management relationship which by definition is not equal? The answer is to facilitate not tell. To facilitate the exploration by the member of the team of the behaviour from a new perspective – and to discover it for themselves, simply because they are now looking at themselves from the outside in. They are perfectly capable of seeing themselves as others do if they accept the invitation to adopt that perspective. Through doing so the manager practises his coaching skills, develops a new dimension to the relationship, builds trust and ultimately a more effective, self-aware and ultimately engaged employee. One advanced level of feedback is more like a commentary – a commentary on what is going on – both in front of you – and inside you. It also creates the possibility of giving feedback that is non-judgemental, by taking responsibility for your own internal processes. For example we often hear things like "she made me angry when she did that" – what this tells us is that it is all about her – there is no acknowledgement that the anger came from their own internal process. Ultimately it did not come from "her".

The statement is quite simply untrue. The correct statement would be something like "when she did that I felt angry" – this is both more neutral and factual, that is exactly what happened. One thing followed another, but it was not her fault. Indeed the revised statement draws a certain curiosity about the person making the statement that when she did this I felt angry – isn't that interesting? What's that about? The process of simply making a statement like a running commentary in effect gives the speaker feedback on themselves, in a neutral way. Feedback done well enables you to build up the quality of your relationships, to facilitate the development of those to whom you relate and most of all to expand your own choices about how to respond and your own personal development.

Decoding language

Some feedback you can easily begin to give yourself is through monitoring your language. The personality is full of out-dated rules and assumptions and the process of becoming aware of these increases personal choice. Those rules can be detected in our language as they are inadvertently sent out into the world. Take this well known saying: "Children should be seen and not heard" – we can recognise that this comes from a more Victorian age where clearly there is a set of expectations about how children should behave and how they are placed in the pecking order of society. It may stand out today as a laden with assumptions, but was just the way things were in days gone by. Likewise today there are many phrases that either explicitly or implicitly communicate what you should do – it is just that they are so familiar to us that we do not recognise the assumptions hidden in the language. Take the phrase "freedom of the press" – there is an implicit assumption that "the press should be free" and that this is a good thing. In South Africa for example there are several aspects where the freedom of the press becomes an intrusion into another's private life. And there is another assumption – that part of your life should be private. Whether implicit or explicit the assumptions are woven into our everyday life in such a way that we do not notice them. Learning to pay attention to the words that people use and the assumptions beneath those words will open up to you a whole new realm of meaning and communication. The words should, ought must, need – and even want – point towards some attitudes and assumptions that were probably fixed in the past and may be outside the speaker's awareness. When we are the speaker we can also pay attention to our own words, listening for the hidden assumptions that may need re-examining. Language also has some built-in limitations. Many words form either/or pairings, which reflect our thinking process – so things are either good or bad, right or wrong, dark or light. The darkness can only be recognised in relation to lightness. The words get their true meaning from being other than their opposites. Our use of these words sheds some light on the thought processes that created them. Most people have been conditioned through life and are unaware of that conditioning. The language carries clues that you can pick up on and get a glimpse of the conditioning. Likewise as you listen to yourself – or as you get feedback from others – you become aware of your own conditioning. We have learnt to become unaware of our conditioning and we can learn to become aware also. With awareness comes freedom. There are four basis mechanisms through which our hidden and often negative conditioning finds its way into language.

Projection

This occurs where something that we think or feel ourselves is put out into the world, rather than recognising our own part in the drama. It can be detected in phrases that use words like "they". For example when talking about "fat-cat bosses" a phrase such as "they are all selfish and greedy" may be used. This is clearly not true. There is a projection onto "them" by the speaker and this is clear from the language. Quite possibly the negative past experience of the speaker of figures in authority or those seen as successful, is projected out into the world and focussed on this particular group of people. A step in the right direction would be to take ownership of this fixed attitude. A more correct statement would therefore be "I think that all "fat-cat bosses" are selfish and greedy". This is a statement which accurately communicates the thought that the speaker is having. It also allows for empirical testing and modification by experience, in a way that "they are all selfish and greedy" cleverly closes down. It is stated as a fact that cannot easily be challenged. So in language projection tends to make use of the words "you", "it" and "they" when what is really meant is "I". One way for you to become a more responsible user of this incredible tool that is unique to humans is to take responsibility for what you say and your own internal processes. Become aware of what you say in relation to "them" and see if you can rephrase your statement to take ownership of your attitude, by saying "I".

Introjection

A second mechanism is introjection. This is where an attitude from someone significant has been internalised. It is like a rule that has been imported into the furthest recesses of a person's mind, outside of their awareness and points out when they fail to live up to the ideal. "I really shouldn't have another drink", "I should lose weight" and "I should work harder" are all indicators of a potential introjection. Someone significant to the speaker has probably in the past communicated one way or another that drinking is bad, that only a certain size or weight is acceptable (well most of the media, advertising, entertainment and fashion industries communicate this to us 24/7) or that hard work is an important way to measure your worth and so to be acceptable and accepted. Introjections are usually the safest thing to believe or accept about the world in order to be accepted by the group – maybe it is a tradition, or it is fashionable. Another way of thinking about this concept is "incorporation" – incorporating a part of someone else's attitudes, beliefs or behaviours into our own by internalising their outlook. It is like we have "swallowed whole" the attitude of another without evaluating, testing and accepting it for ourselves. As a consequence it can be heard in the language of shoulds, oughts, musts and "supposed to's". Other words like "always" and "never" also hint at an introjection, hard and fast rules incorporated uncritically from the outside and residing out of our awareness. Introjections are also quite tricky to overcome. Consider this – the attitude, value or belief that has been introjected – swallowed whole in a trusting way – may well have come from someone whose love and attention was sought, from someone respected, trusted and loved. The act of critically appraising that introjected belief and rejecting it can feel like a high risk option, creating anxious feelings, because in rejecting the belief, you are, in effect, rejecting the person who originated it in the first place. In short rejecting a belief in adulthood that came from a much loved parent may feel as though it is the parent that is being rejected and yet it is their acceptance that we originally craved. Another way to think of introjection is as conditioning. The collection of introjects is how we have been conditioned to think and behave over our lifetime by a wide variety of influences, from our family to wider society. Becoming aware of – and unlearning – our conditioning is an essential step in rediscovering our true authentic selves. In language an introjection can mean that the word "I" is used when what is really meant is "they" – "I believe it's good to work hard", when it's really "they believe it's good to work hard". It is often said that a projection is the opposite of an introjection as a projection is taking something internal and pushing it out into the world, making the external world responsible for it, whilst an introjection is taking something that was out in the external environment and making it part of your inner world, taking responsibility for something that lies outside of yourself.

Retroflection

Retroflection appears in language as a split within the person. The person is both the subject and the object in a sentence – which shows that there is an internal division or internal battle going on. In language this would be something like "I don't know what to do with myself" or "I am ashamed of myself" or "I tell myself not to" – "myself" is a key word that occurs in retroflection.

What is going on here is that action that is meant for the external world is sharply turned back to the internal world, back on yourself. For example it may be dangerous to express anger, so it is bottled up inside, turned back inwards. That energy finds a way to express itself which it probably does through bodily tension and tight muscles – another clue that may be apparent when in conversation. Retroflection means that there is an internal fight – clearly evident in the words used – and it is between a more powerful and less powerful part – the more powerful part "I", suppressing the less powerful part "myself" which must be kept hidden from the outside world (and quite possibly out of conscious awareness too).

Confluence

Confluence arises when an individual has not developed a strong sense of personal identity and chooses to follow the crowd in the hope of being accepted by them. Without strongly held views of their own the individual takes on the attitudes of the majority.

This comes out in language by the use of "we" – making statements on behalf of the group, rather than speaking for themselves. The unfortunate result generally is that the individual in confluence does not get the recognition and acceptance they seek – instead the lack of personal identity means that others cannot easily relate to them, leading to a sense of isolation, the exact opposite of what they sought. An example of confluence is a phenomenon known as "groupthink" – where "we" as a group adopt a certain understanding or way of thinking which becomes set in stone. There is no-one to put an alternative point of view – and if someone does come in from outside to give a different perspective, they are likely to be ignored as "they don't understand us" or "they have strange ideas". In short the desire to hold the group together is stronger than the desire to operate effectively and consider the real situation openly. A certain level of confluence can be useful at times – it is what we might describe as empathy in certain contexts – it has its place, it is just not a useful position to be in permanently.

Self-understanding

With increased self-awareness comes increased self-knowledge. As you become able to spot the clues in the language that you use, you will become aware of your habitual patterns and your internal conflicts. We discussed introjects in language and how to spot them. Now we can consider their impact on us and the need to understand them. If in the past we have swallowed whole a set of values, beliefs and attitudes that came pre-packaged and unquestioned from the outside – from whatever source – it is highly unlikely that all of these introjects are compatible with each other. It is highly likely that they are:

- in conflict with each other, and

- in conflict with our true selves, our natural, innate, intuitive outlook, and

- leading to us actively suppressing some parts of ourselves that the introject says is unacceptable.

Becoming aware of our introjects, what we can call our conditioning, gives us the opportunity to regurgitate beliefs that we swallowed whole and digest them afresh – this time not as unquestioning children, but as experienced adults. Instead of accepting them, we modify and assimilate them – they are no longer a foreign body creating conflict, but absorbed to form part of the coherent whole. Becoming aware of and understanding our introjects and how they operate allows us to change them. It is not necessary to understand where they came from or why they are there, although that may become apparent, it is simply a matter of examining them as an adult in the here and now and taking from them what will be useful for the future. This self-knowledge leads to self-understanding – and this gives us choice and freedom. In each moment we are free to choose how to react to the real presenting world in front of us, rather than to yesterday's world acting out pre-programmed fixed attitudes. It offers up the possibility to live spontaneously, in the moment, creatively applying your accumulated wisdom to the situation before you, free of internal conflict and half-measures.

Self-acceptance

Becoming aware of your own internal processes and in turn gaining knowledge and understanding naturally leads on to self-acceptance. As you become aware of your fixed attitudes, beliefs and values that may no longer be useful to you and you begin to understand that there were good reasons for you to have adopted them, you can begin to see that it is neither good nor bad that this is the way life is – and the way that you are – it is just a natural consequence of living the human experience. Instead of wishing that you were different, you can change not by rejecting parts of yourself that you do not like – which is what leads to these different phenomena of projection, retroflection and so on – but by accepting all of yourself. Accepting yourself leads to increased self-awareness as there is no need to hide parts of yourself as acceptance is pretty much the opposite of being judgemental. The hidden parts can come out into awareness and receive warmth, compassion and acceptance, rather than judgement, persecution and rejection.

The amazing thing is that the route to personal change and development is not rejecting the parts of us that we have been taught not to like or trying to modify or suppress them. Instead it is in accepting them that we can then move on and develop. As Carl Rogers said – "The curious paradox is that when I accept myself just as I am, then I can change."

Who we really are is not who we thought we were or felt we should be. The authentic self is the true self underneath all the conditioning that has been acquired through life's experiences. We are what we are and that is OK – after all who can tell us otherwise? We can get back in touch with ourselves by increasing our levels of personal awareness. We can do this by receiving feedback from others and even by listening to our own language. Our language has the potential to give us clues about our conditioning. From there we can re-evaluate our rule book and look at our true selves with compassion, acceptance – and excitement about our potential and the possibilities. Being in touch with our true selves is about getting real, not living in a fantasy of who we could or should be, but living with what is. Like any situation that needs evaluating or changing, the only way to do so is to first accept how it really is and to start from there. Knowing ourselves fully is no different – it is a pre-requisite for real lasting change and for a satisfied contentment with life.

Ultimately being in touch with your authentic self means that:

- you will have high levels of self awareness. There will be few parts of yourself of which you are unaware and so you are less likely to project onto others. you will accept yourself for who you are. There will be no need to look for acceptance outside yourself and so internalise other peoples' rules. Old introjects have come into awareness and been re-evaluated. Then they have been discarded, unlearned, or modified and assimilated appropriately for today's world.
-
- you will have a strong sense of your own identity. There will be no need to modify yourself to be accepted by the group. You will retain your sense of self in a group rather than experiencing confluence.

- you will be aware of and able to express your true feelings in an appropriate way as a responsible adult. There will be no need to be divided against yourself – with high levels of knowledge and awareness you quickly become aware of internal divisions and can work through the dialogue to a resolution, rather than being stuck in retroflection.

Relating to others

We explored what it means to understand ourselves

and concluded that self-acceptance is the key to personal growth and development. Self-acceptance changes the way we look at ourselves – to see ourselves as we really are. When relating to others, exercising this same attitude of acceptance can transform our interpersonal dialogues and take our relationships to a new level.

Many people feel vulnerable and so have their personality shields up to protect themselves. Showing that you accept others without judgement allows them to dare to lower their shield and opens up the possibility for a real and meaningful contact between two people.

How we see each other

Prejudice

When we meet people for the first time we draw conclusions quickly about them. As a survival mechanism this has served humanity well – are they friend or foe? In most circumstances, although there is no such risk attached to the judgement we make, we still jump to conclusions. It is typical for us to make assumptions about others when we only know a little bit of information about them – this is pre-judging what they will be like – and this is where our prejudices come into play. It is very common when introduced to someone new to ask what they do – "I'm a mother of two" or "I'm in sales" or "I'm an investment banker" may give rise to a range of different pre-judgements about what they may be like. This is based on assumptions and a pre-set list of qualities – either positive or negative – that are associated with that particular group. This list of assumptions mean that a decision is made (a pre-judgement) based on the group to which they belong before the facts are known about this individual. It is clear that much discrimination is built on prejudice – pre-judging someone due to their race or gender for example. Getting to know the individual means that the assumptions are replaced by facts and personal experience. Becoming aware of when you pre-judge someone, based on some kind of generalisation due to the group they belong to, presents the possibility of being able to move beyond that to seeing others more clearly. For example someone goes to a dinner party hosted by a husband and wife. It's unclear who cooked the food and instead of asking the hosts, the guest compliments the wife on her cooking and is surprised to learn that the husband cooked it. This simple example shows how a pre-judgement about a situation leads to an incorrect assessment of a situation and reveals a prejudice about the roles of men and women in the home. Another example of prejudice at work is in the workplace. When a Chief Executive – or your boss – walks into a room it's pretty clear that many will pre-judge the person and be very aware of the role. Indeed it is the role they may see and respond to rather than the person, conscious of the power of that role and how they could personally be affected. So the whispering stops, everyone looks busy, they are a bit more guarded about what they say and so on. To go back to our theatre analogy, when the role of boss enters the stage, the staff members follow the prewritten script of how to respond to a boss, prejudging how this boss is.

The boss may be totally unaware that this is what is going on! The boss may think that everyone is very well behaved and diligent. No matter how much they walk around to get a feel for how the team is doing, they are always changing the environment because of how people are reacting to their role. So roles and prejudices can be a hindrance for relating to others, but can also act as a reassuring way of coping with uncertainty. As the new boss walks into the room, people are likely to respond in a guarded way, protecting themselves from the potentially negative effects of the role of boss. A more real relationship can only be built as the team members see past the role and past their prejudices to see the real person. If you are a manager or leader in your workplace, you may need to think about how people react to you. Do they react to you only in your role? Is that helpful? How do you relate to your boss? Are you prejudged and how do you prejudge others? It is perhaps fairly clear how most people will react to you in a certain role, the most common stereotypes or prejudices are likely to be playing in peoples' heads and this is useful to understand. You can either work with them and go with them, or choose to reveal more of yourself to change their perception by giving them more facts to replace their assumptions.

Projection

In the previous section we talked about projection and

how language can give us clues when this is at work. Your own issues get projected out into the world and projected onto "them", like a movie is projected onto a screen. You see in others what you have created and projected, rather than what is actually there although in reality you are seeing a mixture of the two. Projection is potentially much more difficult to deal with than prejudice as it is generally out of the awareness of the person doing the projecting. So when the new boss walks into the room, as well as the realities of the role and the pre-judgements to contend with, there may also be projections going on. This is unique to each interpersonal relationship and the boss cannot make many assumptions about this. The boss may experience strange irrational responses from a member of staff due to the "unfinished business" playing out in their projections onto the boss. For example if a person had a previous experience of a critical authority figure (like a parent), that made them feel inadequate, then these feelings of inadequacy could get projected onto the boss. This in turn means that the member of staff does not react to what is really going on and what the boss really wants but to the old and outdated projections of their own feelings of inadequacy. So the boss may feel that even though they have given some balanced positive and negative feedback, the member of staff just hears the negative feedback, reinforcing their own feelings of inadequacy, concluding that the boss thinks they are no good. So how to tackle this? All we can do is to take responsibility for our own actions and behaviours. We can become aware of our own projective processes and our own prejudices and in bringing them into our awareness we can re-evaluate the situation and understand our feelings about it. Seeing others as they really are is not as easy as you might think!

Persona

The word "persona" originally meant a theatrical mask and they were used by Roman actors in theatres. When on the stage actors would play a role with a mask on to denote the character. During the performance they could change their mask and so play multiple characters. These personae could also have particular expressions painted onto them to express a particular emotion. Carl Jung used the word persona to denote a social role – it is the social face that the individual chooses to present to the world – it is a carefully constructed mask to project the image that the individual wants. Indeed we may have several personae that are appropriate for different situations, just like the different characters in a play. Once Jack Nicholson, the Hollywood movie star, was asked why he often wore sunglasses. His response was that if he did not he was just another fat fifty year old guy, but with them on he was Jack Nicholson! You can almost imagine him coming to life as he puts them on. We would recognise him as Jack Nicholson without his trademark Wayfarer sunglasses, but with them he indicates that he feels he is more in tune with his public "bad boy" image. He is playing a role, projecting a persona.

This is common with many celebrities – the persona they project, although it is supposed to be themselves, actually is not, it is just another role that they play. This is of course a fairly unique kind of role to play – playing ourselves in the glare of the media spotlight – but how many of us are really playing ourselves, even with the much smaller spotlight shone by the people around us every day?

The most successful personalities have a range of these personae and are able to put on and take off these social masks with ease. Those with only one main mask may become trapped by this character and not have the repertoire needed to respond effectively in all the social situations in which they find themselves. Do you have a persona, or several personae, that you construct and project out to others to establish a social self and protect the real you? We tend to see each other through a wide range of lenses that each distort or colour what we are seeing. As a consequence we do not automatically see people as they really are – and crucially we may not even be aware that we are looking through these lenses as we are so used to them. There are particular types of lenses and we have looked at prejudice and projection. Individuals also wear social masks to protect themselves. They play their roles so well and know the script by heart that they develop effective and convincing personae that mask the real person.

Relating to others at work

Many of us spend more time relating to our colleagues at work than we do relating to our family and friends. When these relationships are not working well and conflict arises this can feel very stressful. Indeed research into what causes stress at work and what promotes employee engagement consistently points to relationships at work – and in particular with the direct line manager and the management team in general. Issues such as poor management, not feeling listened to, not feeling supported and working in a climate of fear are consistently cited as problems.

Roles at work

In the previous section we talked about ourselves as playing different roles – and nowhere is this more tangible than in the workplace. When we join an organisation we are appointed to a role, we receive a role description (or job description) and it may include a person specification. It makes it quite clear and explicit that the role we are to play is not the person that we are. We are primarily paid for the role we play – for what we do and not for who we are. A well-designed role goes through quite a detailed process of design to ensure that there is no overlap with others and that the limits and dimensions of roles and responsibilities are clear. Individual roles carry accountability for certain activities and all resources are allocated to a role to be managed or controlled. This all comes together in a special diagram called an organisation chart – or organogram – that shows the nice straight lines and more complex dotted lines of relationships between roles. It's all very neat – and looks like an efficient system. For it to work like a system everyone needs to play their role well, preferably word-perfect every day, and relate to each other not as people but as the roles. This in theory means that people can be slotted in and out of those roles and replaced without a problem – like a spare part in a car, swap the new part for the old part. Of course it does not work like this at all in practice. People are all different, they prefer to relate to each other as people, not as roles, they probably never learn their script, let alone be word-perfect and sometimes they choose to play other people's roles – or a new one altogether!

All the same issues arise in the workplace as they do anywhere else. Projection and prejudice for example are constantly in play. So in larger organisations where people are grouped into departments or functions, they can develop their own cultures and ways of doing things – and may also attract different personality types. So for example the sales team might be driven and ambitious to make the sale and not focussed on process, whilst the finance or legal team are focussed on the correct procedures being followed. As a result it is easy to see an "us" and "them" situation arising (which is a form of confluence) where one group is prejudiced towards another and individuals may project their unfinished business onto people from the other group. So statements like "finance are always preventing me from making the sale", "finance are nagging me for the paperwork again" or "the sales team never follow any procedures" are all easy to imagine. If you want to truly relate to others successfully at work, to the individual people rather than the roles or the groups, then you need to take responsibility for your own internal processes and communication. Becoming aware of things like your projections onto others, confluence with your own team, and prejudices about other groups will enable you to move past these to see the real person next to you rather than the role they play or the person they might represent from your past. As you do this and use your inter-personal skills that we discuss in the next chapter, you will become recognised as someone with their own approach and will stand out from the crowd as being a self-assured individual.

Management and leadership

Management and leadership are particular roles tasked with running the organisation. An organisation is simply a group of people relating together with a shared common purpose – fundamentally it is a social unit. It is not a machine and it does not exist as an entity in itself separate from those within it – it is those within it, and the way that they relate to each other and do things together (the culture). Managers and leaders have a unique role to play in making this large disparate group of people with different backgrounds, education, technical abilities and perspectives come together to achieve a common aim. The problem is that most of these managers and leaders have never received any specific support to develop the competencies needed to do it effectively. They may have received some training on how to do some of the tasks of management so as to comply with the law and best practice, but this does not help with supporting a complex web of inter-personal relationships. It is perhaps not surprising then that the workplace is not always a happy place!

Management and leadership roles are usually much more public and visible than others and also have power and influence over their colleagues. Relating to your boss – and your boss's boss is therefore quite different from relating to a peer – and probably feels as such. It is certainly an undeniable fact that your boss has power and influence over you, they can, within set boundaries and rules, change your job, require you to work more, reduce your hours, change your salary, terminate your employment – or promote you. It is no wonder that these roles become centre stage – their role is to manage your role. So given this fact, how can you relate to your boss and, if you are the boss, how can you relate to your staff? Two roles cannot relate to each other – ultimately the people need to. It is perfectly possible to see past the role to the person, to relate to the person, whilst respecting the role. Indeed respecting the role works both ways, organisations need all the members of the team to play their part to make it operate effectively. Each person brings to their role a range of skills, experience and attitudes that another person would not and could not. A senior manager or business leader will recognise this, knowing that organisational success depends upon the complete range of technical abilities playing their full part.

In an ideal world your boss will respect the strengths that you bring to your role, but that is not always the case. This may feel frustrating and unfair and it can be tempting to try and change their perspective, however you cannot reasonably expect to change other people – and trying to change your boss is probably unwise! The only thing that you can do is to take responsibility for how you are and how you behave. You may have a set of internal processes going on that create voices that say things like "my boss should show me more respect" or "my boss is unfair". You may have some thoughts and feelings about your boss as you read this. In a previous section we talked about projection and introjection – those rules in our heads that represent fixed attitudes from the past. The more able you are to become aware of these out-dated rules, the more able you will be to see your boss as they really are and relate to them on that basis. More than most other types of relationship at work, you may have two types of reaction going on, one to the person that you perceive and one to the role that they play – and what that role represents to you. If you are the boss, then it will help you to understand that many people will find it difficult to relate to you openly and honestly because of what you represent to them, rather than who you are as a person. The only way to create a genuine inter-personal relationship is to provide the opportunities to build that key ingredient in any relationship – trust. Building trust between staff and their managers and leaders is something that tends to happen by accident and seems to be shrouded in mystery. It is unclear to many what makes a good leader. Put simply a leader is someone who is followed by others willingly, and this will only happen if they trust them.

The phrase "earning their trust" is a useful one for a

manager or leader to reflect on. Earning is strongly associated with working and building trust takes sustained work and effort. It is not just another task that leaders need to perform – it is arguably the task that leaders need to perform! In subsequent sections we will look at how managers can adopt a coaching management style to build relationships with their team and how developing an authentic leadership style will enable leaders to generate trust.

Promotion

If you have just been promoted to your new management or leadership position then congratulations – you have now got a new role to play and a new script needs to be written for the part. An internal promotion means that there is a new dimension between yourself and your colleagues – those who used to be your peers are now your team. You will have to learn that the old ways of behaving with colleagues need to be modified. The reason is simple, with colleagues you could be relaxed and friendly because you were equals, when you are a boss you have power over them. You can tell them what to do, appraise their performance, influence their salary and ultimately recruit and dismiss people. This transition can be a tricky one – not only will they see you differently, but you will see both them and yourself differently. A relaxed approach by a colleague can suddenly become a slack approach when viewed from the role of manager. This change in situation establishes a whole new dynamic to the relationship and gives plenty of opportunity for a whole new set of projections, introjects and confluence to arise!

Take confluence for example – you may have felt one of "us" before promotion – and now you are one of "them"! You may find yourself having to adjust which group you feel allegiance to. Your colleagues will probably be interested to see how you deal with that. Will you become "just like all the other bosses" or will you be different? Will they be able to have an easier life now that you're their boss, or will you change? Will promotion "go to your head"? All sorts of questions could be running through their minds. The way to address this is of course to take responsibility for and become aware of your own internal processes and at the same time to establish new relationships with the team that recognises the fact that you have a new role. One way to build this sort of relationship is to develop a coaching management style.

Developing a coaching management style

There are a range of different management styles. As we saw management theorists have tried to understand what motivates human beings at work and to tap into that for the benefit of the organisation. For example assuming that workers fit a "theory X" profile would lead to a management style that closely supervises staff and puts pressure on them to perform with the only reward being financial. A style that coerces, controls and directs. A "theory Y" profile assumes that workers basically enjoy their work, that they are self-motivated and self-directed towards the end result. The assumption is that these workers want to perform well and progress, they will accept responsibility and value job satisfaction. An appropriate management style to adopt for this kind of worker is a coaching management style. Adopting the wrong kind of style for theory Y workers would result in them experiencing a range of negative emotions, feeling demotivated, micro-managed, blamed and not trusted.

A coaching management style creates an atmosphere of trust and enables employees to develop and grow in their role – and to be able to take on new roles with greater responsibility. Such a style would include things like

- listening rather than just telling

- supporting and understanding rather than blaming

- honest and open communication

- consistency and integrity

- empowering people to problem-solve rather than just giving direction

- giving constructive, balanced feedback rather than just criticism

- and a focus on learning and development rather than just the task in hand.

If you are a manager then adopting a coaching style will enable you to have more effective relationships with your team, enable them to learn and develop more quickly, release more of their potential and increase creative problem-solving. By adopting such a style you can create relationships where you can give feedback that is really heard, and where team members will not feel judged and criticised, but supported and developed. Achieving a coaching management style requires an investment in your own inter-personal skills (which we will examine in the next chapter) and your own personal development. It will be worth it for a number of reasons:

- the improved results from your team

- more effective relationships with your team and other colleagues

- more effective relationships with others outside of work

You will also stand out to others as bringing a special and different quality to your work as a manager, being supportive to the team by investing and developing them, and, at the same time, gaining improved engagement and better results. At work we play roles more explicitly, many of the roles have scripts pre-written and similar roles tend to form into groups and become divided from others. Hierarchy tends to further increase the divisions between us. Bridging those gaps, to enable us to relate to others effectively, particularly becomes the responsibility of managers and leaders. They can adopt and develop a coaching style. In doing so they become role models and through their consistent example can create a coaching culture where all can relate to each other in a much more real way. This culture of mutual respect offers the prospect of people not only feeling engaged and enjoying their work, but finding that there is the space to offer more of themselves and their unique talents to the organisation.

Developing your interpersonal skills

In order to develop real, lasting, authentic relationships with others we need to become responsible users of interpersonal dialogue and develop our communication skills. Authentic communication means expressing what you really think and feel right now and when both parties are doing that, there is the potential for real contact between two authentic selves. There can be no deeper or truer communication!

Listening

Listening sounds like it is the easiest thing in the world – after all we are constantly hearing sounds and processing them. In fact what we are really doing is constantly editing out background noise and just focussing on what we think is important at the time. So our awareness of what is really going on around us varies. Listening is a particular form of hearing and that involves directing your attention towards the person you are in dialogue with. Think of a time when you were in a group discussing someone that you were interested in – how much of the time are you really listening and how much of the time are you really just formulating the next thing to say and waiting for a break in the conversation to make your point? You are either listening to your internal dialogue and preparing your next statement or listening to the other person. It is difficult to do both at the same time and impossible to do them both fully. Effective communication is about one person sending a message whilst the other person is receiving that message, then pausing to digest it and reversing the process.

Without listening properly you can end up making assumptions about what you have heard with the result that the other person can begin to pick up that you have not really been listening or paying attention. Instead of communicating interest, you are communicating disinterest – whether that is true or not. Listening in this sense is focussed awareness and really paying attention to someone is for many an unusual experience and will stand out to them and to others. Feeling heard is important for people to feel valued. If you are in a management or leadership position, then this is a key skill to practise as it is all too easy for people to say "management never listens" – being a manager who does listen will stand out. It is also likely to increase feelings of engagement in your staff. This form of listening only comes with practice. It requires focussing on the other person and letting the internal static of your chattering mind fade into the background – just not paying it attention. However this is easier said than done. If you are feeling anxious and pre-occupied or in a hurry to be somewhere else, this will come across in the quality of attention that you are able to give the other. The internal voices will persist. You mind keeps calling your attention away from your external senses and back to the chatter.

So we could do with finding a way to help us get out of our mind and back in touch with our senses.

One tried and tested technique to manage this is to focus on our breathing. Many of us breathe at the top of our lungs, breathing from our chest in shallow breaths. Sometimes if we're anxious or pre-occupied we may stop breathing for a while! The most effective way to breathe is deeply, from our diaphragm. This means that instead of our chest rising and falling as we breathe, our lower abdomen expands and contracts with each breath. This has a soothing effect, allowing the anxiety to pass and so helps the mind to clear sufficiently to focus on the other person more fully. So, now you have two simple techniques to help you with your listening skills – breathe deeply and focus on the other person with your full attention, undistracted by internal chatter.

Nonverbal communication

Listening focuses on the words that we hear, however there is a great deal of non-verbal communication that we can also learn to become aware of – in ourselves and others – which can greatly enrich the meaning behind our communications. You may not realise it, but your body is communicating all the time, whether you are speaking or not. More than this, when you are speaking, your message might be the same as your words – or the total opposite! Whilst the other person may not quite know why they are getting mixed messages, human beings are well designed to pick up on non-verbal communication. Paying attention to their – and to your own – non-verbal cues will add an extra dimension to your communication. So what do we need to become aware of? In any conversation you can start by listening not just to the words, but to the way they are said, the intonation. A simple example is the question "is that your car?" Firstly you will know that it is a question just from the words, as it starts "is that...", whilst other questions could also be statements depending upon the way that they are said and the intonation. For this particular question it could be said in several different ways with a variety of different meanings. We will examine some different versions below.

"Is that your car?" With the emphasis on the word "that" the question can carry more meaning. Depending upon the intonation on the word "that" it could communicate derision ("I expect you to have a better car than that") or admiration ("I really like your car" or "I didn't expect you to have such a nice car"). Said in a neutral way it could just be for clarification, "is it that one rather than this one?"

"Is that your car?" Again the emphasis and intonation of the word "your" can communicate different meanings – "is that your car rather than someone else's?", "do you own the car?" or even "have you stolen it?"

"Is that your car?" The intonation on the word "car" could suggest surprise that such a thing is called a car and does not meet with the speaker's expectations. Maybe it is smaller than expected, or it is larger, or maybe it is really a van that is used as a car – or maybe it is a luxury chauffeur-driven limousine!

Aside from intonation, there are other clues in the body too – sighing, shuffling on the chair, looking away, changes in breathing patterns, swallowing hard, frowning – the list goes on.

Whilst many books on body language give interpretations of various actions and positions, there is no need to interpret them, as doing so is unlikely to lead to a building up of trust! You may have a hunch about what a particular thing means and you may even be correct, but you do not know until you check. If you see someone swallow hard, you could say something like "I get the feeling that you may be anxious", which is both more truthful and more empowering than saying "you swallowed hard so you must be anxious". It gives the speaker the opportunity to assess what that meant – if anything – and give it a voice. Using this approach you are always encouraging them to take responsibility for their actions and stay in control of the meaning of their communication.

Pauses and silences

If our approach to listening is really about waiting for the other person to be quiet, so that we can say what we have been thinking about when they have been speaking, then silence will hardly ever happen. When someone speaks and then pauses, it does not necessarily mean that they are finished – indeed you may often find that the best is yet to come! Maybe the pause does mean that they have finished, in which case you will soon pick this up. They will probably pick up from your pause that you were listening to what they were saying, that you are giving them both space and time to speak without pressure, rather than just waiting to speak. Silences are difficult for many people to cope with and there is a natural tendency to think we must be saying something, but just leaving these pauses for a few seconds both allows them to formulate that next important sentence and gives you time to digest what has been said and prepare your response. Hand-in-hand with this is the general principle that you do not interrupt if you want people to feel heard – if someone is speaking, let them work through what they are saying. If you interrupt at every pause for breath then you are not letting them complete that phase of the dialogue and you are effectively taking control of the flow. If you interrupt then the message that they will receive is probably that you are bored and want to speak!

Summarising and checking

Given that we know we are unlikely to be perfect at listening to all that has been said and given also that what is said is not always what is meant, and that there is a myriad of non-verbal cues which we are likely to miss and even misinterpret, it is sensible to check with the other person that you have heard and understood correctly. It also sends the message that you are interested and wanting to understand them. There are various ways of doing this and we will examine three of them here.

1. Restating

Firstly you can just check with them, restating something that you have heard for clarification, that is to use your own words to distil what they have said to get to the meaning of it eg – "Can I check I've understood correctly –

if you don't speak to your colleague every morning then they think you're deliberately ignoring them?"

2. *Summarising*

Summarising may be useful if the person has been speaking for some time without being interrupted and you have got an overall sense of the themes emerging. Summarising means drawing those themes out and checking whether that is a fair summary of the key points. It indicates that you have been listening attentively and it allows them the chance to refine the overall message and sense of what they have been saying. It also draws out what you saw as the key points, bringing all the individual pieces of evidence together into one coherent narrative.

3. *Reflecting*

Reflection is used to present feelings and meaning back to the listener as a way of demonstrating your perception of their emotional state. For example "It sounds like you're anxious when meeting with him" or "you feel a little embarrassed by the situation?". They can then confirm whether your reflection is an accurate one or distorted. Ultimately the only person who can tell you if you are good at listening is the person speaking – so checking with them that you have understood is really the only way to know if you have been listening effectively.

Questions

A responsible use of questions can enhance communication by clarifying and getting more data in a neutral way. For example "what are you feeling now?" is a straight request for information. It has a couple of key characteristics worth noting. Firstly it is an open question, rather than a closed question. It cannot just be answered with a yes or no reply, instead it requires the listener to examine the situation and report the answer, which could be anything – including "I don't feel anything now".

Secondly it is not a leading question – i.e. it is not prejudging or suggesting how they might be feeling, whilst "are you feeling sad?" is suggesting a feeling to them and they have to evaluate the situation in the light of that suggestion. Another distortion would be "are you still feeling sad?" which not only suggests that they could be feeling sad, it assumes that they were feeling sad and the use of "still" probably suggests that they should not be feeling sad now. As you can see, "what are you feeling now?" is a neutral request when compared to "are you still feeling sad?" and a much more responsible use of questions. However even this open, neutral question is leading to some degree as it sets the agenda. Inevitably a question demands a response. The questioner has taken some power in the conversation and is directing the thoughts of the other to give a certain type of response. In some circumstances it may be more appropriate to use statements.

Statements

A responsible use of statements can enhance communication. A good neutral statement is factual and free of judgement, reporting how something actually is. For example "after you opened the window I began to feel cold". There may be certain conversations where you do not want to be at all directive and you want to express what you are really thinking and feeling, so a statement can be used. For example "I'm wondering what you are feeling now." This is a statement that may provoke the same response as a question yet leaves the person feeling in control – there is no driving of the agenda, it is merely an honest reporting of what is going on in the first individual – i.e. they are wondering. A responsible use of statements also requires being careful about hidden meanings. One issue to be aware of is the use of the words "but" and "however". If possible try and replace the words "but" and "however" with "and" – in this way you are reporting two facts of equal weighting. The use of "but" and "however" implies a negative attitude towards the first part of the statement – in effect any positive elements of the first part of the sentence are negated by the words "but" and "however".

For example – "your report is very good but I have some amendments to make", suggests that really the report is not very good as it need correcting. Whilst "your report is very good and I have some amendments to make" is simply reporting a fact in a much more neutral way. The use of the words "but" and "however" demonstrate that there is a problem in the first part of the sentence.

The responsible use of language and communication will depend upon the circumstances. For example in some situations it is appropriate to be leading and to drive the agenda – e.g. in a task-focussed work conversation with a more junior member of staff. In a personal development conversation, or a creative meeting with an equal colleague the agenda could be much more free-flowing and you would drive it less. This might include a greater use of statements and fewer questions. At home between partners the use of these more developed interpersonal skills are likely to lead to both people feeling like true partners and able to relate to each other as equals. Honest reporting of what each person is thinking and feeling, in an accepting atmosphere where each pays attention to the other, is much more likely to lead to a positive outcome instead of the use of projection, denial, blame and not listening.

Now that you are aware of these basic tools and techniques you can re-examine how you want to relate to others in your various roles at home and at work. You can begin to try out the techniques and practise them, adopting the ones that suit you well to develop a personal style of responsible communication that allows you to express your true authentic self and enhance the quality of your interpersonal relationships. Finding yourself is probably the most significant thing you can do to improve your quality of life. Getting in touch with who and what you really are will improve your relationship with yourself and your relationships with others, whether they are at home or at work. Understanding ourselves and relating to others is a lifetime's work. Our understanding of ourselves tends to increase naturally over time anyway as we get tested and gain feedback through life's experiences. Making a choice to understand ourselves opens up for each of us a unique journey of personal growth and development. As we understand ourselves more, we can become more accepting of ourselves. We have looked at a range of ways in which we can create greater understanding of ourselves through increased self-awareness. We can become aware of our priorities at our current stage of life, the roles we play, the scripts we follow and what drives our sense of identity. We can seek out feedback and monitor our own language for hidden clues to our out-dated internal book of rules. We can become aware of our prejudices and assumptions about others. As we become more accepting of ourselves, we open up the possibility of being more accepting of others. We can understand that others feel vulnerable too and take steps to protect themselves. They develop a range of personae to present themselves in a certain way, they operate from their own scripts and roles. You can realise that they may not be responding to you but to your role, or their prejudices about you or their projections onto you – you do not need to take all reactions to you personally!

Certain roles, such as management and leadership, tend to bear a greater level of these barriers and distortions than others. Whether you are the manager or the person being managed, actively choosing to overcome these barriers will mean an increase in the level of inter-personal skills needed. A desire amongst managers and leaders to increase staff engagement and unlock potential in others, will often mean adopting and developing a coaching style. All relationships will improve when you take greater responsibility for your communication skills and the quality of your inter-personal dialogue. A range of techniques can help, such as active listening, picking up on non-verbal cues, working with pauses and silence, summarising and checking, knowing when and how to make a statement, and when and how to ask a question. Life is not about pleasing others and playing roles scripted by others, but about being our true selves and exploring the unique potential within each of us. We can all make a choice to follow that path. It is our own unique path, one that has never been trodden before – and will not be again. We make that choice not just now but constantly. Every moment creates a new opportunity to be in touch with yourself and act in line with your authentic nature. As you increase your self-understanding and get back in touch with your true self, you will feel freer to operate as an autonomous individual, fulfil your potential, respond creatively to the changing world and develop deeper more productive relationships. You will operate in tune with yourself whilst being sensitive to the needs of others, expressing yourself in your own uniquely creative way – and this will be recognised by others as the charisma of true authenticity.

THE ULTIMATE VISION

Chapter 2

Who among us could live without computers? It seems they're everywhere – in our studies at home, on our desks at work, in the library, the bank and even the cafe. We get pleasure from them, we get angry at them, we need them. But it's only a recent thing. Just 3 generations ago the Chairman of IBM declared there is a world market for only five computers. As recently as 1977 the President of Digital Equipment claimed there is no reason anyone would want a computer in their home!

The revolution was brought to us in large part by Steven Jobs, the founder of Apple Computers. Steve Jobs was just 21 when he and Steve Wozniak invented the Apple Computer. Until then computers were a monstrous mass of vacuum tubes which took whole rooms. Then the two Steve's managed to take that mass of tubes and incorporate them inside a box small enough to sit on a desk.

Jobs and Wozniak offered their invention to Atari. They weren't interested in big bucks – all they wanted was a salary and the opportunity to continue their work. Atari knocked them back. They offered it to Hewlett-Packard, but Hewlett Packard knocked them back. It seemed Jobs and Wozniak alone could see the possibilities. So Jobs sold his Volkswagon and Wozniak sold his calculator, and with the $1300 that gave them they formed Apple Computers. The company was named Apple in memory of a happy summer Jobs had spent working in an orchard.

By all accounts Steve Jobs is a visionary, and spurred on by that vision he built a successful computer company. But Jobs soon discovered that if his vision was to reach fruition they needed greater management expertise. So Jobs approached John Sculley, then President of PepsiCo. There was absolutely no reason why Sculley should leave a highly paid position in a world leading company to go work with a bunch of computer nerds in a fledgling industry. Not unsurprisingly he turned Jobs down. But Jobs wouldn't take no for an answer. He approached Sculley again. Again Sculley turned him down. In a last ditch effort Jobs passionately presented his visionary ideas to Sculley and he asked Sculley a question that forced him to accept. The question was this: "Do you want to spend the rest of your life selling sugared water or do you want a chance to change the world?" Indeed Jobs and Sculley did change the world.

Carry on with the life you had always wanted: Overcome enough to carry on with the life you had always wanted by your vision and reason rather than the desires and suppositions of others.

When asked to define 'vision', the first thing many say is the act of seeing with ones' eyes. While sight can play an important role in creating a vision statement, one must become more introspective for a deeper understanding of the type of vision being explored here: a prophetic vision or the power of anticipating what may come.

People are commonly influenced by more than one type of vision throughout their lives. For instance, a person may have a personal vision statement, a corporate mission statement, and a vision statement pertaining to one aspect of his/her life (volunteering, parenting, faith, etc.). Some decide to have one over-riding vision statement to guide and direct their lives.

Personal vision and corporate mission statements are similar in that they represent a future picture of you, your business or the company you work for. Setting the framework for future planning and goal setting, vision and mission statements answer the following questions respectively:

What do I want?

Where are we going?

Whether personal or corporate, vision/mission statements are created to help articulate dreams and aspirations. Using your imagination without limitation will help capture your inner passion. Let's get started!

Defining Yourself

Before creating your personal vision statement, first identify who you are as an individual. Though difficult at first, practice will help you better understand yourself and prepare you for the next steps. Start with the following exercise.

Exercise 1: Who Am I?

Introduce yourself to a stranger. Note what you say.

After the introduction, list words used to describe yourself. For example, did you use your name, job title or relationship status?
Review the list carefully. What do you notice?

Next, write an introduction without making reference to the following:

Name

Occupation

Gender

Nationality

Health

Personal appearance

List the differences between your initial introduction and the written introduction.

Most introductions start with something like, "I'm Victor Jakes, Account Representative for ABC Inc." Using the steps above, Sally might redefine herself by saying, "I'm adventurous, spending all my spare time sky and deep sea diving, bungee jumping, and parasailing on the Great Lakes."

The differences will uncover the true you. Remember, use your imagination without limitation. Capture the inner passions that will clearly define who you are while laying the foundation for your personal vision statement.

The exercise above can also be used for business leaders crafting a mission statement for an organization. For step one, include information about the company and the products and services you offer. In step four, describe your company without reference to your products, services, or other identifying characteristics. Once complete, you will be better positioned to start drafting your corporate mission statement.

Core Values

Another crucial element to creating a personal vision statement includes identifying core values. Often referred to as building blocks, core values are the fundamental beliefs of a person or an organization. The guiding principles dictating behavior and/or actions, core values are as unique to each individual as a thumbprint and help to differentiate between right and wrong, good and bad.

Often individuals and companies struggle without understanding why. Typically, core values are at the heart of the problem. Since core values determine our way of life, without them people generally feel lost and conflicted. Core values may change as we grow and enter different stages of life so examine them often so you can reprioritize and adjust along the way.

Like learning to define who you are, identifying core values may seem complicated. The following exercise will help simplify the process and move you one step closer to writing your personal vision statement. Give yourself a minimum of 20 uninterrupted minutes to complete the assignment.

Exercise 2: What Matters Today?

Write at the top of a blank piece of paper, 'What Matters Today?'

List everything that comes to mind without making any judgments about your responses. Take a look at Table 1 for some ideas to help you get started.

Ask yourself the following question for each of the items on your list:

"What does [insert item] mean to me?"

For example, if time made the list of things important to you today ask yourself, "What does time mean to me?" Does time mean flexibility? Order? Peace? The answer will uncover your underlying core values. In this case, flexibility, orderliness and peace.

Look for patterns as you dissect each of the items on your list.

Narrow your original list to the ten items you value most, arranging them in order from the most important to the least.

On a blank piece of paper, list your top three values in order. Write a statement defining what success looks like for each value. For example, if happiness made the top three then ask yourself, "At the end of my life, how will I know I've been happy?"

Once core values are identified, you are ready to take the next step in preparing your vision statement.

Extended List of Values

If you are still struggling to understand what some of your values may or may not be, the following is a non-inclusive list they may help you get started.

Abundance • Confidence • Excellence • Acceptance • Contentment • Faith • Achievement • Courage • Family • Adventure • Creativity • Fame • Aesthetics • Daring • Flexibility • Appreciation • Dedication • Forgiveness • Authenticity • Detachment • Freedom • Balance • Determination • Friendship • Beauty • Devotion • Fun • Bliss • Diligence • Generosity • Caring • Discipline •Good will • Career • Discernment • Grace • Cheerfulness • Discrimination • Gratitude • Clarity • Empathy • Growth • Commitment • Empowerment • Happiness • Compassion •Energy • Harmlessness • Co-operation • Enthusiasm • Harmony • Healing • Loyalty • Sharing • Health • Maturity • Silence • Honesty • Money • Spirituality • Hope • Openness • Spontaneity • Humility • Order •Strength • Inclusiveness • Passion • Status • Insight •Patience • Support • Integrity • Peace • Surrender •Influence • Positive • Success • Intelligence • Power •Tolerance • Intimacy • Prosperity • Trust • Introspection • Purity • Trustworthiness • Intellectual growth • Purpose •Truth • Intuition • Recognition • Understanding • Joy • Relationships • Union • Justice • Respect • Unity •Kindness • Reverence • Wisdom • Knowledge • Sacrifice •Winning • Leadership • Security • Wealth • Learning • Serenity • Love • Service

Read through the list, and select 20 values that naturally appeal to you (not needs, should, role based duties, etc.).

Review the list and narrow to your top 5 values. In doing so ask yourself these questions:

If you NEED it is be happy, it's a need, not a value

If you are doing it in order to get something else, it is not a value

If you want it, but it doesn't come easily, it is probably a "should"

If you did it when you were eight year old, it is probably a value

If it is really exciting and you're afraid of it, it may be a value

This should help determine what you TRUE VALUES are!

Integrity

In the building trade, integrity refers to the integration of the bricks, mortar, foundation, plumbing, interlocking pieces, and strength of materials. When built and assembled properly, the building has integrity and does not require propping.

Integrity in people refers to the design of our personal life system whether it works easily and effortlessly or with great struggle. Without integrity, we spend much of our time propping ourselves up, which is costly, exhausting and distracting.

To be our best, we must be whole: responsible for our actions and inactions, responding fully to the lessons being offered to us, honoring our bodies and ourselves, and respecting the realities of the physical universe.

Integrity is a measure of personal wholeness, describing how well your actions align with your core values and represent your purpose. You define your level of integrity by vigilantly developing the fit between calling and conduct.

Integrity is dynamic. Integrity is not a state you try to achieve but a reflection of who you are in any moment, and the dynamic relationship you maintain between purpose and path. As you progress through these lessons to build a stronger personal foundation, you will also find your integrity increasing. Your wholeness is based on a strong personal foundation made up of many parts working in harmony.

"Self" work and "integrity" work. "Self" works involves increasing awareness of how you interact with yourself, others and circumstance – mostly on an external basis. The objective is to see yourself reflected in many multifaceted ways and dimensions in order to increase your "self" knowledge and awareness and to strengthen your relationship with yourself. The "integrity" work of personal foundation begins to look at the alignment between who you are and the behavior you engage in. Integrity work allows you to make the shift from operating from an automatic pilot, reactive state of decision making to a well thought out and well explored plan, based on what really creates your uniqueness in the world and serves you the best.

Personal levels of integrity. Everyone has a unique degree of integrity required to be who he or she is intended to be. We are all at different points along the path of development. There are distinct integrity requirements at each point that permit us to grow to the next one. And until we are living in the integrity required to be at any given place on that path, we will not grow to the next place. We begin to see that all of life gets easier as we move along, and the integrity levels will naturally increase.

The Integrity Equation. Integrity is the result of having the following conditions in life:
No unresolved matters
Alignment
Responsibility
Each of these are discussed in various lessons, but you should be aware of them now. Briefly you are in integrity when:

You are clear of the past and in the present. That is,

you have corrected any wrongs, fully communicated any censorships, holding back or disturbances with another, made personal changes to make sure life works well and fully handled every task and job.

Your life is aligned and balanced. That is, your goals are aligned with your core values, your actions are based on what is true, not a fantasy or delusion, and your commitments are aligned with your vision or purpose. Your life is aligned with something bigger than your ego.

You are responsible for all that occurs in your life. This does not mean responsible as in to be blamed for having caused the problems – rather, responsible as in handling whatever occurs and then making necessary adjustments so this type of problem does not occur again. Being responsible does not mean complaining; it means handling and resolving.

Follow these 10 steps to restore integrity and wholeness:

Make a list of 10 ways you are currently not in integrity.

Get to the source of each and every item; resolve all fully.

Make a commitment to start living in integrity, as you see it.

Let go of at least 10 "should, coulds, woulds, oughts, wills."

Involve a coach or other strong, able person to help you.

Start getting 50 percent more reserve than you feel you need.

Utilize additional resources.

Stop associating with people who are poor role models.

Eliminate adrenaline and other unhealthy "rushes" in your life. 10. Let go of everything you know is not good for you.

Crafting Your Vision & Values

Now you will begin organizing what thus far have been abstract thoughts, the results of using your imagination without limitation.

Developing a Vision

When developing a vision statement, focus on the future in a positive and inspirational way while keeping the statement simple and easy to remember.

For a personal vision statement, reflect on strengths

and talents when asking yourself the following questions:

Why am I special?

What makes me happy?

What do I love about me?

What am I best at?

Where do I excel?

For a corporate mission statement, ask your team the questions above and include the following:

Why do we exist?

What is our purpose?

Vision and mission statements set the framework for future planning and goal setting by describing the future in present and powerful terms. Whether for yourself or your company, the statement should be...

...written in present tense. ...positive.

...aligned with your core values. ...specific and include action.

Defining and Understanding Wants

People are eager to talk about what they want... more money, more time, more flexibility. Developing your vision statement includes identifying what you want and, just as importantly, discovering what you don't want from life.

When writing your statement, consider the following to help you define exactly what you want.

What do I want more of in my life?

What do I want less of in my life?

If money were no object, what would my career look like?

What relationships do I need to nurture? Let go of?

What is my relationship to money?

The dream I never mention because it's too big to think about is...

What are my fears?

What must occur during my lifetime to call my existence well lived with few or no regrets?

What would bring more joy into my life?

What am I grateful for?

As you reflect on answers to the above, review your core values. Are the things you want in alignment with the values originally chosen?

Make Your Vision a Reality

Ensure your vision statement represents you. If you discover that what you want fails to align with your original core values, start over. What you want must be fully aligned with your core values in order to live in harmony with your vision statement.

After refining your statement, follow the suggestions below to help make your vision a reality.

Measurements Define and development measurements for success. Visions typically include ambitious ideas so organizing your thoughts will help to manage the tasks at hand. Break your vision into bite sized goals and celebrate each triumph leading you towards achievement of the bigger vision. Like the old saying goes, "How do you eat an elephant? One bite at a time!"

Accountability

Find someone you trust to serve as an accountability partner. A partner will be honest and unbiased when questioning the systems developed to measure success. Together, you and your accountability partner will identify potential roadblocks and develop a plan to guide you when challenges arise. Finally, your partner will remind you to celebrate the victories while keeping you mindful of the bigger vision.

Planning

What do bite-sized pieces of your vision look like? In what order does each step need to be complete? Outline an action plan with small steps that must be accomplished in order for the bigger vision to be realized. Plan to celebrate each success along the way.

Rewards

A reward system can keep you on track and give your accountability partner another tool to guide you on your journey. For instance, if health is a core value and your goal is to lose 100 pounds, perhaps you establish a mini reward of a manicure for each 10 pounds you lose. When you reach your entire weight loss goal, then you might reward yourself with a vacation or a spa weekend.

By now, you have an excellent start on your vision statement and a clearer understanding of what you want. What's next?

Clarifying the Vision

To ensure your vision aligns with your core values and beliefs, test the statement again using the exercise below. Creating a plan and setting goals only to discover later that you were not vested in the original vision can be discouraging. Avoid the pitfall and test your vision again. This is often referred to as gap analysis.

Exercise 3: WIIFM (What's in it for Me?)

Ask yourself why you want the vision. What's in it for you?

-- If your vision includes a statement about being healthy and fit, ask yourself what that does for you. Perhaps you answer 'A better quality of life.'
Write 'Why' before each item on your list.

-- Why will I have a better quality of life? Because I will have more energy and physically feel better.
Review your answers to verify the vision created is one you can live with. The reassessment will also help you better understand why the vision is important and identify areas where changes can be made to guarantee your vision is in alignment with your core values.

Once you have completed this process you are able to make the necessary adjustments to your vision statement and you are ready to begin getting organized.

Limiting Beliefs

Limiting beliefs refer to negative thoughts and stories individuals tell themselves that ultimately discourage achievement of one's goal. Essentially an opinion (yours or someone else's), limiting beliefs often prevent people from taking crucial steps forward. The good news? With a little work, limiting beliefs are reversible!

Limiting beliefs are frequently excuses in disguise. "I can't lose weight because I never have time to work out and health food is just too expensive." Riddled with limiting beliefs, what can this person do to achieve her weight loss goal?

Rearrange schedule, making exercise a priority

Reexamine budget, eliminating unnecessary expenses

Reconsider lifestyle, adopting new habits to support weight loss

The example above demonstrates how limiting behaviors can prevent individuals from making necessary behavioral changes, changes essential to the achievement of one's goal.

Limiting beliefs can also cap one's achievement. "Without a degree, I probably won't make more than my current income." A common assumption, consider how the above statement limits individuals. How does one overcome this limiting belief?

Consider higher education, trade school and other educational courses

Apply for a promotion

Work for a different company offering higher wages

Start a business

Explore additional revenue streams

Limiting beliefs are sneaky. Like the examples above, they often include negative self-talk peppered with excuses. Limiting beliefs can also be disguised as fear, perfectionist thinking, beliefs conditioned from one's culture and justifications.

If limiting beliefs are hindering your success, or if you are unsure how to identify your limiting beliefs begin by asking yourself the following questions:

What rules do I live by that limit my ability?

Example: To be successful, I need to stay with a company until retirement.
What recurring negative thoughts prevent me from pursuing my dream?
Example: I don't have the money necessary to start my

own company.

What unnecessary assumptions do I make about committing to this goal?

Example: I'll never secure the needed financing for start-up costs.

What clichés, quotes, aphorisms or other catchy phrases limit me?

Examples: No one's perfect. Better luck next time. If life gives you lemons…

What stereotypical beliefs or cultural myths am I allowing to hold me back?

Example: I don't have the right [education, appearance, background] to successfully do the job.

How do standards about "what" and "how" things should happen limit my abilities?

Example: Is there only one correct way of doing things?

What values might interfere with achievement of my goals?
Example: Do I value something that contradicts what I need to move toward?

What self defeating behaviors do I engage in? Examples:

Eating fast food after committing to a healthy lifestyle. Submitting to your child's demands after saying no.

What reoccurring stories, narratives, or mental scripts do I play over and over again in my head that disempower me?
Example: I'll never be able to do that because...

What philosophies keep me frozen in a passive way?

Example: Mistakes equate to failure.

If a pattern of limiting beliefs starts to emerge, isolate one you feel most encumbers your success. Let's examine the belief further using the exercise below.

Exercise: Dissection of a Limiting Belief

Identify one limiting belief.

Choose a belief impacting your ability to take action, one intruding on your personal and professional growth. Example: I don't have enough money. Why do you have this belief?

What contributes to the seeming deficiency in financial resources? Examples: I don't make enough money, I have too much debt.

What evidence undermines the limiting belief?

You may feel destitute however, the belief may simply not be true. Examples: You have basic needs met (food, shelter, clothing).

In what ways are you not fully alive and engaged in life?

How does your limiting belief restrict you from enjoying life? Example: I don't have enough money to take a vacation.

How do you feel about these missed opportunities?

Give special attention to the feelings you have knowing what life should be like and the ways your belief has prevented you from experiencing it fully. Write down your feelings.

What would you do with your life if you no longer had this limiting belief?

Imagine the belief disappeared instantly. How would this change your perceptions of what you can do? What goals would you set for yourself?

Is there any current truth to this limiting belief?

What actual circumstances support your limiting belief? Example: I didn't go away for vacation this year because I'm broke.

What can you change about the circumstances listed in your previous answer?

Many limiting beliefs are disguised as excuses. Once corrected, circumstances are less limited than we thought. Example: Are you broke or will a few minor changes in your budget allow you to travel (eat out less, open a vacation savings account, break an expensive habit)? Are there alternatives to a luxury vacation that would offer rest and relaxation at little or no cost (camping, hiking, visiting friends and family)?

What outcome do you fear most tied to this limiting belief?

What is the worst thing that could happen if you take no action? Example: I worry about suffering from stress and depression.

What you do you think the odds are of the worst things happening?

Release the limiting belief and take action. How comfortable are you with the ambiguity of feeling fear and uncertainty but taking action anyway?

All change involves risk, even when one calculates every possible outcome. You must take risks in order to grow and create a better life. Become comfortable with the presence of ambiguity and uncertainty.

How does the limiting belief impact your relationships?

Often we compromise our relationships when we remain stuck in a false belief. Can you see how any of your close relationships have been impacted? Example: Time that could be spent bonding with family is being spent in frustration.

Write your limiting belief on a small piece of paper and seal in an envelope.

Put the belief "on hold" for a week. Assign the belief a number between 1 and 10, with 10 being extremely limiting and 1 being not very limiting based on how you feel today.

Of all the things you've wanted to achieve but avoided due to your limiting belief, which one stands out as the first you'd like to work toward?

What are 3–5 small, manageable actions you can take towards the goal identified above while your limiting belief is sealed away?

Acting as if you have no limiting belief, create a few actions you will commit to take towards the achievement of your goal and write them on a calendar.

Once the barriers to positive thinking are identified, you will start creating a new belief system to replace your previous limited thinking. The biggest challenge will be to catch yourself engaging in negative self-talk or self-defeating behaviors and changing how you communicate with yourself. Create new mental scripts promoting a positive perspective:

Mistakes are the stepping stones to mastery.

Choice will determine my success.

I am alive, everything is possible.

Now that you have isolated a limiting belief and sealed the negativity in an envelope, use this time of freedom from the belief to take action. Commit to the actions outlined with actual deadlines, repeating the new positive mental scripts created for yourself.

Finally, remember to share your beliefs (old and new!) with an accountability partner to help you maintain focus as you shift from limiting thoughts and behaviors to unlimited possibilities.

Getting Organized

We know certain tasks must be accomplished in order

to reach our goals however, disorganization can waste countless hours. Wasted time hinders progress and creates doubt regarding the mission. To avoid this, try the following:

Create a list of things to do in support of your vision statement. The list should include short and long term goals. Research suggests a daily task list in support of a larger goal (or vision) can be highly motivating.

Establish a designated work area, free of clutter and distractions.

Use the POSEC Method:

Prioritize your time and define your life by goals.
Organize the things you have to accomplish regularly to be successful.

Streamline the things you may not like to do, but must do.
Economize the things you should do or may even like to do but that are not pressingly urgent. Contribute by paying attention to the few remaining things that make a difference.

Plan what you do and do what you plan. To stay organized, follow through with your entire plan throughout the day and set boundaries for distractions you can plan on (i.e. cell phone, email, children/family, etc.).

Goals

Break your vision into bite-sized pieces by setting smaller goals along the way and diligently work towards achieving the bigger picture. Goals should always be SMART.

Specific – Objectives should address the five W's…who, what, where, when, why. Use action words such as create, design, establish, implement, produce, etc.

Measurable – Goals should be quantifiably defined in such a way as to gauge progress, giving a clear indication of when the goal has been successfully met.

Achievable – Challenging and rewarding yet still within reach.

Relevant – Goals should be instrumental to your personal mission and align with your core values.

Time-based – Identify a definitive target date for completion.

Following the outline for SMART goals above will greatly increase your likelihood for success.

Additionally, before you set a goal, there are some key steps and considerations you should consider.

Make sure the goal you are working for is something you really want, not just something that sounds good.

Does your goal contradict any of your other goals?

Write your goal in the positive instead of the negative. For example the goal should not be "Stop being fat" but instead "Lost 20 pounds in 90 days"

Daily Habits

Another simple way to accomplish your goals involves creating new habits. Habits are defined as a regular tendency or practice and often occur with little or no thought. For example, when you wake up in the morning you may take a shower, brush your teeth, dress and eat breakfast.

If you are working on goals that require new habits, using a chart similar to the one below can be helpful. Perhaps you want to include flossing as a regular part of your morning routine. List 'FLOSS' at the top of the chart and track your progress throughout the week.

Print weekly and display someplace you are certain to see the chart, like a bathroom. The constant visual reminder will help you stay focused on developing your new habits When items on your list become routine, change your chart to include new habits you want to develop.

TIPS:

Choose habits you want to do. There is no place for "should" or "could" in your daily habits. Instead, select habits that you look forward to and give you pleasure.

Choose habits that give you energy. Most of the daily habits that actually work for people are the ones that add to the person's well-being or energy flow. It might mean that you do something like having 5 or more vegetables each day, or that you stop something such as watching television. A ratio of 2:1 of doing and stopping works well.

Modify your habits as needed. If you find yourself not doing one or two of your habits, change or replace them with ones that come naturally.

Use visual help.

Public Commitments

Another method used successfully in goal setting involves making a public commitment. Written goals shared with a friend increases the chance of successfully achieving a goal than those who simply made a commitment to themselves. An accountability partner can help you reach goals while providing an opportunity to be far more successful than you might have been individually.

Positive Mental Attitude/Letting Go of Fear

To accomplish a goal, you must let go of fear. Start by staying positive about your goals. Focus on the benefits and achievements your goals will bring. When you start to feel anxious, remember...this is normal. Most fears are related to change. The resulting change your goals bring will have a positive impact on your life. Avoid "dream stealers", individuals seeing the positive changes in your life yet insist "it is never going to work."

If you are still struggling to maintain a positive attitude try these steps:

Live for yourself.

Understand that even if you can't control outside circumstances, you can control your reaction to them.
Leave your work at the office, at least mentally.

Slow down.

Learn something new every day.

Make a list of the positive aspects in your life.

Help others.

Show gratitude.

In today's society fear is common. Fear of terrorism, fear over financial problems, fear is a dominating figure in most of our lives. Although fear can help us make necessary preparations, fear can also become quite debilitating. Fear can lead to physical and emotional challenges; fear stops us from living our lives fully. What can you do?

Turn off the news/television. Although it is important to be informed the news media's job is to bring about an emotional response to every story. Your senses are being bombarded with visual and auditory stimuli meant to evoke fear. A less intense way of staying informed is reading the newspaper or by getting your news online. If you do choose to watch the news send a prayer to those who are suffering.

Meditate or Pray. Meditation quiets the mind, body and spirit. A simple what to being is to find a quiet spot where you won't be disturbed. Lie down or sit in a chair.

Close your eyes. Take a deep breath in through your nose and feel the breath travel down into your belly.

Hold the breath for several seconds and exhale through your mouth. Repeat three times.

Then begin counting backwards from 10 to 1.

After you are in this relaxed state, imagine yourself blowing up a balloon, placing all your fears in the balloon, and then releases your fear filled balloon to the universe.

Once you have released your fear, visualize the highest outcome for any situation you are fearful of.

Spend time outside. Nature has a wonderfully calming effect on the body, mind and spirit. Take time when you are fearful to visit the beach, a forest or the mountains. Watch the sunrise, the sunset, or simply take a peaceful walk through the park.

Listen to music. Turn on your favorite music, or a favorite song. Crank it up and sing along.

Read. When you are experiencing fearful thoughts find inspiration in books of poetry, personal growth, motivation or whatever inspires you.
Seek positive people. Avoid "dream stealers" and seek out people who inspire you to be better whether at a place of worship, bookstores, community centers, social groups, wherever you can find them.

Seek help. If you are still experiencing fear, or the inability to let go of fear, seek professional help. Spiritual counselors, life coaches and psychologists can empower you with tools to help you let go of your fear.

Savor every moment. Life is perfect right now, right at this moment. Perhaps this is the most important element in eliminating fear. None of us knows our fate . What we do know are the gifts that are present in our lives at this moment. Every day make time to find the perfection in your life.

The power of our thoughts, intentions, and actions can greatly affect the outcome of our lives. By implementing some of these strategies you can learn to let go of fear and being to live your life fully.

BUILDING GOALS

Chapter 3

What does it take to succeed on a big scale? A tremendous god-given talent? Inherited wealth? A decade of post-graduate education? Connections with the top people in your field? Fortunately for most of us, what it takes is something very simple and accessible: clear, written goals. A study of Harvard graduates found that after 20 years, the three percent of those who had written goals achieved more financially than the other 97% combined! "An average person with average talent, ambition and education, can outstrip the most brilliant genius in our society, if that person has clear, focused goals."

At whatever point you need to accomplish something, keep your eyes open, focus and ensure you know precisely what it is you need. Nobody can hit their objective with their eyes shut.

Setting your own goals is an investment in yourself and your future. You owe it to your FUTURE self to be thinking NOW about what you want him or her to be doing in 5, 10, 20 years' time. Will your future self thank you for investing time now in order to secure a better future? You bet (s)he will!

The first thing that you must commit to doing at the very outset is to set aside time to work on your goals – they won't just happen by themselves. The stages I'm setting out for you here are ones that I've followed myself, that I've coached other people to use and that work...if you invest the time to actually DO them, and do them consistently.

Setting aside some time may take a certain amount of self-discipline, but it shouldn't be a chore – you shouldn't look forward to it with dread – after all, these are YOUR goals we're talking about. It should be fun, because you'll be working on things that YOU actually want to do, for your own future. Besides, think of the return on investment of that time spent NOW that your future self will reap.

Spend time thinking

Part of the time invested in your goals will be spent thinking about what it is that you want to achieve. What EXACTLY it is that you want to achieve. Knowing 'roughly' what you want might not be enough. Knowing what other people expect you to want is definitely not enough.

DO something

You'll spend quite a lot of time thinking, especially at the beginning while you're working out your goals. It's critical, though, that your goal setting doesn't stop there!

This might seem a statement of the obvious, but it's vital that you DO something to achieve your goal.

Be prepared to put in a bit of spadework, put your plan into action, and take action to move towards accomplishing your goals.

Otherwise that dream is going to remain a daydream.

A crucial starting point

Before you even begin to think about your goals, you must recognise and accept the fact that you have the right to shape your future. You just do. In my mind, there is no question about it whatsoever, and there must be no doubt in your mind either.

I'm guessing (it's certainly true for me) that throughout your life, other people will have made decisions for you. To start with, it will have been your parents or guardians. Obviously, this is entirely appropriate in childhood...however, many people allow childhood patterns to follow them into adult life and find that, without realising it, they are allowing other people, circumstances and outside factors to decide on big parts of their lives for them.

I was talking to someone recently who told a rather sorry story about his career (which, incidentally, is a very worthwhile one – he's a teacher). He began by saying that he has always enjoyed maths and science at school, and decided that she would like to be a doctor. He went on "but they told me I wasn't clever enough to do that, so I thought I'd focus on the maths side and be an accountant. But they said I'd have to go all the way to X University to study for that and it would take years to qualify, so I settled on becoming a teacher instead".

It's a shame that these people, even though they meant well, advised this man not to follow his goals and encouraged him to aspire to something else. It's even more of a shame that he allowed them to do so.

So who are YOUR goal stealers? Who might – even with the best of intentions – be making your goal choices for you? Think carefully.

Your teachers might have been encouraging or inspiring...or might have crushed your hope altogether and told you that you'd never make it as a doctor, actress, astronaut, vet...whatever you were aspiring to at the time. One has to wonder sometimes whose interests they have at heart when they advise in this way.

Your parents and your wider family might, while

meaning well, be pushing you in certain directions, and showing their approval or disapproval of your life and career choices.

A friend of mine is an artist and art teacher. He commented recently that most parents are keen for their children to experience and take part in as many activities as possible...until they reach a certain point at secondary school when their focus turns towards future jobs. From there onwards, there's a tendency for parents to push their children towards certain subjects (usually science and maths, etc.) and away from others (usually arts and creative subjects), purely on the basis of their beliefs as to how job-worthy these subjects are.

I'm advising my children to find something they love, and do THAT. If that turns out to be creative writing or art rather than accounting or business studies, so be it. If they find something that they love and set their goals accordingly, they will find their niche and they'll always be able to make a business out of it. Either which way, they will choose their own goals.

Your friends and peers might be subtly pulling you towards certain life choices. Are there things that 'people like us' do/don't do? Are there things that you enjoy that you wouldn't necessarily share with your friends and peers because they might show their disapproval, or throw you out of their clique?

In the workplace, you might be tacitly waiting for your boss, colleagues or the organisation in general to give you permission to move on up the company hierarchy, to change careers or to make a move.

It's NOT up to your teachers, your family, your peers, your boss, your company or anyone else. Your goals are up to YOU!

As a fundamental starting point on your journey towards your goal, please understand this:

GOAL MINDSET #1

YOU DO NOT NEED ANYONE ELSE'S PERMISSION TO CHOOSE YOUR OWN GOAL YOU DO NOT NEED ANYONE ELSE'S PERMISSION TO SUCCEED

IT REALLY IS UP TO YOU...AND ONLY YOU

If you've accepted this and made the decision to choose your own goals, then it's time to start building the path that will take you there.

Establishing Your Goal

Working out what you want to achieve and focusing on your goals is fun. Unfortunately, it's where most people start and finish when it comes to goal setting, in a 'wouldn't it be great if I could...oh, well, back to reality' sort of way.

We're going to start with a blank piece of paper (literally – so get your notebook ready) and think of your overall goal first of all, before breaking it down into its component parts.

Both at this early stage of the goal setting process and as we move through the book, we'll be following a principle (and what will become a recurring theme) of 'define the goal, break it down' before moving on to devise a plan of action that will take you closer to your goal...and then put that plan into action.

By the end of this chapter, you'll have a much clearer idea of your goal AND the key factors that contribute to it. You'll also have a much better understanding of WHY these are your goals, and this will become important later on when you start to make your plans and put them into action.

Choose your goal

I'm sure that you'll have heard a lot of clichés when it comes to goal setting: Think big. Aim high. The world's your oyster.

These are all absolutely true...up to a point.

At this stage, use your imagination and don't put limits on yourself. This might SOUND unrealistic, but at this point in the process it's imperative. Don't worry – we'll be focusing on the practical aspects of putting your goal into action in later. For the moment, it's important that you use your imagination and let your creative brain come to the fore.

For those of you with a more practical or logical mindset, this might prove more of a challenge. You might find that no sooner have you begun thinking about your goal that you're thinking, "I can't do that because..." or, "that means I'll have to..." STOP! At this early stage, you will need to consciously put your 'editor' or 'practical' brain to one side. We'll need it later, but not now.

A small caveat here: Challenge yourself to 'think big'...if that's what you want.

GOAL MINDSET # 2

THINK ABOUT WHAT YOU WANT, AND NOT ABOUT WHAT OTHER PEOPLE EXPECT YOU TO WANT

I cannot stress enough how critical this point is, and it links back to some of the goal stealers and goal influencers that I mentioned in the introduction.

So many people who have focused their energies – in some cases their entire working lives – on other people's expectations, and have turned round one day and realised that they've denied themselves opportunities which now, in retrospect, they wish they'd taken.

Please don't let this be you.

It's actually very easy to get swept along by other people's aspirations and expectations of you. We're constantly being fed images and ideals of the sort of lifestyle that we're supposed to aspire to by the media: a large house in the countryside with a sweeping drive up to the front door: a fancy executive car, and perhaps a sporty little number to sit alongside in that driveway: exotic holidays with smartly dressed hotel staff at your beck and call...

For me, much of the above represents a complete nightmare.

If what you'd rather work towards is a cottage in the countryside, a retro Volkswagen, and camping holidays in the great outdoors of the Highlands...then focus on that.

It really is YOUR choice. After all, YOU are the one who's going to live it...or live without it.
Start with the 'big picture'

While running a workshop for teenagers, I was encouraging them to set some life goals. In their case, it was a question of saying "imagine that you're 35" – to them, this represented a great age.

Predictably, the boys all said that they would be premier league footballers married to supermodels. The girls demonstrated a more mature response, and described the type of house they'd like to be living in, the family and career they'd like to have, the community they'd like to be part of and so on.

Here's where you and they are the same: the choices that you make in ten years' time will be governed by the choices that you make today.

GOAL MINDSET #3

START WITH AN OVERALL PICTURE OF YOUR GOAL
AND THE POSITIVE IMPACT IT WILL HAVE

Your goal can be absolutely anything you like, from a life or career goal, to a specific project at work, to a personal challenge. As I've already said, start with the 'what' at this stage. We'll focus on the 'how' later on: at this stage, gaining absolute clarity on what you want to achieve is essential.

Imagine you're booking the holiday of a lifetime. You'd make pretty sure you knew exactly where you were going and what it was going to be like, wouldn't you? You'd browse the internet, read reviews of the location, investigate some of the sights that you wanted to see, plan a few excursions and activities... you'd figure out what you'd need to take with you – some things you'd already have, others you might need to go out and buy especially. You'd pick who you were going with – friends or family, and so on.

You'd not spend large sums of money just knowing ROUGHLY where you were going. You'd not risk spending your valuable fortnight's holiday in some dive that looked OK online, so you didn't really check it out...and you forget to bring mosquito repellent...all with a bunch of people you don't care about, would you?

How much more important are your goals? Make sure that you invest time NOW to focus on exactly where you're going.

Goal...or fantasy??

Whilst it's important to daydream and allow your imagination a pretty free rein at this stage of the goal setting process, it's important that you're not setting your sights on something that doesn't actually exist.

GOAL MINDSET #4

MAKE SURE YOU'RE FOCUSED ON A GOAL AND NOT A FANTASY

Here's the thing: when you focus on a goal, make sure it really is a goal, and not just a pipe dream, and that it's based on the reality of achieving that goal. For example, imagine someone is intent on becoming lawyer and, having watched various dramas on TV, they picture themselves freeing innocent people wrongly convicted, arguing their case in front of an enthralled courtroom, and earning a fortune and the respect of their peers.

Is this an accurate picture of the life of a lawyer? Probably not. There will be lost cases. There will be times where you're defending people you're pretty certain ARE guilty; there will be times when you work long hours to complete a case in time.

Do some research if you need to, and make sure that the goal you're focused on is the real deal, and not just some sugar-coated media construct, or something you've read in a novel.

Useful techniques for defining your goal

The 'Forward Focus' Approach

This approach simply involves focusing on and thinking carefully about your goal, as it is, in the future. Again, and just to state clearly this important point, focus your attention on WHAT you want to achieve at this stage. The how will come later.

Ask yourself the following questions (and challenge yourself to be really thorough in your response):

What is it that you want to achieve?

Be as specific as you can. What is the thing? Make sure that it's a specific GOAL and not an aspiration.

I was delivering a 'Life Choices' to some young people once, and one of the participants said that his goal was "To make a difference in the lives of young people".

Of course, this was an admirable sentiment and one that came from the heart. However, it wasn't a specific enough goal. He needed to add a sentence or two to say, for example, "...by travelling to the developing world and carrying out voluntary work for a children's charity", or, "...by sharing the expertise I've gathered during my career with youngsters at school who are just starting out in life", or, "...by being a football coach on a local programme set up for local kids with nothing else to do in the evening"...or whatever.

In short, he needed to be MUCH more specific about what that goal would actually involve, and what he would be DOING.

What EXACTLY is it?

Really challenge yourself on this one. It might take a day or so to flesh out your initial idea, but make sure you do. To put it bluntly, the clearer you are on exactly what you want to achieve, the more likely you are to get there.

What will your LIFE actually look like when you've achieved your goal?

Consider what it will be like when you've achieved your goal. What will success look like? Where will you live? What will you eat? What will you wear? How do these differ from what's going on now?

How will you feel when you've achieved it?

What will it actually mean to you to complete this goal...and conversely, how will you feel if you DON'T achieve it?

How will others respond to you once you've achieved it?

How might others react when you achieve your goal? How important is this to you? Many people will say, "Oh, I don't care what other people think of me". This is rarely true. Most people DO care about the opinions of people who they love and value.

Think about how they might respond when you are successful...don't think about whether or not they'd approve of your goal – remember, it's not up to them.

Which parts of this goal are in your control? Which can

you influence? Which are out of your control?

It's important that your goal is something that you can control or at the very least influence. If its completion is totally out of your control...like winning the lottery, for example...then you really need to choose something else!

Make a note, though, of which factors you can actually control, which can you influence, and which factors might you have to leave to chance. The more you can control and influence – even indirectly – the better.

WHY is this your goal?

Understanding the reason and motivation behind your goal is an important factor. There will be times as you work towards your goal when you'll wonder whether it's worth the effort...and at times like those, it's useful to remind yourself WHY you're aiming for your goal.

In some instances, your 'why' might be a positive motivator: to make a better life for your children, for example. In others, it might be negative: "My headmaster always told me I'd amount to nothing...I'll show HIM!!"

Either is valid. Just make sure that your reason why is geared towards the achievement of success and not the avoidance of failure: you're thinking about 'having a prosperous lifestyle' and not about 'I don't want to be poor'. We'll look at this a little further on when we consider how knowing what you don't want can help clarify what you do want.

Understanding your 'why' is useful if for some reason you need to change direction, and cannot complete your original goal.

I've mentioned before that when I was younger, I wanted to be an actor. When I look back and consider WHY this was, I realised that there were two very important underlying reasons :

I didn't actually want the uncertainty of an actor's life – what I actually wanted, and my reason why, was to work in a creative environment, with creative people. I also wanted an audience – I find it easier in many ways to relate to and communicate with groups of people than on a one-to-one basis, unless I know them well

Whilst I'm quite active in amateur dramatics, just for fun, these two factors – working creatively and working with groups – have become a key feature of my life in learning and development.

I don't regret not being a professional actor, because I've fulfilled the underlying reasons 'why' in other things.

So think carefully about your goal...why is it exactly that you want to pursue THAT goal in particular? What is it about that goal that draws you?

Challenge yourself to write down ten reasons WHY this is your goal.

The 'Already There' Approach

Whilst covering the same ground as the 'Forward Focus' approach, this method takes a slightly different starting point.

It relies on your ability to visualise, so set aside some time to really think about your goals, and what achieving them will mean to you.

Start by thinking about your whole goal AS THOUGH YOU HAD ALREADY COMPLETED IT. REALLY think about it. And write your answers in the present tense.

What exactly have you achieved?

Writing in the present tense, tell yourself what you've achieved.

This might feel a little bit uncomfortable, but no more so than writing your CV, and reading it back to yourself and thinking "Hey – is that really ME?! I sound quite good!!" (I'm sure I can't be the only person who's done that!).

What have you overcome to get there?

Think more deeply about the answer you've given. Here you should go into more detail about what you've achieved, the obstacles and challenges that you've overcome in order to reach your goal.

Usually these are personal challenges, for example, "I've overcome my fear of public speaking, and am now often called upon to speak..." and so on.

What else have you done in order to get here?

In your imagined future, what else have you managed to do in order to achieve your goal? Successfully persuaded venture capitalists to invest in your business idea? Gone back to varsity and taken exams that will set you on a fresh career path? Moved to Cape Town to open a beach bed and breakfast??

How does it feel to achieve your goal?
How do you feel about yourself? About other people? How do you respond differently to challenges and difficult people now?

What does your ideal day/week look like/feel like?

Describe your lifestyle – what do you do in a usual week/day? Bear in mind what I've already said about a goal versus a fantasy: make sure you're looking at what it will REALLY be like.

What do you think about...not think about?

If, for example, you've been working towards health goals, you might spend more time thinking about which mountain you'll climb next, and less worrying about your cholesterol level.

What do you do/not do?

Again, what do you no longer do? Perhaps you wander into the garden with your laptop, rather than facing a two-hour commute through rush hour traffic to an office.

Who have you become in order to get here?

This can be a tricky question to answer: moving towards a new goal is going to mean making some changes to yourself. (If you didn't have to do that, you'd already be there, right?!)

Think carefully, in your imagined future state, about how you've changed. Have you become more self-disciplined? More tolerant of others? More open to new ideas? More willing to take risks? What??

So, how do you feel about the prospect of achieving your goals? Excited? Optimistic? It's important that you have some sort of emotional attachment to your goal. As you face challenges along your way, reminding yourself of the impact that achieving your goal will have on you and those close to you will help to motivate you to continue.

Establishing Your Goal

Thinking deeply about your goal in order to clarify it is all very well...if you actually know what that goal is in the first place.

Sometimes people don't actually KNOW what they want, which can make pinning down a goal more of a challenge.

If you're not sure about what your goals are (especially if these are life and career goals), here are some techniques and approaches that will help you.

GOAL MINDSET #5

BE PREPARED TO REALLY FOCUS ON YOUR GOAL, AND THINK DEEPLY ABOUT IT.

The 'Menu' Approach

Actually, once you've opened yourself up to the idea that you can set goals for just about ANYTHING, the choices open to you can become almost overwhelming.

I remember once staying in a very exclusive hotel, and being told by the reception staff that if I required anything at all, I should just call room service, and they would see to it that I got it. Anything?? Anything at all? I began to wonder what I could ask for: freshly pressed juice from some exotic fruit? A sandwich made with delicacies from the four corners of the globe? Baffled by the possibilities, I began to think about just sticking to my comfort zone of a plain orange juice and a biscuit.

To be honest, having SO much choice was almost TOO much choice. So I looked at the room service menu and picked from the extensive list there.

If you're new to goal setting and don't quite know where to start, here is the menu.

Knowing what you DON'T want

Sometimes it's easier to pinpoint what you DON'T want than what you DO want. Needless to say, this isn't precise enough for proper goal setting! However, it CAN provide a useful starting point. Focus on some of the things you know you don't want. Then think of the positive alternatives for each of these.

Take a piece of paper, or a page in your notebook and draw a line down the middle, from top to bottom. On one side write down some of the things that you know you don't want.

On the other side of the line, challenge yourself to pin down what you DO want instead.

For example:

What I definitely DON'T want:

to be working 16 hour days for a boss/organisation that doesn't appreciate me and can make me redundant at any time

to be stressed out meeting impossible targets set by someone else who has little idea what I actually do

to be working weekends and ignoring my family because I'm running to stand still chasing the next paycheque

Therefore, what I DO want is...

I'm working in an environment where I have a work life balance (I'll need to think about what exactly that means). I leave work at a reasonable time and have time to have a life outside work. AND I'm fit enough to enjoy it and DO something with my time outside work...as opposed to doing more work or collapsing at the end of the day .

I'm challenged at work, but not pushed to perform the impossible.

My boss/clients appreciate what I do and I can make what I feel is a valued contribution to the business. I feel valued, and not just a 'cog in the wheel'.

You get the idea. In the next chapter we'll take this theme further as we look at what would constitute an ideal situation for you, what would be acceptable, unacceptable and so on.

For now, focus on working out the 'big picture' of your goal. If you know some of the things you DON'T want in your future life, challenge yourself to think of some positive alternatives that you DO want.

Tapping into your emotions

Sometimes, the best way to look forward is to look back. If you're unsure about what goal you want to focus on, or perhaps unsure whether it's actually YOUR goal or someone else's expectation, focusing on times in the past when you've felt happy and fulfilled can provide some useful pointers to your future goal.

If you invest the time to think about some past scenarios and situations, you'll start to see patterns emerge; patterns that tell you about your personal values and aspirations.

Spend a little time thinking about the following:

Think about times in your past when you felt really happy and fulfilled. write down as much as you can about each situation, and try to think of at least five situations in detail:

What exactly were you doing?

Think about the details: where were you? What was it about the project or task you were working on that you enjoyed?

Who else was involved?

Were you working alone or with other people? Who did you enjoy working with? What was it about their contribution or the working relationship that you enjoyed?

What were you aiming to achieve at the time?

What were you working towards? Why?

How did you feel when you achieved the goal?

What did it mean to you to accomplish your goal? How did you celebrate your success?

What other circumstances were important at the time?

What else made it the great situation that it was?

Harness negative emotions too

Even negative emotions can be useful in figuring out

your goal: not only do they give you a strong indication of situations that are negative and unacceptable to you, but they also help you to pinpoint your values, which are likely to be an important factor in your overall goal moving forward.

Bear in mind as you focus on some of the less positive aspects of your life and career, that thinking of negative situations in our past is not a pleasant experience – you're likely to experience some of the negative emotions that you felt at the time as you do so.

Consider also, though, that we are taking a logical – not an emotional – approach to goal setting, and that your negative emotions are in this instance working for you in a positive way, highlighting what you don't want in your future, and drawing attention to your values.

Consider the following questions:

Thinking about a situation/situations where you did not feel at your best, ask yourself:
What was going on? What were the circumstances?

What were you doing? How did you react to those circumstances?

What did you do?

Who else was involved?

How exactly did you feel?

WHY did you feel this way?

What specifically made you feel bad?

Once again, you should see certain patterns starting to emerge in response to these questions, and these patterns will help to highlight your values, and conversely, situations that are unacceptable to you.

Again, by way of personal example, I once worked in an organisation with some very dubious management styles. They were referred to as 'strong management techniques'. Given that people were stressed out, wanting to leave, demotivated and depressed, I called it 'bullying'. I was aware that as a manager I had two stark choices: conform to the bullying culture at work...or leave. I left.

I might have been able to build a great career in other respects at that organisation, but I wasn't prepared to conform to the company culture and expected behaviours in order to do so.

I left: at the time it was a difficult choice, but in retrospect it was the best career decision – LIFE decision, even – that I've ever made.

Harnessing your feelings about other people

How you feel about other people and their achievements will also give you some clear indicators as to what YOU actually want.

Consider the following:

Who do you admire because of what they've achieved? Why?

Often, though, it's the reasons why that are most illuminating. Invariably, the person who admires Mandela for his ability to influence people and his persona of authority would like to be able to influence people and appear more authoritative themselves.

Who do you admire...and what does that say about you and your aspirations?

Are there people who others admire for their success, but you don't? Why not?
Conversely, there are people that some admire, but you don't. A successful businessman, perhaps, (naming no names – I don't want to be sued!) who commands vast wealth but is seen to trample on others to achieve success.

Again, what is this telling you about your own aspirations and your values?

Is there someone you feel slightly jealous of, in terms of what they're like, what they have, how they behave, what they've achieved?

Yes – even jealousy can be useful. Have you ever felt envious of someone else's success? Well, instead of feeling a bit guilty that you feel that way, ask yourself what this emotion is telling you.

I remember a year or so ago feeling pangs of envy on hearing that a friend of a friend had had a book published. Why? Because deep down I wanted to have a book published! Having figured that out, here I am, writing a book.

By now, if you've thought about the questions I've posed and invested a little time thinking deeply about your goal, you'll have a better understanding of:

Your overall goal, and what it will mean to you to achieve it

WHY you want to achieve this goal

Refining your goal

Our starting point will be something with which you may well be very familiar – turning your overall goal into a SMART goal.

GOAL MINDSET #6

BREAK YOUR OVERALL GOALS DOWN INTO SMALLER GOALS.

BREAK THESE DOWN INTO EVEN SMALLER GOALS

UNTIL YOU HAVE A DAILY 'TO DO' LIST.

Making your goal SMART

Start by writing your goal down in a sentence or two: stick to the high level overview here.

Let's use, as our working example, Jacob, who expressed the following goal "within the next 3 years I will set up by own business, based on my hobby of crafting and embroidery."

This is a clear goal, with some obvious parameters: it's not like the aspiration that I mentioned, of 'making a difference in the lives of young people' which gives little indication as to what the person with this aim will actually DO.
However, to make that goal more robust, it must be SMART, that is

Specific

Measureable

Attainable and Action orientated

Relevant

Time bound

Jacob can make his goal more specific by considering details of his business:

What exactly will he do? Teach his skills to others? Sell his products...and if so which ones and where – online, offline?

How big does he want this business to be...to take over from her existing job, or to run alongside it?

...and so on.

He can introduce some measurable elements by being clear on, for example:

how much she would like her business to bring in

how many hours a week she's working in her business

what the milestones are that will tell her she's on the right track to meet her specific goal

To be fair, there might be some things which Jacob can't actually measure: maybe he wants 'to be taken seriously as a business, not as someone playing at a hobby'. How do you measure that?! In cases like these, what he could be looking for is positive and negative 'indicators' that will tell him whether or not he's being successful in this area.

Positive indicators might include being invited to speak at a networking event about business, or being featured in a newspaper article about new business start ups.

Negative indicators might include an absence of the above, but also things like a business development agency pointing him in the direction of a craft association for help and advice.

Only Jacob will know if his goal is really attainable – it certainly looks on the face of it as though it is. Goals must be a challenge, but there MUST be a realistic chance of success occurring. His goal is also action orientated – it involves her doing something to make it happen.

Jacob's goal must be relevant to him and to his values. It clearly is.

This point about being 'relevant' becomes all the more...well...relevant when we come to break down your overall goal into sub-goals: each sub-goal should be relevant and contributing to the overall goal. If it's not, it could be a distraction.

Jacob does have a time-bound element to his goal: he wants to be up and running in 3 years. However, he could go into more detail here:

where exactly does he want to be in 3 years time...just launching, or already up and running?

What exactly does he mean by three years? Three years from today, or 'by the end of 2020' or something else?

If he intends to launch in 3 years, what milestones need to be in place between now and then? If he doesn't put these into place and put together some sort of schedule, it might never happen.

Look at the goal you've written down and ask yourself:

Be SPECIFIC

If your goal is still a little vague, now is the time to sharpen it up and clarify what you're aiming for

What exactly do I want to achieve?

What will it look and feel like?

How will I know I've got there?

Which parts of it are measurable?

What aspects of my life will be different to what they are now?

Which parts of it are under my control? Which can I influence? Are there any that I will have to leave to chance?

Make your goal MEASURABLE.

You'll need to know whether or not you're on the right track and making progress as you move forward towards your goal.

Ask yourself:

Again, how will you know when you've succeeded?

What are the milestones along your way that will confirm to you that you're moving in the right direction?

If these can't be counted numerically, what will indicate to you that you're heading in the right direction (or not)...remember Jacob's positive and negative indicators of being taken seriously as a business
HOW will you measure your progress?

How will you celebrate these milestones as you reach them?

Is your goal ATTAINABLE and ACTION ORIENTATED?

Aim high with your goals, and be prepared to DO

something to achieve them.

Ask yourself:

What knowledge and skills do I need to achieve this?

What's holding me back?

What's REALLY holding me back (is it...ME?!)?

Who can help me achieve my goal?

What's the first thing I need to DO?

On a scale of 1–10 how willing am I to put in the work to get there?

Make sure your goals are RELEVANT to your own personal values

It's important to ensure that your goal doesn't conflict with your personal ethics and beliefs. If it DOES in some way...is it actually your goal, or someone else's expectation?

Ask yourself:

Why do I want to achieve this goal?

What will be the benefits to me and those around me?

What am I prepared to do to meet my goal?

What am I not prepared to do?

As you move forward, consider each sub-goal, and weigh up how relevant it is to your overall goal.

Make sure your goal is TIME-BOUND.

This is often the biggest single point of failure in goal setting – people simply don't set themselves deadlines....in which case, more often than not, time drifts on, and nothing happens.

Set yourself some timescales, even if you have to be flexible later on. Aim for something. Put it in your diary.

Ask yourself:

When do I want to achieve this by?

When do I need to start?

Where am I now?

Where do I want to be by the end of the year?

Where do I want to be by the end of the month... week.........day?!

What's the consequence of not setting some deadlines?

Setting smart goals – and writing them down and putting them somewhere where you can see them – is a major step forward.

It's important that your goal is exciting to you – that you're motivated by it and that you stop every so often to review your progress and check that you are where you need to be.

Some useful techniques for refining your goal

Mind Map approach

Drawing a mind map of your goal provides greater clarity as to what exactly is involved, and it helps you to visualise what you need to do. For both of these reasons, it's a useful precursor to your actual planning, which we'll be looking at in the next chapter.

It's particularly useful because it's NOT a list….it's a shape which you can add to in the coming days without having to re-arrange the rest of it.

Take a large piece of paper and some coloured pens and write your goal in a circle the middle of it. From this central point, draw branches and add themes that are linked to your goal as you think of them. Mind mapping works best with colours and images – here's an example,

Using Jacob's business goal from earlier in the chapter. In essence, what you're doing is mapping your train of thought, rather than trying to put together a list.

Mind mapping is also useful for considering other aspects of your life that will be affected when you achieve your goal and as you move towards it.

Remember the 'menu'? I'd like you to move on to consider other aspects of your life that will see the positive benefits as you move towards your goal.

If you haven't already considered these, then it's worthwhile doing so here and now.

Great – acceptable – unacceptable

With both of these mind maps, allow yourself to think pretty freely about what you would like to happen: we're not at the actual planning stage for your goal yet – that will come in the next chapter.

When you've completed your mind map – and bear in mind that you might want to put it aside and come back and add to it in the coming days, look closely at what you've written.

With the key sections (you'll know what they are) think to yourself:

What would be great – the best possible result?

What would be acceptable – I could live with that and still feel that I had succeeded?

What would be unacceptable – if this happened, I'd feel like I'd NOT succeeded?

Being more certain of these things will help you to tighten up the 'measurables' in your SMART goals... and also give you a much keener sense of EXACTLY what success will look like, in your own terms.

GOAL MINDSET # 7

BE CLEAR IN YOU OWN MIND: WHAT CONSTITUTES FULL SUCCESS, WHAT'S ACCEPTABLE...AND WHAT'S UNACCEPTABLE

How well do I really know my goal?

Make sure that you know and understand your goal, and that you're not aiming for a fantasy that doesn't actually exist. countless websites exist promising a multimillion Rands income on a four hour day... something which (in my opinion) simply does not exist. Aim high – but be real. If you need to know more, do some digging and research your goal. Look up people who have already achieved what you're aiming for, and learn from them.

What have I already tried, in pursuance of my goal?

What's worked so far? What hasn't worked?

In all probability, unless you're going for a complete career change or have only just begun to think about what you want to achieve, you will already have begun to make steps towards it. Look at your goal and consider how far you need to go on any one of the factors you've considered and how far you've already come.

What will I have to change in order to move forward?

This is really important: what will you need to change as you move forward towards your goal? There's a well known saying "if you always do what you've always done, you'll always get what you've always got".

If you want to 'get' something that you haven't already got...you'll need to do something different – it's no good hoping that you can achieve new things by doing the same things. It won't happen. So what needs to change?

What might I miss about the current situation when I move on?

With what will I replace these 'losses'?

Change and moving forward will mean that you gain many new things. It might also mean that you lose some. What might these things be, and with what will you replace them?

What am I prepared to invest?

Closely linked to this is the question of compromises, sacrifices and investment. Don't worry – it's not as drastic as it sounds.

For example, if you want to start a business, you'll need to make some investments in that area in terms of your time and finances. What will you be prepared to sacrifice... and what won't you? This might be something as straightforward as 'I'm prepared to lose my evenings relaxing in front of the TV, and will do a couple of hours work instead...but I'm not losing out on time with my family'.

It might mean reining in your spending in one area so you can spend it on your business – are you prepared to skip that overseas holiday this year and go somewhere closer to home?

The decisions you make now will help form your plans as you move forward.

From where I am now, what barriers are stopping me from moving forward?

Are they real or imagined?

As I discussed in the first chapter, it's vital that you don't fall into the trap of thinking 'I can't because...' when it comes to your goals. Think carefully, what is stopping you?

Is it really?

How do I move closer to 10?

Before you spend time planning your goal and then following that plan, ask yourself now how much you want to achieve it. On a scale of 1–10, if it's anything less than and 8, you'll need to question whether or not you actually want to achieve it. If not, you might want to focus on another goal. Unless you're really self-motivated, it might not happen.

What are the core values that I will carry forward?

As I've said before, your goals – and the means by which you achieve them – should be in line with your values. This is one for you to judge: what values will underpin how you achieve your goals?

What happens if I stay where I am?

This is always worth considering: what happens if nothing happens? How happy are you being where you are at the moment? What is the 'burning platform' that is spurring you on towards your goals?

What's the impact of doing nothing?

Why am I doing this?

Remind yourself why you're doing this – what will it mean to you to achieve your goals. What will it mean to those around you? Think carefully about this – having a clear reason why to focus on will help you overcome the challenges that you might face along the way.

Make a 'Goals Board'

I have one of these and it's fun to make. Basically, it involves getting hold of a pin board and collecting images that relate to the achievement of your goal – pictures of the holiday destinations you'd like to go to, the type of house you'd like to live in, the type of lifestyle you'd like to lead.

This is more than just a wish-list of dreams, though; you've spent some time now really thinking about your goals and what you want to achieve, and this is a visual representation of those things.

When you have challenges to overcome in the coming months, looking at these images and reminding yourself where you're going is a powerful motivator.

And finally...

Remember, that as you move forward towards something, it becomes clearer. Ensure that you start with as clear and SMART a goal as possible, but be prepared to learn new things about your goal – and what success will mean to you – as you move forward towards it.

Bear in mind also that as you look closely at your goal, it might be bigger than you initially thought. Worry not. That's normal.

Devising a plan

Having gained clarity over your goal and reasons and values behind it, this section will be a 'how to' on breaking your overall SMART goal down into manageable and realistic chunks, and building a practical plan to achieve it.

To some people (myself included) who are more action orientated and would rather just define their goal and get on with it, this planning phase can seem a little dull.

To others, who have a more thoughtful and process-driven approach to life, it will be easy, as it's all about taking your ideas and aspirations and turning them into the practical steps you need to take to achieve your goal.

For those action-orientated people who want to skip the planning stage and start running towards their goal now…pause for a moment. Planning is vital and in this chapter, you'll be considering factors that will in the end help you to get to your goal quicker.

For those who enjoy thinking and planning – ensure that you remain focused on achieving your goal, and not in planning for planning's sake.

Once you have your plan, it will be a question of sticking to the plan and being self disciplined if the goal is to be achieved.

A plan on paper is worthless. A plan in action is priceless. And with that in mind consider also that you should start taking your first few steps towards your goals as soon as you have clarified your first few steps: don't wait until the whole master plan of your life has been drafted out in full...begin to walk the path as soon as you can.

GOAL MINDSET #8

PLAN. DON'T JUST DIVE IN.

Make a list

Start by looking at your overall SMART goal, and start with what you want to achieve and your timescale (the S and the T).

Think carefully about all the things that need to happen if you are to meet that goal in that timescale, and make a list. To start with, just write things down in any order, and bear in mind that more things might occur to you in the coming days.

It's also extremely likely that things will be added to

this list as you move forward: at this starting-out point there will be things about your goals that you don't know you don't know...you'll find out as you journey towards it.

At this stage, be as thorough as you can though – the more detailed your overall 'to do' list is, the more robust your plan will be.

Let's take the example that we saw of Jacob, whose goal is to set up a business based on her crafting skills.

Jacob's initial list might look something like this:

Find workshop premises

Develop website

Make more products to sell

Start with soft furnishing and clothes
Buy / source more raw materials to work with

Think about farming work out for completion

Think about design services, completed elsewhere...

Branch into home décor and 'how to' resources online

Join craft networks to share ideas

Learn business skills

Contact the bank to set up an account

Sell product range on TV shopping channels

Run craft workshops and residential weekend programmes

Find an accountant

Find someone to help with marketing

Contact the local enterprise agency for business start-up advice

Join and attend business networking groups

...and so on

Work through the list

Clearly with each of these, further thought is required.

The first consideration is what needs to be tackled first?

Looking down Jacob's list, it's fairly safe to say that things like;

Visiting the local enterprise authority for business start

up advice

Setting up a bank account

Finding an accountant

Start with soft furnishing and clothes

(and some other factors)
....are going to have to happen before, for example,he starts selling things via TV shopping channels.

Considering the factors on his list like this might make Jacob think about some factors that he might not have considered before:

How big do I want to start – go for major bank investment, or fund it myself and work from home to start with?

And leading on from this:
What sort of start up businesses do the banks lend to?

How much do they lend?

What are their terms?

What are the implications for me?

These questions in turn might lead him to think about researching funding options before choosing a bank and setting up her account.

In terms of his overall goal, Jacob might reflect that he wants a successful business in three years time, so he will need to invest heavily at the outset to get the ball rolling.

Or he might decide that, in terms of his lifestyle and other commitments outside his goal, he will make his ideal business a ten year plan and grow more slowly.

As for your own list, it's important that you take each point on it and ask yourself:

Where does this sit in relation to other things on my list?

How important is this thing, in terms of my overall goal?

What is involved with getting this particular thing done

When does it need to happen – right away? In six months time?

When EXACTLY will I do these things?

Who do I know who can advise/help me with this?

What else do I need to find out about this? Where can I go to find out?

What will I need to do to achieve that step?

Following on from this, once you've organised your list into some sort of timeline order, each thing on your list will need to become a mini SMART goal.

Set mini SMART goals

By now, you should be familiar with SMART goals if you weren't already.

You'll already have expressed your overall goal as a SMART goal. Here. We're looking to turn each of the factors on your list into a SMART goal in itself.

Specific – be as accurate as you can about exactly what it is that you need to get done.

Measurable – what are the measurables, in terms of what you're actually doing and in terms of the results you expect to see? Make sure that at least some of your measurable factors are results based: don't fall into the trap of being busy, but not seeing any return on that investment of your time.

For example, on his list, Jacob has written that she wants to join networking organisations, and attend at least once a month. These things are easy to measure – he is either been or he,is not. He needs also, though to put a measurable on what he wants the outcome to be – to make 3 new contacts and follow them up, per event, say.

If he finds that, six months in, he's been attending events but has made no useful contacts at all – he'll need to rethink the events he's attending, what he's doing and who he's talking to at the event etc. Otherwise he's in danger of going through the motions, but not getting any results.

Achievable – don't make excuses, but are the things you've set yourself achievable with the resources and time that you have? It's important to challenge yourself, but remember your well-being and work-life balance!

Action orientated – as you move forward with your goal, your actions might involve motivating someone else to do something for you, Jacob might check, for example, that his web designer has everything he needs etc.

Relevant – this becomes really important at this stage. As you explore your mini-goals, are they relevant to your overall goal...or are they distractions?

It's all too easy to rationalise things and give them a place on your plan, but sometimes it's really worth asking yourself if the things you're doing are fundamental to your goals, or will take you away from them.

Timebound – put a date in the diary for when you'll do these things, or when you'll have them done by.

This will become particularly important when you consider the dependencies between the factors on your list: Jacob can't go out and buy raw materials from suppliers until he has a bank account set up and has worked out his budgets....so the longer he takes to do these two things, the longer the delay in purchasing the raw materials...in making the products...in selling those products and so on.

This might seem like overkill – after all, haven't you already spent time making your overall goal into a SMART goal and listing down all the things you'll need to do to get there?

It's not. SMART goals prompt action – especially if you write them down.

GOAL MINDSET # 9

IF IT'S NOT A SMART GOAL, IT'S NOT A GOAL.

Challenge yourself at each point:

What exactly do I need to do here?

How am I measuring whether it's been done well or not?

Can I actually do this?

Is it taking me towards my overall goal?

WHEN will I do this?

Brainstorming for ideas and solutions

It's possible that there will be some elements of your goal that leave you thinking 'how on earth am I going to do that?!'

Brainstorming is a useful technique to tackle those challenges.

Generate ideas

Set aside some time for this, and be prepared to think about it over the course of a few days. What you're aiming for is to come up with as many ideas as possible that might take you towards your goal or sub-goal.

Aim for at least ten, and don't worry too much if the ideas you're coming up with seem a little far-fetched at a first glance, just write them all down anyway. If you're struggling for ideas yourself, ask for the input of friends, family or colleagues who can provide ideas without judging your rationale.

What can often happen is that people will come up with two or three ideas, and then try to work through them. The thing is that the first few options you come up with will be the blindingly obvious ones that they've been chewing over for months.

Challenge yourself to come up with new, less obvious possible actions...however ludicrous those might seem: at this stage it's about getting as many ideas as possible out in the open.

Come up with as many ideas as possible as to what you're actually going to do to achieve your goals, BEFORE analysing and discounting any of them. Why? If you move too quickly into analysis mode, you'll miss out on some good ideas that come from lateral thinking, and inadvertently close down your possible actions, rather than opening them up.

Analyse your ideas

Once you have your list of ideas (at least ten, remember) place them aside for a day or so. Then set aside some time to analyse them. At this stage, don't be too quick to write off any that you think you can't do – there may be ways round that.

Understanding the reasons why you want to achieve your goals can be an influencing factor here, and help to eliminate some ideas, and push others to the top of your action list: some of your options will align with that reason why, and some won't.

Consider each of these options carefully, and then narrow them down – I find that categorising them as 'no' 'yes' and 'maybe' is fine.

Make sure that you're not discounting ideas because you don't have the skills to do them (you can learn) or because you don't think you can. Make sure also that your options tie in with your values, and the reasons why you are aiming for your particular goal.

Let's imagine that Jacob has been brainstorming some low-cost publicity-generating ideas, and his list includes:

A pop-up craft shop

Workplace workshops

Sending marketing material out on fabric not paper

Being a 'rogue crafter' pinning up her work in public

Designing and wearing an outrageous outfit to a networking event

In his analysis, he might decide that sending out marketing material on fabric not paper isn't practical or cost effective….but it could lead to him sending out something more interesting in terms of her direct marketing.

Running the risk of arrest by posting her work up in

public places might not be an option.... but getting permission to do so in an office building, to promote craft workshops as part of a large company's well-being program might be a more realistic possibility.

In essence, some ideas will receive an outright 'no'. Some are obviously a 'yes'....and some might seem ridiculous at a first glance, but could lead to something very productive.

Decide on your course of action

Make sure that your thought processes so far don't just stay as thoughts – work out what your first steps need to be, and make plans to actually DO them (setting yourself another SMART goal in the process).

At this level, you're starting to come up with a focussed action plan or to-do list, and that action plan will be prioritised: by now you'll know what you need to do first, and what your timescales and measurable factors are.

Think about some contingencies too – if this particular course of action isn't doing what you need it do so, at what point will you call time on it and try something else?

Contingencies and scenario planning

Inevitably as you journey towards your goal, you'll come up with certain obstacles, and it's worth doing some scenario planning at an early stage to try and plan ahead.

Be aware that there's a balance here though – it's useful to consider a few options where you genuinely think you might face a challenge: it's not useful to plan and plan and plan again and try to cover every eventuality, because you won't be able to, and you could end up spending so much time planning that you don't get round to actually doing anything...and if you don't actually do anything all your planning has been a waste of time.

Whenever you come across challenges – even if it's in this scenario planning stage – it's important to think back to your overall goal and the reasons why you want to achieve it. At which point ask yourself "am I going to let this barrier/challenge/inconvenience prevent me from achieving my goals?". I'm sure I hardly need say that the answer really should be 'no'.

You might want to consider some of the bigger 'what if's' simply to get used to the idea that you will sometimes have to come up with a 'plan b', and you may well also have to hone your problem solving skills as you go along.

Let's imagine that Jacob, in setting up her business, is going to ask the bank for funding...but is concerned that they might not lend to a business like his. His 'plan b' might be

To fund his business start up himself...and accept that it will take longer

To look for investment from independent funders

To see if the local enterprise agency has a funding scheme

To give up altogether

Of course I've put that last one in to make you think 'obviously he's not going to do THAT!'

One would hope not. Every day, though, people give up on their goals because of some issue that they might well have been able to overcome or think their way round... they have just chosen that 'give up' option instead.

Please don't let this be you. Learn to problem solve. Become resourceful. Develop your ability to stop and think to overcome a challenge, and not to let your frustration about the challenge stop you in your tracks. We'll be looking at some of these skills in later chapters as we look at how to maintain momentum and motivation.

For the moment, hold yourself to account – you are responsible for your goals, and how and when (and indeed if) you achieve them.

GOAL MINDSET # 10

LEARN TO PROBLEM SOLVE. BECOME RE-

SOURCEFUL. DEVELOP YOUR ABILITY TO STOP AND THINK TO OVERCOME A CHALLENGE

What to do now

Spend a little time looking back at everything you've written down as you read this chapter. You should have quite a bit: a list or mind map of all of the factors associated with your goal, further details about what each of those points involve, a clear idea of which things need to happen first, and which things depend on other factors on your list...and now your possible contingency plans.

Look closely at what needs to be done...and what needs to be done first; you may already have made these actions into SMART goals – if you haven't now is the time to do that, and to build up your 'to do' list.

Focus not only on the large scale plan of what needs to happen in the next 6 months, but on what needs to be done now to get the ball rolling.

Set yourself tasks that you commit to achieving within the next week. Write them down and put them somewhere where you will see them.

Tick them off the list as you do them.

Hold yourself to account, and get them done! Your goal depends upon it!

And remember to reward yourself along the way as you move forward towards your goals.

Ask yourself:

Do I need to break my goal down further?

Which bit will I focus on first? Why?

What can I do to move this forward? What else can I do? What else? What else? What else?

Who else might I ask for suggestions?

Where else will I look for information?

If anything were possible, what would I do?

What's holding me back, in a practical sense?

What psychologically is holding me back?

What am I going to DO first? When?
THEN GO AND DO IT!!!

It's absolutely vital (I cannot stress this strongly enough) that you have the confidence and self belief that you will achieve your goals. Faith is crucial to success. If you don't believe you can make it, then you probably won't

– even if there are other people who do.

Depending on how ambitious your goals are, this might sometimes mean flying in the face of those who don't think you will achieve. And that can take some bravery.

Developing the confidence to succeed

There will be times when you have to ignore the voices of those around you and dig deep into your inner resolve and believe you can succeed.

I cannot overstate how vital it is to have self confidence, and a strong faith (which is why I'm repeating myself again so soon). The same goes for teams and organisations: if you don't actually believe that you can achieve your goals, or – worse still, that you aren't really worthy of them – then it's pretty much 'game over' from the start.

I'm not talking about becoming arrogant, ignoring feedback from others and thinking you're infallible or invincible – I'm talking about a balanced view of yourself that doesn't indulge in false modesty and self-pity, and an inner view of yourself that is strong enough not to be crushed and defeated when someone challenges you.

I've worked with a lot of leaders over the years, and I'm astonished at how many of them have 'impostor syndrome': they almost don't believe they are worthy to be where they are, and some of them focus upon issues that really are non issues. One of them was deeply concerned that his accent and tone of voice grated on people: another very senior leader fretted about his writing style, which he didn't think was as good as his colleagues. Yet another one felt guilty that he had risen to a senior position, and didn't have a university degree. Not helpful baggage to be carrying around!

Here's the thing. You must develop the mindset and confidence to achieve your goals. If you really want to reach your goals, you cannot afford to wallow in thoughts of 'I'm not good enough'.

Don't think "is that statement (about your accent, writing, lack of education etc.) true or not?" Think to yourself "is it helpful to focus on this?" If not, ditch it.

Confidence techniques

Self Talk

What is your inner voice telling you? Is it your best coach...or your worst critic? It's been said that we often talk to ourselves in a way that we'd never allow anyone else to. If your inner voice is always telling you how stupid you are, how you're not as thin/beautiful/clever/wealthy as someone else...then it's time to shut it up.

I used to know someone whose standard phrase used to

be "it's very difficult for me because...." And guess what. He seemed to struggle with everything. He was constantly telling himself how difficult life was for him, and it became a self fulfilling prophesy. He could have made a slight – but profound – change by focusing on a solution rather than a problem 'I face challenges head on' is a lot more useful than 'Woe is me, everything is so difficult'. Are you talking about brain surgery here? Rocket science? No? Then how hard can it be?!

If you find yourself making negative statements to yourself, think of a positive statement you can say instead. Discipline yourself to say this positive statement whenever you catch yourself thinking the negative. Every time.

I'm quite clumsy, and have often found myself dropping a sheaf of papers all over the floor, spilling my coffee on my desk.

Here's the thing. If I say '"I'm such a klutz, I've got to be careful not to drop/spill/smash anything" it's going to result in nervous behaviour that will probably lead to those very things happening. I choose to tell myself "I'm every inch the successful leader". Believe it or not, this makes a huge psychological difference.

GOAL MINDSET #11

TALK TO YOURSELF. IN A GOOD WAY.

The Behaviour Cycle

What you think about and what you say to yourself has a profound effect on your behaviour and on what happens to you. I'm sure we've all known someone who has been worrying about something they have to do – make a presentation at work say – and has constantly spoken about how badly they think it's going to go. When it does go badly, they'll turn round and say 'I knew that would happen!'.

They probably don't realise that they created their own self-fulfilling prophesy.

Our thoughts, attitudes and behaviours…your thoughts, attitudes and behaviours towards your ability to achieve your goal…have a profound impact on your expectations of the situation.

In turn, your expectations will impact on the way in which you behave in a given situation.

People obviously can't actually see what's going on in your head, they respond to your behaviours, and this can become a negative cycle.

Imagine that Jacob is on his way towards his goal of setting up his craft-based business, and is invited to speak about his start-up experiences at a business networking meeting.

Imagine he thinks to herself "oh good grief, why did I offer to do this? I hate presenting in front of people. It's going to be awful: I'm going to be so nervous my face is going to go all red and blotchy, I'll forget what I'm supposed to say no-one's going to take me seriously…it's going to be a disaster!!"

What impact does this thought process have on his expectations of the situation? He's not expecting it to go amazingly well, is he?!

His expectations of the event not going well are going to impact on his behaviour: he might not prepare as well as he should, because at the back of his mind he's thinking "what's the point – it's going to be a disaster anyway!!"

He's expecting to feel nervous and flushed, so he's likely to be focussed on how nervous he's feeling, and this will come out in his body language and his voice. People will see that he is nervous.

They might show some sympathy for a first-time speaker and respond well…or they might think that, because of his nervous approach and poor delivery that he's not a very convincing business man. It could go either way.

Instead imagine Jacob – although he's nervous about giving a presentation in public – saying to himself "this is a fabulous opportunity to share my business, and I've got a great story to tell!". Literally every time he has a negative thought, he consciously says this to himself instead.

What will his expectations of the event be? In this case now, that he's going to tell a great story and share his business.

His expectations will have an impact in the way he comes across. It just will. He will be nervous, but his focus will be on giving a good presentation and telling his story.

Again people will respond to him positive approach, and have a much better impression of him.

Tell yourself that you will succeed. That nothing is going to stop you. That you deserve success . Tell yourself until you believe it.

Ask yourself:

In relation to my goal and my ability to achieve it, what am I saying to myself?

How has the behaviour cycle impacted me in the past?
Moving forward, how can I focus on positive mental statements?

Be accountable for the achievement of your goal

Being confident means accepting responsibility for

your goal, and believing that one way or another you have the wherewithal to achieve it.

A confident person with faith will think their way round problems to achieve their goal – someone lacking in confidence might be prepared to give up in the face of obstacles.

Focus on the things you do well

One of the things that can help to boost your confidence is doing a bit of an 'inventory' of the skills and attributes that you already have that will help you on your way.

We're going to analyse these further in chapter 5, as you work out what new skills you need to learn, but at the outset of your goal journey, reminding yourself of what you're good at, what you can do and what you've achieved in the past can be motivating and confidence building.

Ask yourself:

What am I good at?

What do people value me for?

What have I received compliments and positive feedback for in the past?

What have I achieved in the past that I perhaps didn't

think I could?

What challenges have I overcome in the past? What skills helped me to do this?

Write your answers down so that you can refer to them later: there may be times when you need to remind yourself of your capabilities as you move towards your goal.

Whilst it might feel a little uncomfortable, it can be worth asking the opinion of a trusted friend or family member what they think you're good at. There may well be achievements that they respect you for that you've forgotten, and it may be that they recognise a core skill of yours simply because they don't have it and you do (if this is the case, it's easy for you to think that everyone has this skill…and they don't).

Make a note of these second opinions too. Take them at face value: don't devalue them by saying "well I asked my dad and he's bound to say nice things about me".

Look for patterns in your own responses and in what other people are telling you: this will give you an insight as to your strengths AND will boost your confidence.

When you have moments of self doubt, refocus on these things. Review your list, and your past successes, and tell yourself – however cheesy it might feel – "I CAN do it… and I deserve it!"

Be inspired by others

One of the things that has always inspired me and given me the confidence to succeed is looking at other people who have succeeded.

Sometimes the person in question has a rare or special quality that I don't possess, and this has taken them to the top.

Nine times out of ten, though, I can't help noticing that it's their perseverance, attitude and determination to succeed that have taken them to the top, not necessarily the extent of their abilities. Nine times out of ten, I end up thinking to myself "if they can do it…so I can".

Find yourself some role models whom you admire, and whose story of success inspires you. What can you learn from them in terms of:-

Their attitude and approach

Where they started from (some of the most inspiring people had the most humdrum beginnings)

How they overcame challenges

How they made the most of their abilities

How they leveraged the skills of others along the way

How they handled their success

Remind yourself that these too were ordinary human beings who, once upon a time, had an idea and a hope and a goal, and set about determinedly to achieve them and didn't give up until they had.

GOAL MINDSET # 12

REMEMBER THAT ALL SUCCESSFUL PEOPLE STARTED OUT AS YOU ARE STARTING OUT – WITH HOPE AND WITH AN IDEA. IF THEY CAN DO IT, SO CAN YOU.

Take on the 'mask of the expert'

In layman's terms, this means 'fake it till you make it', and acting as though you are the thing that you want to be. In the past I've found it a useful technique for situations which I'm new to: I'm literally saying to myself 'now what would so-and-so do in this situation?' and acting as I'd expect them to act.

Earlier in the chapter I wrote about how important it is to think positively about what you're doing. I also said that people don't know what's going on in your head, they merely respond to what they hear and see you do – your behaviour.

Luckily, we can leverage this if we take on 'the mask of the expert'.

To begin with, focus on a role model who inspires you, and watch people who appear confident. How do they behave? What do they wear? How do they carry themselves? How do they talk?

Begin to notice these things consciously, and absorb some of the techniques into your own behaviour. This is not about trying to ape someone – this is about emulating successful behaviours that you see in others.

I used to be terrified of networking situations – walking into a room of strangers and trying to strike up a conversation. To my mind there's nothing worse (there still isn't!).

I used to watch my leader walk into a room with his head held high, and start talking to someone, effortlessly. I started to copy his body language...make no mistake, I was just as terrified as before, but I'd think to myself 'what would my leader do' and I'd just do that.

Amazingly, I had broken into the 'behaviour attitude cycle.' I had deliberately changed my behaviour, by taking on the 'mask of the expert' and copying someone else. Somehow, this changed people's attitude towards me – they thought I actually was confident. This changed their behaviour in response...which began to change my attitude.

It became a virtuous cycle.

I still don't enjoy walking into a room full of strangers and striking up a conversation...but I've got to a point where I can actually do it reasonably well, appear confident, and get results.

Empower yourself to succeed

I mentioned this important point right at the very beginning of the topic – you do not need anyone's permission to succeed. It really is up to you.

Whilst this, in effect, offers few excuses for not succeeding, holding on to that thought will also give you the confidence to move forward towards your goals.

There will, of course, be times when permission to do something must be sought. What I'm talking about here is when we actually give up responsibility for our own actions and potentially give up on our goals and aspirations.
At this point in your journey towards your goals ask yourself again...whose permission are YOU asking to succeed...and why?

The Government's?

If you're waiting for the economic tide to turn before you start a business/sell your house/plan for the future... you might as well give up now. The best time to start moving towards your goals is now.

We have to work on the basis that this is the 'new normal'. We live in an uncertain world. We must make bold decisions anyway. We must raise our aspirations anyway. We must move forward anyway.

Your bosses or clients?

I was talking with someone a while ago who had felt that her career had run into the buffers because her boss wouldn't let her attend a training course that was necessary for her to progress, because he felt she wasn't ready for it. She'd been inspired by something she heard in a song on the radio: Labi Siffre's 'Something Inside So Strong'. The words that caught her attention were 'When they insist we're just not good enough...just look them in the eyes and say "I'm going to do it anyway". Without her bosses consent, she funded the course herself, and was able to move forward in her career.

The decision to progress is an individual one.

Your family and friends?

Usually your friends and family have your best interests at heart. They don't want to see you get hurt. They don't want to see you fail. They don't want to see you make a fool of yourself.

And sometimes, they can unwittingly put a halt to your plans and aspirations.

Challenge yourself: WHY are you asking the wrong people for permission? To my mind, there are 3 key reasons...all of which can be fixed.

Fear. Fear of getting it wrong, fear of what people might say, fear of looking like an idiot. Asking someone else's permission (whoever that might be) can indicate that you're looking for reassurance. Which is fine...but what if you don't get it? Do you have the courage of your convictions to just get on with it anyway? Is it really a confidence thing that's holding you back?

Procrastinating. Asking for permission allows you to delay decision making and put off taking action. The ball is in someone else's court. You can't move forward until they get back to you, or until they give you the go ahead. Is this really the case...or can you move ahead anyway? Is this more about your motivation levels than anything else?

Lack of personal accountability. Asking someone else's permission absolves you of responsibility for the outcomes, and provides you with plenty of excuses why failure wasn't your fault. Is it really fair to blame someone or something else...or is it more about you?

So whose permission do you need to succeed? It's a question you really need to ask yourself.

In conclusion, ask yourself:

What am I good at?

What do people appreciate me for?

How have I used these skills successfully in the past?

What am I saying to myself in my head?

Where are my negative self beliefs coming from?

Whether they're fact or fiction, are they useful?

What positive messages or mantras will I say instead of the negative things?

Who inspires me?

What can I learn from them?

AM I looking for someone else's permission to succeed....if so, WHY?

Your skills, and what you need to learn

Inevitably, striving towards a goal will mean learning new things. If it didn't, you'd already be there.

On this point, we'll look at how to evaluate your skills, make the most of the ones that you have, and figure out how to either develop the ones you haven't, or leverage the talent of other people to plug the gaps.

It's important to think as broadly as possible about your skills, and to ask other people for their thoughts as to where your abilities lie. Often, when it comes to our own core strengths and abilities, we are so familiar with these and they are so much part of who we are that it becomes impossible to imagine that other people can't do the same thing.

Think about the things that you do, how they are unique to you, and how you can leverage them as you move forward towards that goal.

Think about what other people value you for, and perhaps asks the opinions of trusted friends and family as to where your key strengths lie.

Your Skills

As I've already said, it's important to consider your skills in several areas.

Often, we may find that society is geared towards recognising the first two intelligences below: an ability with words and numeracy skills. However, your broader talents will be just as important – possibly even more so – in getting you to your goal.

Bear in mind also that whilst you might have very

strong abilities in one area above all others, it's likely that you have a range of skills that fall into several intelligence categories.

Make a note of which ones apply most to you.

Linguistic

Are you a good communicator, verbally and/or in writing? Think carefully about this: because so much of our education and work system revolves around being able to communicate at some level, you may well think that everyone can communicate.

Whilst everyone can communicate some people do it better than others. Are you one of them? How will a way with words be useful to you as you move towards your goal?

Signs that you are particularly strong in this area might include:

You like word games, crosswords and so on

You enjoy reading and telling stories

You have a good memory for information

You may be good at public speaking, debating and reasoning (although some linguistic people prefer written communication)

You may be good at learning languages

Strong linguistic skills are common amongst authors, journalists, writers, politicians and editors.

Logical-Mathematical

Are you organised and methodical? People with strength in this are typically very good at analysing data, and following a logical thought path. This strength will be an asset to you as you figure out how best to achieve your goals, and as you move towards them step by step.

Typically, people with abilities in this area are likely to:

Be good at maths, logical reasoning, and calculations

Like abstract thinking

Like being organised and precise

Like analysing data

People with strong skills in this area are likely to be drawn towards careers in science, accountancy, IT, law, the police and so on.

Kinaesthetic

People with a bodily-kinaesthetic intelligence are, in a nutshell, physically co-ordinated and gifted in terms of precise movement. Sportsmen and women are perhaps the most obvious to fall into this category however, others include surgeons, dancers and those working with precise mechanics.

Do you:

Have good timing and reflexes

Enjoy sport and physical activity

Tend to fidget if you're required to sit still for a length of time

Prefer to act, to DO rather than to analyse

Remember what was done, rather than what was said or seen

Respond to the physical environment

Like models and machines

Mentally review while you're doing something else – working out, housework, or whatever

Don't relegate your kinaesthetic skills to the hobby bin.

How will you use them to reach your goal?

Interpersonal

People with interpersonal intelligence have strong social skills, and might describe themselves as 'a people person'. These are skills often found in politicians, teachers, public relations and human resources professionals among others.

Do you

Mix well with others and find yourself able to relate to them

Read other people's intentions accurately

Work well as part of a team, and enjoy co-operating

Empathise with other people

Recognise your impact on other people

Whatever your goal, it's extremely likely that you're going to need to involve other people at some stage. This skill is therefore, arguably one of the most important ones you possess.

Naturalistic

This particular intelligence is often overlooked in the grand scheme of things, yet you might find that it's central to your goal or your ability to achieve it.

Are you someone who:

Keeps pets

Enjoys nature and being outdoors

Feels an affinity with nature

Feels strongly about environmental issues

Enjoys gardening

Sometimes prefers animals to people

Where does this have a bearing on your goal? Think how you might use your skills to move forward towards your goal.

Intra personal

Intra-personal intelligence revolves around self awareness and intuition. In any circumstances, a strong sense of self is going to be important in your achieving your goals.

Are you someone who:

Has a strong sense of self knowledge

Doesn't feel the need to 'follow the crowd'

Has a sense of your own purpose in life

Has a keen sense of your own values

See yourself as a 'deep' person

Is inclined to be introspective

Can motivate yourself

Is intuitive about others

How might you capitalise on this sense of self as you move forward?

Visual/spatial

Do you have a good memory for images, and tend to remember things in pictures? If so, it's possible that you have strong visual and/or spatial skills.

Where does this play a part in your goal or in your achieving your goal? Where MIGHT you be able to use it to fullest advantage?

Having a visual/spatial intelligence doesn't necessarily

mean that you're good at art: it may be that you are good at visualising concepts.

Do you:

Think in pictures

Use metaphors to explain concepts and ideas

Like art/drawing/painting

Prefer looking at charts and diagrams to abstract data

Have a good sense of colour

Enjoy going to the cinema or watching TV

Visual and spatial skills are often LESS recognised – and even valued – than other skills, but this is a mistake. They are incredibly valuable in a wide variety of contexts.

Musical

If you have a musical intelligence, you'll know it. Again, it can sometimes be sidelined as a hobby, but it still has the potential – like ANY intelligence type – to take you towards your goal.

Musical people are likely to:

Be sensitive to pitch and rhythm

Be sensitive to the emotional power of music

Find it easy to study to music

Relax or workout with music

Play a musical instrument or sing

Write music

Music has a powerful psychological impact in many areas that we don't even think of. Where might you be using it to your advantage to meet your goal?

Your Knowledge

In addition to your underlying skills and intelligence type, there will be a wide range of knowledge at your disposal: things that you've learned and that you know about.

Think carefully about what you know: there'll be more than you think.

What knowledge do you take so much for granted that you almost forget that you have it?! It could be one of your strongest assets.

Ask yourself:

What do I have qualifications in?

What do I do as a hobby?

What do I read?

What do I watch on TV?

What am I interested in?

What do I do in my spare time?

Where do I go on holiday?

What do I do at work?

What am I asked to help other people with?

What subject areas really motivate you?

Your attitudes and approach

There are innumerable quotes that point to the fact that even if you don't yet have the skills to succeed, if you have an attitude and a mindset for success, it will weigh heavily in your favour.

Your underlying personality traits

These relate to your personality type. There are no rights or wrongs – it's just how you are. As you move towards your goal however, it's worthwhile being very aware of who you are, and of who you need to be in order to achieve your goal.

Analyticals are logical and process orientated. They like to analyse data, and to be clear about the facts before moving forward. They are likely to prepare carefully and thoroughly and will opt for planning above spontaneity.

Amiables are a 'people person' who thrives on working with others. They are keen to promote harmony and for this reason are more likely to conform. They value loyalty, and prefer work to be relationship orientated.

Expressives are creative and spontaneous. They are flexible, work at a fast pace and are keen on new ideas (perhaps more than following them through). They enjoy recognition.

As a start, consider the following pairs and which is most interesting to you.

People or things?

Practical or theoretical?

Thinker or doer?

Spontaneous or planned?

Sequential or random?

Positive or negative?

Extrovert or introvert?

Logical or imaginative?

Change or status quo?

Starter or finisher?

Disciplined or haphazard?

What does this tell you about your personality, those of the people around you, and how you relate to them?

How might your personality traits impact your goal and how you achieve it?

The tipping point

I mentioned earlier that too much of any one trait can actually work against us. Those who have a strong tendency towards a particular style tend to find it much easier to think of all the positive aspects of their own style, and also easy to think of the negative aspects of other styles.

Conversely, they are sometimes surprised at the negative aspects of their style highlighted by people of a different style.

For example, Drivers will often see themselves as focused on achievement, getting things done, and moving forward – all of which are good things. An Amiable person might see them as 'ruthless', 'heartless' or 'would stab their own grandmother to get ahead'. NOT so good.

Expressives might see themselves as fun, creative and full of energy... Analyticals might see them as lightweight, shallow, and not thorough.

On the premise that, at some stage, other people will become involved with or affected by your goal, it's worth bearing this in mind. Where are your strengths most useful to you...and at what point do they start to work against you?

Beware aware also that you can have too much of a good thing...

Your core quality is your strength – in this case, the characteristics of an Amiable person, but you can substitute in whatever is most relevant to you.

You pitfall is what happens if you have too much of that quality: perhaps in this case you're so concerned in promoting harmony and making sure that everyone else is OK that you adopt passive behaviours and let people walk all over you.

Your challenge is the area that you need to work on: in this case, learning to be more assertive.

Your allergy is what you're afraid of becoming, and it's usually the polar opposite of what you are. The harmony promoting Amiable does not want to become what they perceive as the ruthless driver who'll stop at nothing and not consider the feelings of others as they storm relentlessly towards their goal.

The Analytical's 'allergy' might be becoming the sort of person who acts spontaneously on a whim rather than weighing up all the options in advance.... Conversely, the Expressive might hate to be the sort of person who analyses everything to death before taking a single step forward.

In fact, you're not ever going to become the person you are 'allergic' to. The key point is that all too often fear of becoming that person prevents you from making steps forward in your development area.

GOAL MINDSET #13

RECOGNISE THAT YOU NEED TO LEARN

So where does all this self analysis lead us?

It's important to recognise that there will be much to

learn as you move towards your goal: the knowledge, skills and attributes that have got you this far, but you will have to develop new ones to take you further.

Ask yourself: what does your goal require of you?

Think back to the earliest of this chapter when I asked you to imagine that you'd already achieved your goal... what did you imagine that you had actually done?

Imagine yourself in that place again. What does your goal require of you in terms of your knowledge, skills and attitudes...and how can you leverage your natural personality?

Consider this in the light of each of the headings we've just looked at, and consider where the gaps may lie: what standard is required for you to reach your goal, in terms of your skills knowledge and behaviours...and where are you now? How will you develop and learn?

Bear in mind that once you've identified a gap in skills or knowledge, you'll need to consider how you might address these: it might involve building your own knowledge, reading a few books on a given subject or attending classes...or you might decide that you'd rather use someone else's talents to plug your gap.

For example, let's consider Jacob, from our example in previous chapters, as he looks to set up his own business based on his talent for crafts. His talents lie mainly on the creative side and he might be less comfortable with the numbers aspect of his new business. He might prefer to hire a book-keeper rather than to undertake all the finances on his own.

(Just a word to the wise, though, especially where finance is concerned: if you really don't like working with numbers by all means bring in an expert...but make sure you know enough to know what's going on. You hear too many horror stories about people who have left big aspects of their goal in the hands of someone else, and it's all gone horribly wrong.)

Unlock your potential

Leveraging the skills of others is not an excuse to be lazy or to avoid doing the things you must – it's about playing to your strengths in order to achieve your goal.

Consider again that at some point your strengths will reach a tipping point and start to work against you.

For example, being a logical sequential thinker who's deeply analytical is extremely useful in many situations and lines of work. However, it can work against you if you are trying to come up with new ideas and fresh approaches: you'll find yourself trying to analyse ideas and possibly kill them off before you've fully explored them.

Or you might find that you get into 'analysis paralysis' – so busy going over the data that you have that you don't actually get a move on and DO something.

Conversely, the person who is confident and bases their self esteem on their own opinion of themselves might actually veer towards arrogance, ignoring the feedback of others and choosing to believe that they are consistently right.

And now back to your plans...

Once you've identified any development areas – and indeed any ideas that might make even more of the abilities that you already have – you'll need to work these into your plans, and develop some SMART goals.

What exactly do you need to learn?

How will you know when you've developed these skills enough?

Do they involve you actually doing something, rather than things just happening?
Are these skills really relevant to your overall goal?

WHEN will you learn this?

Once you've added what you want to learn and your development points to your overall plan, it's a matter of working the plan.

Maintaining momentum and motivation

It goes almost without saying that in order to reach your goals, there are times when you're going to have to be determined, resourceful and motivated to get there.

Everyone is raring to go when it comes to starting their journey towards their goal. Many falter along the way. Sadly, many give up and settle for something less than they set out to achieve.

Those who DO give up are likely to rationalise this to make it feel like the right thing to do. Common rationalisations are:

Thinking you got your goals wrong in the first place (if you've spent as long working on defining, researching and building your goals as I've suggested in this book, you won't have) -- Thinking 'it just wasn't meant to be'
-- Thinking 'my obligations to my family/spouse/kids/job make it impossible to continue -- Thinking (subconsciously) 'I'm not sure I deserve it'

If you ever get to a point where you're seriously considering letting go of your goals, do not do so lightly.

GOAL MINDSET # 14

DEVELOP RESILIENCE FOR THE LONG HAUL

Know why – the bedrock

As I've already said in previously, knowing WHY you want to achieve something and thinking back to your desired outcome can provide a reason to go on when difficult challenges arise.

Revisit your goals often to remind yourself where you're going, and why. If you've gathered images of your goal, look at them often, just to remind you what you're aiming for.

Pick the right journey

If you've defined and investigated your goal as thoroughly as I've suggested, you'll have a clear idea of what's involved in getting there, so hopefully the stumbling block of "I didn't realise it was going to be like THIS!" won't be one that trips you up.

It has to be said, though, that there is a difference between giving up and changing direction. You might reach a fork in the road along your journey and decide to take one path rather than another. You ultimate goal and your reasons why you want to achieve it, though, will probably remain unchanged.

There might be other factors which mean that you aren't able to achieve your goal or you wish to change direction: circumstances change, your life goals change...stuff happens.

However, if you have really thought about the reasons WHY you wanted to achieve that goal you'll be able to find another route that takes you to a different destination that meets the same needs.

Change direction by all means, but do not give up. Take a step forward every day. Every single day.

Ask yourself am I going to let this hurdle destroy my dreams? It might sound melodramatic, but it can work.
Know your 'triggers'

There's a well know quotation that states "it's not the mountain that will stop you – it's the stone in your shoe".

Ask yourself: what's the stone in your shoe? What's the little, annoying thing that might just have you throwing your hands up in frustration and saying "Oh just forget the whole thing!!!"

Seriously, think about things that annoy you. If you are aware of what your triggers are, then you're more likely to recognise them when they come along, and to be able to deal with them logically, rather than make emotional response.

Recognise when you start to become angry or frustrated and ask yourself "am I going to let this thing/ person/circumstance stop me?"

If it's a person who's annoying you, you're certainly not going to let them get the better of you.

In the light of this question, a jammed printer when you're trying to produce an important report or a traffic jam on the way to a meeting becomes less significant. You're more inclined to find a way round it than to sit down and give up.

(And let's face it, do you really want to be saying to yourself in years to come "I gave up because the printer jammed and I'd been having a bad day"??)

Develop resilience

The concept of 'mental toughness' in sports psychology is one which is well worth further study.

It's NOT about developing a ruthless streak that strips you of your values and means that you'll stop at nothing to reach your goals.

It is about ensuring that your mind works FOR you in all circumstances.

Coping with challenges

Recognise the signs

Become aware of what your body is telling you. When you face challenges and hurdles and your start to become tense, try to identify where physically you become tense.

I tend to clench my teeth: I have a friend who starts drumming his hand on the table. Other people might feel a tightness about the chest, or feel a prickly heat on their scalp.

If you can recognise these early physical symptoms of stress and bring them from the subconscious to the conscious, then you'll be able to do something about them

Starting with breathing and relaxation techniques is best. Take a few moments. At the very least, stop, breathe and think...in that order!

Stop...breathe...THINK!

Challenges will arise. And you can overcome them, or work round them.

Re-frame the negative thought into something more useful: I'm not suggesting you go from "I just can't get to grips with this issue!" to forcing yourself to think "hurray – I'm an expert in this". If it's an unconvincing lie, then there really is no point.

However, you could re-frame this negative thought into something more useful like "I'm going to learn how to do this" or "I can figure this out" or "I'm going to get through this".

My personal favourite is to consciously ask myself: "Is it rocket science? No. Is it brain surgery? No. Then how hard can it be?!"

When your commitment is tested

Sometimes it's easy to lose sight of the mountaintop that you're heading towards when you find yourself slashing through the undergrowth unable to see more than a few feet in front of you. Step back from time to time to refocus on your goals and remind yourself of why you're aiming towards them. Remind yourself of how far you've come. Above all keep moving forward. Do something every day – even if it's a small thing that you don't really feel like doing – that will take you a step closer to your goal.

You've invested a lot of time by now in defining your goals, refining them and devising a plan. Now just follow the plan.

Beware bright shiny distractions

As you move towards your goals, be aware that 'opportunities' might well come your way. Weigh them up carefully – are they opportunities that will contribute to your goal or to your journey towards your goal in some way...or are they distractions?

Maintaining your confidence

Self talk

Remember what we said about self talk? Bear in mind that changing habits – whether mental habits or practical ones – requires repetition. Positive self talk isn't something to be done once in a while it's something to practice constantly.

Remember:

If you're used to saying something negative to yourself, CONSCIOUSLY choose something positive to say instead.

Whenever you catch yourself saying something negative to yourself or talking yourself down choose to say something positive instead. You might not feel like it, but just do it.

Make a choice to be your own cheerleader. Strange though this might sound, sometimes when the going gets tough, you need to hear a voice saying "You're doing OK"! Keep going!!"

Sometimes, that voice has to be your own.

Steer clear of negative people

Some people have an innate ability to sap the life out of people around them. Some people seem to think it's funny or fashionable to grumble about anything and everything. For some people, the glass will always be half empty.

Steer clear of them all as far as you can. Obviously, if they're in your family then that's a bit more difficult – make sure you offset their negative opinions with a circle of friends who are positive and supportive of what you're doing.

Visualisation

This is a straightforward but very effective technique that warrants your investing a bit of time in it. It's perhaps useful to think of it as structured daydreaming.

In essence, what you are doing is visualising in your mind's eye your achieving your goal or some aspect of it. Psychologically, you're focusing on there being a positive outcome: I'm sure all of us at some point have allowed ourselves to think of a forthcoming challenge and pictured the worst possible outcome. How helpful is that?!

Self motivating actions

It's important, as I've already mentioned, to know what your triggers are, and to recognise when you're starting to become demotivated or distracted. Sometimes thinking through the issue is the best way forward. Sometimes, it's better to DO something to take your mind off the problem or challenge, and to allow your subconscious to work on it.

Draw up a list of self-motivating actions: things that will pick you up when you're feeling a bit down.

Whenever I ask course participants what motivates, them, I'm always surprised at the range of their answers, which have included:

Listening to music

Going for a run

Remembering my faith in God

Playing a computer game

Going to sleep – it's never as bad the following morning

Talking to a friend

Reading something inspiring

Watching my favourite film

Playing with my kids

Cooking or baking something

Going to the shed and doing a bit of woodwork

What might you do? Rather than focusing on a challenge or problem and remaining in an unproductive frame of mind, what quick-fix will enable to you to shake off negative feelings and re-focus on moving forward?

Ask yourself:

WHY do I want to achieve this goal?

What will it mean to me when I get there?

What really motivates me?

Who really motivates me?

In the past, what's caused me to give up?

Who drags me down?

What actions can I take to motivate myself?

How will I aim to respond if things don't go the way I planned?

Go for it!

By now, you'll have a notebook full of goals, ideas, plans, observations of your strengths and development areas, a note of people whose help you could use, and lists of tasks to accomplish.

You'll have set yourself SMART goals that relate directly to your goals, and which are the blueprint that will enable you to achieve them.

And of course, you've got this book and the questions in it to refocus at any point as you journey towards your goal.

I'm already on my journey towards my life and career goals. I'd be delighted if you'd join me, right now. There's nothing stopping you...is there?

Ask yourself:

What will I do first?

When?

How will I track my progress?

...what will I do...NOW??

Don't wait any longer – it's time to fly now.

I wish you every possible success.

THE POWER OF HABITS

Chapter 4

A gentleman was once visiting a temple under construction. In the temple premises, he saw a sculptor making a statue. Suddenly he saw, just a few meters away, another identical statue was lying. Surprised he asked the sculptor, "Do you need two statutes of the same". "No" said the sculptor. "We need only one, but the first one got damaged at the last stage". The gentleman examined the sculptor. No apparent damage was visible. "Where is the damage" asked the gentleman. "There is a scratch on the nose of the statue." "Where are you going to keep the statue". The sculptor replied that it will be installed on a pillar 20 meters high. "When the statue will be 20 meters away from the eyes of the beholder, who is going to know that there is scratch on the nose?" The gentleman asked. "The sculptor looked at the gentleman, smiled and said "God knows it and I know it". The desire to excel should be exclusive of the fact whether someone appreciates it or not. Excellence is a drive from "Inside" not "Outside".

Your convictions turn into your considerations, Your considerations turn into your words, Your words turn into your activities, Your activities turn into your habits, Your habits turn into your qualities, Your qualities turn into your fate.

You are driving in the dark. Thoughts of work are slowly disappearing as your favourite music takes over. You are only a few minutes from home when suddenly a drunk driver crosses the centre line at high speed. You brake hard, but the crash is inevitable. You regain consciousness two days later in hospital. You can no longer walk and you are convinced that your life is over.

Is the drunk responsible?

Clearly, he's responsible for the accident. Would he be responsible for your failure to make the best of your new circumstances?

Let's look at what's useful. Blaming the drunk might give us some satisfaction, but it wouldn't help us develop a positive outlook or help us find new opportunities. Other people can help, but ultimately we must do it with or without them. It would surely take extraordinary willpower to do it, but it is the only positive choice.

Many people think it's superficial to suggest that being

successful or not is mostly a matter of choice. The debate may go something like this.

'What if I'm someone who has no confidence?'
'That's a choice.'

No it's not, it's conditioning.'

'Possibly it began that way, but does it matter now? Sitting in the corner, or not speaking up at a meeting, not taking a study course, not taking risks in business are all choices. You would be choosing to give in to your fear of failure.'

'It's like you're patronising people with a simplistic solution. The way they are is a result of their upbringing and their opportunities in life and the genes they inherited. You're making it sound like it's their fault.' Even to dismiss 'choice' as too simplistic is a choice. And we have an inescapable fact: Seeing choices where others don't is an outstanding characteristic of successful people.

The rewards of knowing that we are in control and have choices are not just in motivation, but in better health, better relationships, more optimism, more resilience and less stress. Taking control means looking for choices in every situation. It means thinking carefully about our setbacks to see what we can learn, listing ways of recovering from them, choosing the best and putting them into action.Often we don't exercise our power to choose because we don't think we have any choices, but it can be an invigorating experience to seek them out, especially when we've encountered a setback or face a particularly testing challenge.

Of course, we all make choices every day, but let's divide choices into three categories. The most basic choice is whether to do what's required to survive. It usually relies on needs so, for instance, we eat and sleep and avoid life-threatening situations, but we could choose not to. The second level is broad. It ranges from the basic day-to-day choices: to go to work today, which breakfast cereal to buy, through to those that are more values-based, such as to hand in the money we found in the restaurant or to campaign for a noble cause. Choices in the third category are also value-based, but their particular virtue is the power they give us to make the best use of our talents. I call them liberating choices. The most basic liberating choice is to take charge of our own lives.

Become the captain of your ship

There is a talk about our locus of control, meaning the extent to which we believe that our own behaviour influences events in our lives. It's a sliding scale and can vary from day-to-day and changes in our circumstances. Choosing to take control of our own lives gives us an internal locus of control. We accept that success is up to us, that we have options and can overcome setbacks. It's just a matter of finding the best way. People with a mostly internal locus of control are the captains of their own ships. People who have an external locus of control believe that their success depends on luck, fate, powerful people or other factors beyond their control. Externalizers are the ships – tossed around by the sea.

An externalizer may tell you that his business is suffering because of the government's mis-handling of the economy, the exchange rate or a system of government , and simply sit and wait for something to change. An internaliser might be just as annoyed with the government, but would still believe that his success is up to him. The sense of control we have over our own lives has significant implications for our health. There's also strong evidence that because internalisers are less prone to learned helplessness, they are more optimistic, more persistent, less inclined to suffer depression and more resistant to stress and anxiety.

We develop our locus of control early. Parents who emphasise the value of effort, learning, responsibility and thinking about choices, encourage a healthy internal locus of control. They also tend to model internal beliefs and deliver on any rewards they have promised for achievement. Let's call the decision to take charge of our own lives the Supreme Liberating Choice, because once we have made that choice, we can make others that liberate us to achieve more.

Choose to be courageous

Literally, courage is the ability to face and endure danger, even being immune from fear. For most of us, courage means overcoming fear. Maybe that's real courage – sensing or knowing the frightening possibilities and choosing to take action anyway. It takes judgement to use courage effectively. Adopting a macho courage that drives us to strive for one unattainable goal after another suggests impaired judgement or slow learning. Even so, we'd have to acknowledge that some remarkable people persist long beyond the point where most of us would have decided the goal wasn't worth the effort. The most common effect of losing our courage is stagnation. We create comfortable habits: the same job, the same fixed opinions and the same interests. There's something to be said for being resistant to change. It's not as if all changes are for the better. But sometimes we are simply choosing the apparent security of stagnation. I meet many people who complain that their co-workers are reluctant to learn new computer software, can't bear public speaking and resist new ideas with lofty cynicism or eloquent silence. The people complaining are usually in training workshops. They're ready to change and want to know how. Many of them find changing old habits and learning new skills daunting, but they're doing it. That's courage too.

Choose To Be Proactive

It sounds easy enough, but it's a demanding discipline to be constantly anticipating problems and acting before they develop. It can be as simple as preparing a wet weather and a dry weather plan for your picnic. It can be as complex as having plans to match all the 'what ifs' in a takeover battle – then acting on them appropriately. Being proactive can take determination, energy and courage. If you sense that the share market is about to fall, or your teenager is becoming interested in illegal substances, it would be easy to wait to see what happens or deny the evidence. As we'll see when we look at handling stressful situations, people who take control are much more likely to emerge better for the experience. They also build their resilience for the next crisis. Less resilient people are inclined, not only to passivity and denial, but less robust mental and physical health. Being constantly proactive reminds us that we have choices – that we are in control of our own lives. One caution with choosing to be proactive: We can overdo it. We can become constantly anxious as we search for threats. Choosing to be proactive should mean facing reality and taking action before problems escalate.

We can choose our attitude – always.

Viktor Frankl reports a television interview with a Polish cardiologist who showed how far we can take the notion of choosing our attitude. The cardiologist had helped organize the rebellion against the Nazis in the Warsaw ghetto and the television interviewer was clearly impressed by his heroism. 'Listen,' replied the doctor, 'to take a gun and shoot is no great thing, but if the SS leads you to a gas chamber or to a mass grave to execute you on the spot and you can't do anything about it – except for going your way with dignity – you see, this is what I would call heroism'.

We can always choose to be positive and look for solutions, or at least to accept our situation in a positive way. Choosing our attitude frequently allows us to preserve our valuable relationships. Lashing out with angry, contemptuous words is only satisfying for a moment. Successful people choose their attitude and express their anger in more constructive ways that preserve their relationships.

Choose to be unembarrassable

Think about the last time you were embarrassed and ask yourself what was achieved by it. Does fear of embarrassment make you less inclined to speak up at a meeting, sing a song you enjoy or be outgoing at functions? What would it do to your life if you were to choose to be unembarrassable?

Most people I've associated with have never thought about being unembarrassable. They've thought that being embarrassed was something that happened to you. 'Nice idea,' some would say, but 'I'd just go red and prickly. When you are landed in what other people might see as an embarrassing situation, being embarrassed won't change your circumstances. It can only make you feel worse. It's a choice to give in to it. Choose not to. Avoiding potentially embarrassing situations might ease your fears, but it's a cop-out. If fear of embarrassment is holding you back, prepare a strategy so that if the worst happens you'll know you can handle it.

Let's say you are giving a presentation to 500 people. Your confidence is building to the point where you feel comfortable about leaving the lectern and your notes to step towards the audience a couple of metres. You are sensing the beginnings of a rapport. In the blur of faces you see people nodding, even smiling. They seem to be ignoring your nervousness, or even unaware of it. The words are flowing. You ad-lib a one-liner. They laugh. There's a pause. Suddenly, you've lost it. Five hundred people are waiting for your next point and your mind is blank. How embarrassing is that? Try this: Choose not to be embarrassed and say, as if in a conversation with a friend, 'Let me just check what I was going to mention next.' Go calmly to your notes, take a moment to find your place and come back with energy, 'Ah yes, I wanted to talk about the marketing strategy…' Embarrassment wouldn't have changed anything, just made you and your audience feel bad. Relaxing and recovering with energy will impress them with your confidence and enthusiasm for your message. Liberating isn't it?

What if you were to speak up at a meeting and not a single colleague agreed with you? You might plan to say in a relaxed way, perhaps even with a smile, 'I can see I'm not getting much support on this one, but I just want to make it clear where I stand.' We tend to overestimate the extent to which others even notice our embarrassing moments. If somebody makes unflattering comments about us in public or the security alarm in the library goes off because we forgot to check out a book, it's natural to assume that everybody is noticing and will remember. But observers are much less focused on the embarrassing event than the person it happens to. The observers tend to be charitable through empathy, or because they can imagine doing something similar themselves.

I encourage people who have a high fear of embarrassment to try 'decentering' – which involves questioning whether other people really are evaluating them. We can also choose not to need the whole world's acceptance or approval. We can choose not to be concerned if we don't perform perfectly on every occasion and after all, we're in control of our lives, not the people around us. Some people tell me they are uncomfortable about the effect that unembarrassability might have on society generally. They fear that it will become a licence to embarrass other people simply to show how unembarrassable we are. Drunks do that at parties and it does nothing for their relationships. Being unembarrassable is simply about liberating ourselves from fear so that we can make the best use of our talents.

We can be unembarrassable and still say sorry – maybe often. If we say something hurtful or inconvenience other people, we can apologise, make amends if necessary and decide not to make the same mistake again. Even so, we can move on from any embarrassment, especially that crippling, guilty embarrassment that drags us down weeks and months later. How could that help anyone?

Choose to be happy

Here's a simple question. Which of these events, if they happened tomorrow, would make you happier a couple of years from now:

winning a substantial prize in a lottery

being disabled in an accident

staying at home and reading a book?

It may seem a ridiculous question to ask, but the average outcome of those three events may surprise you. In resaerch comparing people who had won between 50,000 and a million rands in lottery, people who had been disabled in accidents and 'regular folks' who had not had either experience. The only real difference was that on average the regular folks were a little happier than the people who had been injured. Clearly, some lottery winners in that study were miserable and some accident victims happy. It is support for the notion that events are neutral and we choose our reaction to them. There's evidence that many people are born with 'happiness genes'. It doesn't mean that they drift through life in a euphoric haze, only that they have a pre-disposition to be happy.

Liberating choices

Not having the genes doesn't stop the rest of us being

happy. Happy people view life and cope with setbacks, and they are all attitudes or skills we can choose to learn.

Happy people think more positively about themselves and have a network of supportive relationships. They recover from setbacks more quickly and have better problem-solving skills. They have a sense of humour, even when the going gets tough. Happy people are inclined to think of the positive side of negative events. Unhappy people dwell on the negative, even with events that we could easily see as positive: 'That holiday put me behind with my work'.

Develop your happiness

We can choose the approach to happiness: to find it in everyday events as simple as a smile, our children's milestones, the first signs of spring, intimate moments with our partner or a calm sunny morning – rather than some pot of gold. You could say that all we would be doing is creating short-term pleasure from everyday things, and you would be right. It's when it becomes a way of life and we look back over perhaps years, that we can say we are happy or happier.

Want a long-term focus for building happiness? People with the most satisfying lives choose to focus on causes beyond themselves. For many, it comes from volunteering in the community. For others, it's striving to be an excellent parent, friend, colleague or leader while living according to their values.

Let's be realistic

Happy people are able to appraise situations well and when the stakes are high, or their self-esteem is at stake they feel disappointment, sadness, anger, and frustration like everyone else.

Even if you make it to the top 10 percent on the happiness scale, it won't be all bliss. Although happy people can see more positives in negative events, they often need time to do it. Even so, their healthy reaction to negative events sets them apart from less happy people, more than anything else. Happiness is a way of life rather than a permanent state of mind.

Choose to love unconditionally

Loving unconditionally makes love a gift, not a deal. We expect nothing in return. In reality, we benefit too, but that benefit may be no more than believing that we are better people. More likely the love will be returned over time. In strong relationships people express love partly by contributing to a reservoir of goodwill, whether the other person is contributing or not. Loving unconditionally doesn't mean tolerating unacceptable behaviour. We can question, even object vehemently, to rudeness, selfishness or idleness and demand changes, but the love is never in question. We choose to believe that people are lovable, despite their faults.

Many relationships suffer because the partners react to bad behaviour or criticism with contempt. They see the behaviour not as a lapse, but an ingrained characteristic of someone who is no longer worthy of love or even respect. The response becomes an attack, not on the behaviour, but the person: 'That's typical! You're always looking after number one. You're a loser! That's rich coming from someone who always...' Contempt is a key feature of relationships that fail early. Even if the bad behaviour really is ingrained, someone who loves unconditionally still sees it as separate from the person. Let's acknowledge that we can't love everyone, but if we see love as more than romance or love for our family, we could extend it to our friends, even colleagues or team mates. You and I might have different views of how far we can extend unconditional love. We might express a general love of humanity, because we like most people we meet, but to give all of humanity unconditional love is to choose the demanding path to sainthood.

Choose to think and act independently

Imagine you are sitting at a table with six other people. In front of you are two cards and I am asking everyone in turn which of the three vertical lines on one card is the same height as the single vertical line on the other card. It's supposed to be an experiment in 'visual judgement'. At first, it seems a pointless exercise. Then I keep on introducing new pairs of cards and everyone agrees which line in each card is the same height. The answers are obvious. After the sixth pair of cards something odd happens. You are near the end of the line and everyone else has given the wrong answer. Would you go along with them, or stay with the answer you know to be right? What about the next time and the time after that?

Clearly, if you had made the choice to think and act independently, you would say what you believe, but more than one in three people would go along with the majority opinion. We need to acknowledge that going along with the majority makes sense much of the time. Clearly, it pays to drive on the same side of the road as everyone else and it's essential to the democratic process that we accept a majority decision. There are conventions that seem reasonable to most of us. Dressing in your best for a wedding says, 'I'm taking this seriously. I'm respecting the occasion'.

There are some conventions that don't make much sense, but we might not think it worth the hassle of rebelling against them. Wearing a tie to work with our shirts buttoned to the throat makes little sense, beyond adding a little colour, and wearing the same outfit on a tractor, as some men do, makes no sense at all. We could dye our hair green, but it's an unusual statement of independence to do it.

Successful people choose to think and act independently when it liberates them to do more with their lives.

They refuse to be controlled by what other people might think when it stops them achieving their goals and living their values. They can distinguish between conventional thinking and what they believe to be right, and they refuse to fulfill other people's expectations when they conflict with their own values or aspirations.

Choosing to be released from the past

It's like driving by looking at the rear vision mirror, but very human. Past resentments, guilt, anger and destructive habits can be overwhelming. But releasing ourselves from the past is a choice we can make. When Nelson Mandela emerged from prison after 26 years on South Africa's notorious Robben Island, he had every reason to be bitter. Instead, he chose and advocated forgiveness. In his autobiography he says, that when he left prison he made it his mission to liberate both the oppressed and the oppressors, '... for to be free is not merely to cast off one's chains, but to live in a way that respects and enhances the freedom of others.'

Letting go can be difficult, but a range of techniques can help. If it's guilt over something you have done or not done, you may be able to put things right with an apology, an offer to make amends, or simply talking it over. If it's anger or resentment holding you back, you may be able to resolve it with some assertiveness. If it's embarrassment, remind yourself that you are human and that you choose not to need the world's approval for everything you do. If you can't do anything about the cause, it's time to put the events and the disruptive thoughts behind you because there is nothing to be gained by prolonging the guilt, anger or resentment.

Prepare a standard distraction you can use when you sense upsetting emotions welling up – perhaps a tune or favourite thoughts. Therapists who work with people with recurring disruptive thoughts recommend that they yell stop! or hit a desk or wall, the moment they sense the thoughts returning. That's easy in a therapy room, but maybe at work or out shopping you'll prefer their less public alternative – perhaps snapping a rubber band around your wrist. Whatever you choose, you'll be interrupting the disruptive thought, which makes it easier to think about your favourite dining spot or run the catchiest tune you can think of through your mind one more time.

Redefine your identity and tell yourself regularly. 'I'm one of those people who never dwell in the past.' or 'I'm the kind of person who never harbours a grudge'. Do the same with your other choices. 'I'm someone who knows there's always a choice' or 'I'm not someone who's easily embarrassed. I'm an optimist. I'm a happy person who finds pleasure in everyday events'.

Your Brain

This part is about the most trainable part of your brain.

It's vital in achieving your goals, managing your emotions, building your relationships, leading, negotiating and any other way you might define success.

Many people have difficulty reacting in any other way to emotionally-charged situations. I know a chief executive of a very large organisation who admits to striking another motorist in the middle of a city street. His anger had hijacked an intelligent brain, shutting out the possible consequences to his career and reputation.

Get to know your prefrontal cortex

Fortunately our brains have what we might call an executive centre that takes the raw emotion and says, 'Hold on a moment, maybe there's another way of interpreting and responding to this one.' Your executive centre is in the prefrontal cortex and if your hand is on your forehead as you are reading this, you're almost touching it.

There is a link between the front of the brain and emotions and personality.

In 1848, Phineas Gage entered the history of medical science and psychology professors around the world still tell his story. Gage was on a railway construction project in Vermont. He was the contracting company's most able and efficient foreman, described as having a well-balanced mind and being a shrewd businessman. September 14 was not his best day at work. As he was laying an explosive charge, it ignited and sent a tamping iron one metre long point-first into his left cheek bone, through the front of his skull and out again. It landed 10 metres away. It seems incredible, but he survived. The tamping iron had performed an accidental prefrontal lobotomy.

Months later Gage felt ready to return to work, but his personality had changed dramatically. The railway company described him as, 'fitful, irreverent and grossly profane, showing little deference for his fellows'. He was 'impatient and obstinate, yet capricious and vacillating', unable to settle on any of the plans he devised for his future action'. The tamping iron is now an exhibit at the Museum of the Medical College of Harvard University.

Typically, people with an impaired prefrontal cortex have difficulty forming strategies, even for simple tasks. They become irresponsible, lack emotion and have no concern for the present, let alone the future. It's clear that the brain's executive centre helps us make decisions, concentrate, plan and stick to our goals. It also gives us an emotional working memory which allows us to learn from our emotional experiences and anticipate how we might feel if the same thing happened again. The prefrontal cortex helps explain some significant differences in the way people respond to emotional events and the time it takes to recover from events that generate fear or anger. Most of the key emotional skills depend on our ability to respond in emotionally and socially appropriate ways, rather than react impulsively to anger, fear or want. Some people have highly developed executive centres. I've been with taxi drivers as other motorists have cut them off and shut them out and heard them say in an unruffled way things like, 'Well, I guess it takes all sorts to make a world'.

Ready for some training?

Kirk Brown and Richard Ryan from the University of Rochester have been researching a simple strategy that seems to develop the power of the prefrontal cortex.

Mindfulness has become popular in the last few years and taught in businesses. It involves training ourselves to focus on what is happening right now.

When listening to our partner or child, we could increase our mindfulness by being particularly attentive to both the words and the subtle emotional content, without judgement. We could take a walk and pay attention to the range of sounds under our feet and around us. We could savour the taste of our morning coffee – perhaps identifying which parts of our tongue are affected most by the lingering flavour. We could focus on our emotions and put names to their subtle changes.

So, what's the pay-off for increasing our mindfulness? Better self-regulation, more positive emotions, less pre-occupation with negative emotions, less absorption with the past and fewer anxious fantasies about the future.

Socialising teaches most of us to resist impulsive behaviour, but impulsive behaviour is increasing.

The harm of impulsiveness

So how much damage does impulsiveness do to your life chances?

Even those of us who generally cope well with life, battle with impulsiveness from time-to-time. A negotiator who reacts to a hostile comment with a single outburst of retaliation may ruin her chances of success. A leader who can't resist an impulsive putdown comment may destroy the trust he has built with his team. The consumer who wants, but doesn't need, a new car, house or suit may live to regret his tendency to buy on impulse.

Instead of acting on impulse, we can pause and focus on the long-term benefits of a considered response. At work, we might strive to be the consummate professional, at home, the model parent. It sounds simple, but our ability to regulate our emotions, both positive and negative, and to learn from our experiences is at the heart of success in business, study, sport and relationships.

There is strong link between children waiting, and their ability in adulthood to delay angry reactions long enough to develop some cooling strategies. Grabbing the chocolate bar is impulsive. So is the angry lashing out of the adult who feels frustrated or hurt by criticism in a meeting.

Pre-schoolers can learn to delay gratification with 'fun thoughts' (for example, what it was like when we went to the beach) or reframing (perhaps, imagining the marshmallows are rubber). Adults who refuse to give in to children who 'want it and want it now' are laying the foundations for a range of vital emotional skills.

Taking time to consider our responses, rather than reacting to our initial emotion is a major theme of the rest of this book. That self-regulation is, of course, a choice and based on the supreme liberating choice – to take control of our own lives.

Being Optimistic

Use the simple method you'll see in a moment to develop your optimism in a focused way. Hang on to it. Make it a way of life. Optimistic people have enormous advantages. Optimism is strongly associated, not only with motivation and achievement, but more rewarding relationships and significantly better mental and physical health. It's healthy optimism we need not: 'It can't happen to me' or 'Don't worry, be happy, everything will be okay' (and doing nothing). That's denial.

Unbridled optimism is as useful as striving to be relentlessly positive. They are related ideas and they're both exhausting and unrealistic. Despite what many of the motivational gurus say, the research shows that you'll be less resilient and achieve less. Healthy optimism means facing the facts, but believing that we will cope, or succeed in the end. Healthy optimism doesn't mean being totally realistic or objective about our ability to overcome our setbacks. The idea that to be mentally healthy we need an accurate picture of reality, isn't supported by the research. Depressed people have the most accurate view say, the probability that they will have a serious accident or a fatal disease. Their realism doesn't make them successful.

I believe that our achievements and our mental and physical health depend on 'positive illusions' such as evaluating ourselves more positively than the facts justify and believing that we have more control and skill than we do. A flattering selection of facts and memories about ourselves is more healthy than objective reality because it gives us the confidence to continue facing challenges. Positive illusions seem to be more common and perhaps more useful in western cultures. In Asia, where belonging and relating to other people is valued more than independence, seeing ourselves as average could be more adaptive.

Think of healthy optimism as the zone between denial and the depressed person's view of reality. Healthy optimism is a key to motivation and resilience. Take selling. Even if you've never made a living from selling, you can probably imagine the challenge of facing rejection every day – rejection that could vary from a polite, 'No, thank you,' to being chased off the premises.

How long and well do you want to live?

Optimists live longer, healthier lives – and not just a little longer or a little healthier.

Of almost 100 men who had graduated from Harvard University between 1939 and 1944. The men had been interviewed and physically examined every five years and the researchers were able to conclude that their optimism or pessimism at 25 predicted their health at 65. By the time they reached just 45, the pessimists' health began to deteriorate more quickly. Researchers from the Mayo Clinic studied the health of 839 patients over 30 years. They found that the optimists decreased their chances of early death by 50 per cent. They were also happier, more peaceful, more relaxed and had less pain and suffered fewer physical and emotional problems. Some researchers have studied 'learned helplessness'. It's a product of conditioning that starts when we are very young, but we can learn to replace pessimism with optimism. So how do we account for the repeated findings that positive people and optimists live longer? It could be that the real issue is avoiding negativity and the harmful effect it has on our autonomic nervous system which keeps our body aroused to handle threats.

Positive emotions have a healing effect. Pessimists' bodies have even more to cope with than constant arousal. They are more likely to believe that nothing they do makes any difference, so they drink and smoke more than other people, and exercise less. They are also less likely to visit their doctor for a check-up. They are significantly more depressed and depression is linked with early death. There's also evidence that a pessimistic outlook damages or inhibits the body's immune system. Pessimists suffer in their relationships throughout their lives. They have more relationship break-ups, have more family troubles, fail more often in their education and are more likely to be lonely – probably because all the doom and gloom talk turns off people with a more balanced view of life.

Longer, healthier, happier lives with more rewarding and enduring relationships. It puts the effort to train ourselves to be more optimistic into perspective, doesn't it? If you think that your outlook is generally pessimistic, don't despair. You won't have to wait decades to see the benefits of retraining yourself. This time you will have two very important advantages: You'll be focused on change and you'll be in charge of the training process.

Getting specific about optimism

I think of optimism in two ways: a generally optimistic outlook (a trait) and an optimistic 'explanatory style'. Explanatory style is the way we usually explain our successes and setbacks to ourselves.

Develop your optimistic explanatory style

You can develop your optimism by changing or enhancing your explanatory style. It can be a challenge to change old habits, but the process is simple. The successful people attribute their failures and setbacks to something other than their ability or potential. When they succeed, it's the opposite – confirmation that they have ability or potential.

A student with an optimistic explanatory style would believe that her poor mark in an exam had a temporary cause, say, not studying hard enough. She would still believe in her potential. A student with a pessimistic explanatory style would believe that the cause of her poor mark was lack of talent- something she couldn't change. The mark would be evidence that she had no potential and should abandon the subject.

If it seems easy to avoid that kind of pessimistic thinking, let's note what many people say about their setbacks. They tell themselves that it shows they have no talent: 'I'm just no good at this. I should stick to things I can do.' They will also see the barriers to success as permanent or inevitable: 'It's impossible.' They avoid challenges and give up easily because any setback is evidence that they were right about their talent or the barriers to success. They set easy goals to avoid being crushed by more failure. They may believe that success is a matter of luck or fate, not effort, persistence or choice.

An optimistic explanatory style

You tell yourself that it's an opportunity to learn. It's a setback, not a failure. You still believe in your potential to succeed. If the event is not something you can control, you recognise that you could not have done anything about it, that it will not always occur and has a limited effect on your life.

A pessimistic explanatory style

You tell yourself that it's a failure, all your fault and evidence that you don't have the potential to succeed. You may even tell yourself that you fail at everything you do and always will. In its most severe form, pessimism or learned helplessness is expressed in self-talk such as, 'I'm hopeless at this, and everything else and I always will be.' This refer to those three elementsas internal ('It's me. I failed because I don't have the ability.') stable, ('I'll always fail.') and global ('I'll fail in everything I do.'). That pessimistic self-talk is also a characteristic of people who are depressed. Pessimists cannot win because when they do succeed, they dismiss it as just luck: 'I was just in the right place at the right time,' or, 'The boss must have been in a good mood,' or 'I should quit now before they find out I'm no good.' It's all very humble and there is a place for, 'I was lucky' when we are considering other people's feelings. What really matters is what we tell ourselves. Let's not miss out on the benefits of seeing each success as confirmation of our potential or ability.

Let's look at the process in a little more detail.

1. Choose to be on your way to being a first-class leader, parent, sportsperson etc.

It puts you in growth mindset, which is likely to make you more adaptive and focused on what you want to become and achieving your personal best each time. You may be worried that you would be avoiding reality by choosing to be on your way to being first-class, but we don't know the reality of your potential. Let's consider the alternatives. You could choose to say to yourself, 'I'm no good at this and never will be'. How real is that? It might be true, but more likely it's just the easy way out.

So how true is your belief that you are on your way to being a first-class leader, parent or golfer? We won't know until you've developed a pattern of healthy self-talk about your successes and setbacks and learned from them. Maybe, by the end of your life, you'll only be competent rather than excellent, but it surely beats quitting at the first hurdle. Why shouldn't you be on your way to being a first-class almost-anything-you-like? If you are motivated and prepared to learn from experience why should you be limited by the way you and other people have seen your abilities up till now? Carol Dweck of Stanford University, has some strong views about the notion that our current performance dictates our long term potential. It's in her list of 'beliefs that make smart people dumb'.

2. Strive to act the part.

Once you have made your choice, strive to act the part of someone who is already first-class in that role. A first-class speaker for instance would appear to the audience to be totally confident, not giving in to fear of embarrassment. A first-class parent would strive to be fair and consistent and create opportunities for his child to develop new skills – amongst many other things. Striving to act the part of someone who is already first-class helps us focus on high performance, and because we are in a growth mindset, we can accept our setbacks as simply part of the process of learning.

Think of acting the part of an optimistic, confident, first-class performer as heroic. You'll feel the fear of trying something new, of being someone you're not yet, but you'll choose to do it anyway. Does acting the part seem false or insincere? Maybe it is, but we have obligations to ourselves and other people that are far more important. The opera singer who acts the part of a confident performer from the moment she sweeps on stage is setting herself and the audience up for a first-class performance. So are Olympic athletes, professional footballers, swimmers, business people and politicians around the world. The British prime minister Winston Churchill suffered deep depression, but chose to act the part of the confident, optimistic leader throughout the Second World War. There's no hint of pessimism in, 'We shall fight on the beaches. We shall fight in the fields and in the streets. We shall never surrender!'

3. Attribute any setback to something other than your potential.

If you have an optimistic explanatory style and encounter a setback, it obviously won't be anything to do with your potential, because you're on your way to being first-class. It will be something you did or didn't do, probably something you can learn or improve next time. Maybe it'll be something about the circumstances that won't arise again. It's the most challenging part of the process and not just a matter of cheering yourself up. You'll be actively separating your disappointment and any temptation to dismiss your potential from your need to look for ways of doing better next time.

You often need to become a sceptic as you examine your own reactions to setbacks. For instance, let's say you have just come away from a party you haven't enjoyed. Your natural inclination might be to think, 'I'm just no good at parties. I've always been shy and always will be.' Imagine being a supportive friend who likes to ask sceptical questions. Your friend might ask, 'What about the party last Easter? You enjoyed that, and talked to Jane for an hour. Haven't you enjoyed parties when you've made the effort to start conversations? How many conversations did you start this time? What are you going to do next time?'

Your sceptical friend can help you see failures as simply setbacks and bad events as temporary and controllable. Even if the bad events are beyond your control, you can use your disputation to help you maintain your belief in your potential. We could blame other people or find reasons or excuses and we would still be explaining our setbacks as nothing to do with our ability or potential. We could say that an exam wasn't a valid test of our ability, it's not a goal worth worrying about, or that it was someone else's fault.

Reasons or excuses become particularly tempting when our failures are public. Sometimes finding excuses we can live with is useful because it leaves our belief in ourselves intact. But if that's what we usually do, it becomes a way of avoiding reality and we miss opportunities to learn from the experience. It also suggests that we have not yet made the Supreme Liberating Choice – to take control of our own lives.

4. Attribute your success to your potential or ability.

Top achievers see their success as evidence of their ability or potential. 'It shows that I'm on my way to being a first-class speaker,' or 'I always knew I had the potential.' Okay, maybe you can't share your thoughts with the world, but you can, and should, tell yourself. You can say similar things out loud when your children succeed. Make it genuine. These days, even a ten-year-old recognizes flattery. You might want to be more restrained with your colleagues, partners and friends. Overstating your explanation for their success makes it seem artificial – just a technique and even manipulative. Your affirmations should be credible and genuine. The conversations might go something like these.

You: 'How did the competition go?'

Friend: 'I got gold.'

You: 'Thought you might. Congratulations.'

'Thought you might' states your belief in your friend's ability or potential in a low-key way.

You (as team leader): 'The directors were impressed by your presentation.'

Team member: 'That's a relief. I was really worried.'
You: 'I wasn't. You were well prepared and you're a confident speaker.'

You could add a suggestion to help your team member do even better next time (provided it doesn't come across as a criticism and the real point of your comments). It's important not to attribute your success entirely to what you did. It may be that specific, practical things you did helped you succeed and obviously it would be useful to note what worked, but the key issue is your ability or potential. If you were to say to yourself, 'I did well because I studied hard', it would encourage you to study hard next time, but its value in building your optimism would be temporary. The world's top achievers learn to believe in themselves, not simply what they do to succeed.

How's your mindset?

Do you believe that people are either intelligent or talented or not and can't change? That's evidence of a fixed mindset. It's unhealthy and the consequences are serious.

If you have a fixed mindset, it's likely that you will be less inclined to take on challenges and be less resilient. You will be less likely to be a top achiever and you'll probably focus your efforts on trying to impress other people, or at least avoid their criticism. People with fixed mindsets are likely to see themselves as failures, not just their attempts to meet the standards they have set. Their fear of failure makes them more inclined to take easy assignments rather than challenges. They lack resilience because even a setback is evidence that they don't have the talent or intelligence.

Fixed mindsetters avoid practising and learning skills. To be seen doing either would suggest they didn't already have what it takes.

Do you believe that people can develop their intelligence and talents? Do you see life as a series of opportunities to experiment and learn? You have a growth mindset. Growth mindsetters enjoy the journey. They willingly take on challenges. Setbacks may be frustrating, but they are opportunities to learn. Growth mindsetters are resilient achievers.

Motivating children

Mindset and explanatory style have much in common and both are vital for raising healthy, resilient, motivated children. You can help your children to motivate themselves by believing in their potential, no matter what mistakes they make or what setbacks they encounter. Help them develop a growth mindset by seeing setbacks as learning opportunities and a natural part of working towards a goal. You might need to suggest that they should work harder or concentrate more, but that's healthy too, because that effort is within their control. Even suggesting that the effort is worth it, implies that you believe in their potential.

The effects of your belief can be dramatic. A tutor gave nine-year-olds a set of word puzzles and responded to their failures by criticising their effort and implying that they should work harder – which suggested that he believed they could succeed. With another group he focused on how wrong they were – suggesting that they didn't have much ability. Half the puzzles both groups were given were impossible. Only 25 per cent of the children whose effort was criticised believed that they failed because they lacked the ability. In the group that had heard how wrong they were, 75 percent reported that they failed because they didn't have the ability. It took only one hour to create the difference in beliefs at the heart of motivation and health.

Encourage your children to be independent and set high standards for themselves. You are implying that you know they have the ability or potential to succeed. Bernard Rosen and Roy D'Andrade tested 9 to 11 year old boys for motivation. Then they visited those at the top and bottom of the scale at home to watch what happened when they tackled challenging tasks such as building a tower from irregularly shaped blocks while blindfolded. Both mothers and fathers of the highly motivated boys were very involved and set high standards for them to achieve on the frustrating tasks. They offered hints and were very ready to praise their sons' success at each stage.

The parents of the boys who had scored poorly on the motivation test were very different. The fathers, especially, didn't encourage independence or set high standards. They often told them how to do the task and became annoyed when their sons had any setbacks.

Staying on track to our goals

Before we begin, we must make sure that the goals are our goals. Most of our goals are influenced by other people. It's almost inevitable that the people who raised us, the people we admire or with whom we have shared experiences, will have had some bearing on the goals we set for ourselves.

Concordant goals are those that match our own long-term interests and values and which give us a sense of satisfaction as we make progress towards them. Being clear on what we want to achieve does check out as an effective motivator. That's hardly surprising, but even writing our goals and displaying them prominently isn't enough. Our goals are much more motivating if we think carefully about what our success will look like. Create a vivid mental picture and keep returning to it.

Here's a refinement. After you have imagined what success will look like, consider what you don't like about the way things are. Create a contrast between the way things are now and how life will be once you have achieved the goal. Write them – both of them. Review and revise them regularly.

Achievers focus on action, not optimism about their goals. There's some evidence that the most optimistic goal-setters are the least resilient. They are crushed by setbacks they didn't expect. Focusing on action means setting short-term, maybe daily, goals that describe what you will do – and getting on with them. It's important to make sure that your daily goals relate to your long-term goals. Day-to-day 'relatively-urgent-but-not-important' tasks can easily take over and our long-term goals become relegated to the status of something we must get around to sometime. There are significant mental health benefits when our goals are our own, we relate our daily goals to the big picture, make the striving fun and make an effort to work on all our goals.

There is a trap in goal-setting. We can aim too low so that all we are doing is reassuring ourselves that we have a plan. An effective goal is a stretch.

Never link your sense of self-worth to your goals.

Deciding that you'll be a worthwhile person when you pass an exam, buy your dream home or find your life partner is unhealthy and unproductive. You are less likely to achieve those goals and may pay a significant price as you strive for them. Social Research surveyed more than 600 students and found that more than 80 per cent based their sense of self-worth on their academic achievements. The students who made that link did not receive higher grades, despite being highly motivated and studying more. They were more likely to feel stressed and more likely to be in conflict with the academic staff. Linking their sense of self-worth to their grades made them more sensitive to failure.

There wasn't even an upside to compensate. When they did do well, they just moved the goal posts. Their sense of self-worth didn't increase any more than the other students who weren't depending on the outcome to feel good about themselves. We can choose not to need to justify our existence to the world and feel worthless when we have setbacks. People who agree with the statement, 'In order to be truly happy I must prove that I am thoroughly adequate and achieving in most things I attempt,' are not only dissatisfied and more sensitive to their failings, but much more inclined to be depressed. Achievers are more likely to find their self-esteem internally. The students in the University of Michigan survey, who based their self-esteem on internal sources such as being a virtuous person or adhering to their own moral standards, received higher grades.

Top achievers enjoy the journey, setting goals and giving their best effort certainly, but believing in themselves, not just in what they achieve along the way.

Control Your Emotions

You are at a function. You've been looking forward to this one. You've taken the trouble to dress up and the evening has been all you had hoped. As you cross the room to thank your hosts, you pass a woman who has been talking loudly for the last hour. Suddenly, she lifts a wobbling hand with a full glass of what looks in your peripheral vision alarmingly like red wine. You react too late and the wine spills down the front of your jacket and her dress. She looks menacing and shouts, 'Why don't you watch where you're going? You're a disgrace. Who invited you? Get out of here!' Everyone turns to watch.

What's your reaction?

Just as important, what are you thinking? If it's, 'This is humiliating,' your reaction might be embarrassment, perhaps followed by depression. If it's, 'She's asking for trouble, I have to show her that I'm not the kind of person to be treated like this,' your reaction may be anger. If you are thinking, 'She might attack me,' your reaction would probably be anxiety or even panic. Those thoughts would reflect your beliefs and something about your personality, but each would probably be inaccurate and the reactions unhealthy. There's another way of thinking about the same predicament. 'She's drunk. I'm not. I'll react calmly and everyone will know that she's the one behaving badly.' That kind of thinking reflects the belief, 'I'm a good and confident person,' and the action (reacting calmly) helps you to soothe yourself and the situation.

When we are at the centre of a public 'scene' or some other highly emotive event, we respond in ways that we've learned over the years and they are frequently automatic. But even if our immediate response is unhealthy, we can change it with some simple strategies. Ideally, we should deal with our problems directly. If we are anxious about a business slump, we can prepare a plan and put it into action. If it's a family crisis we can sit down together and work our way through it. People who deal with their problems directly are the most adept at reducing their disruptive emotions and feelings of stress. Problem-focused coping also increased their sense of control in their lives and their self-esteem. It works even when we are already depressed, anxious or angry. A partner who is under pressure at work might decide that his problem was that his wife doesn't support him in his career, so he would complain and make demands for more support. The real problem was stress at work.

Dealing with the problem might be the best strategy, but clearly, it's not always possible. So much of life is like the spilled wine: It happens before we know it and there's nothing practical we can do about it. Instead, we need strategies to manage our emotional reactions so that, although whatever caused them continues, we preserve our own mental health and our valuable relationships. Resilient people combine reframing with a commitment to finding a solution and they also see stressful events, especially change, as a challenge. They see their successes or setbacks as things they can control, so they will agree with statements such as, 'What happens is my own doing,' and 'Capable people who fail to achieve have not taken advantage of their own opportunities'.

I find resilient people very effective at gathering information and reviewing a range of possible solutions. They may also ask friends, family or colleagues for practical help. Notice how their attitudes reflect an internal locus of control – the belief that they are the captain of their own ship and that they have choices. People who handle life's stresses least well blame themselves, indulge in wishful thinking or try to avoid facing their problems. Men are more likely to abuse alcohol or drugs to avoid problems. Women are more likely to do passive (and less harmful) things such as watch television, drink coffee, eat, rest or go shopping.

There's one outstanding characteristic of people who do better under stress and it's optimism. Optimists are not only more motivated, they're more confident, resilient, resourceful and problem-focused, both in a crisis and with everyday hassles. Optimists live less troubled and more rewarding lives. But it only works for those who are healthy optimists, who face reality – not those who dream, deny or avoid their way through life. Optimists emerge as individuals who follow the idea espoused in the well-known 'serenity prayer' – accepting those things that can not be changed and working to effect change where possible'.

Try some therapy

Do-it-yourself, cognitive therapy is useful even for people who are not particularly troubled by everyday negative emotions or irrational thoughts because it provides a focus for healthy thinking in times of stress. The challenge of self-therapy is to stay on track. As with dieting, it's unrealistic to expect instant success. You'll have short-term successes, but the real value comes from being dedicated to retraining yourself long-term.

We will look more closely at how you might apply your self-therapy to depression, anxiety, anger and stress soon, but first, we need to note the essential steps in cognitive therapy.

What to do

The first step is to recognise the emotion and name it. Just being aware of which emotion is disrupting us is a valuable skill and researchers have found that people who are able to identify and name their disruptive emotions are able to recover from them more quickly. Think about how your body is reacting. Is it flushed with anger, or heavy like a weight in the stomach? Think about what may have led to your disruptive mood and your usual way of reacting. Is this reaction similar? I encourage you to keep a diary to monitor the disruptive emotions and record the events that lead to them.

Sometimes the symptoms are mixed, but it's important to recognise the symptoms and name the emotions as best we can.

What am I saying?

You must recognize what you are telling yourself about the upsetting event. Think of it in two stages: 'Is this event really a threat?' and if it is, 'What can I do about it?' Slowing the process down and thinking deliberately and sceptically helps to break unhealthy thinking habits.

You can hear thinking errors every day, even from people who cope well with disruptive emotions, but don't give much thought to what they are saying. 'Wet days really depress me' or 'My cousin makes me so uptight,' suggests that our mood is controlled by the weather or another person. What about, 'Exams make me really nervous' or 'Mondays make me gloomy' or 'Parties always make me feel anxious'?

Those statements cannot be true. They refer to neutral

events. Our reactions to them may have been influenced by our experiences throughout life, but today those reactions are a choice. Believing that events, or people or days of the week, or the stars, control our emotions suggests that we are not the captain of our own ship.

That can't be right!

Apply some healthy scepticism. Give yourself time to look at the situation and be sceptical about the beliefs that have led you to your initial reaction. Thinking that the drunk with the wine glass is the one who is behaving badly and that everyone knows it stops you thinking that the situation is insulting, threatening or humiliating. You may still be annoyed, but it's healthier than responding with rage, panic or depression.

Scepticism helps us to be more objective and that's not easy when we are caught up in a depressive fog, or feeling anxious or angry. The emotional state distorts our perception of reality. Depressed people are especially quick to spot any signs of strained friendship. They exaggerate the slightest criticism and are much more likely to interpret remarks as critical. Healthy scepticism can be a challenging discipline, but ask the direct questions, 'Did she really mean to criticise? Isn't he just a bit tired and grumpy this morning? We have a strong relationship don't we? Is there any evidence that she really thought that? Would it matter? Wasn't it just a passing comment?'

The pioneers of cognitive therapy assumed that their clients were distressed because they had irrational beliefs or were systematically misinterpreting information from the outside world. Since then Australian researchers have used it successfully with people whose distress seems perfectly rational and based on accurate information – patients with advanced cancer. Sarah Adelman and Anthony Kidman from the University of Technology in Sydney report that while the cause of the patients' stress may have been real, they were still making the classic thinking errors. Those patients learned to reframe their thinking. 'If I can't do the things I used to life is not worth living', became 'I can't do some of the things, but there are many things I can do to make my life worthwhile'. 'If there's a chance that something bad might happen, I should focus on it now', became 'I will deal with it when the time comes'. They also encouraged the patients to work on problems they could solve, such as better medication for pain and resolving conflicts with other people.

Reframing in action

'There's no such thing as bad weather – only the wrong clothes.' -- Billy Connelly

Useful comparisons

If you are distressed because your team lost an important game, try comparing your success with those teams that didn't even make the quarter-finals. If your business is worrying you, try comparing yourself with someone who is bankrupt. Even when the situation seems desperate, some people manage to find a useful comparison that makes them feel better.

Express emotions

There's strong evidence that expressing emotions does help us to recover more quickly, but as you'll see, expressing them is not the same as acting them out or being preoccupied with them.

If processing and expressing emotions helps us to understand more about an upsetting event and leads us to develop plans to move on or feel more positive, we benefit both mentally and physically. Numerous studies have shown that writing about traumatic events, especially a current trauma, can be a very effective healing process because it helps us assimilate and understand the event better. Putting the event into words seems to prevent intrusive, distressing memories. It has worked for people in a variety of distressing situations, including post-traumatic stress disorder and breast cancer.

Let's look at the main disruptive emotions and some strategies in more detail.

Manage depression

Depression is the fourth most prevalent disease in the

world. It seriously damages the quality of life of millions of people and drains economies through the costs of mental health services and lost productivity. We may have more freedoms, more wealth and more opportunities, but it seems that in the world, the last one hundred years has brought more depression, not less.

Are you dwelling on negative thoughts about yourself, or your future for prolonged periods? Depressed people tend to think in absolute terms about loss, hopelessness, worthlessness and fatigue, and they think they'll always feel that way. Depression is common in adolescence, during pregnancy and after giving birth, but it is not the inevitable outcome of loss or failure or hormonal changes. It's perfectly normal to grieve, feel sad, feel rejected and go through life's transitions without the long-term suffering and distorted thinking associate with depression.

Most people recover from depression whether it is treated or not, but if you have had one depressive episode, your chances of having another are increased to about 50/50.[58] Depression can be a very serious disorder. You may be able to manage mild depression with cognitive therapy, but talk to your doctor if you think you have something more serious or managing it yourself doesn't work.

First, as you sense you are heading towards an emotional slump, you must recognise the symptoms of depression and call it depression. You'll find that many of the suggestions for managing mild depression will help with sadness too.

Usually, the event that triggered your mood will be abundantly clear, but not always. Sometimes small things can set off a depressive reaction so that you lose track of the cause. If you do know the cause, you may be able to deal with it directly, but let's assume that you can't or that solving the problem hasn't been enough to take away the symptoms of depression.

Stop the rumination

People who ruminate worry excessively about their depression. They often isolate themselves to think about their symptoms and ask 'What if I don't get over this?' It's a passive reaction to depression. Ruminators are not thinking about action they could take or reframing, they are simply stuck in a state that's easy to slip into and can be difficult to escape.

Clearly the more they ruminated, the longer their depression. Ruminators are on a cycle of distorted thinking and unrewarding relationships. They need support from others, but believe they are getting less of it than they should have. It may be just their perception, but because constant rumination is draining for friends, family and colleagues, it may be true. After a while, everyone else wants to see some action.

Women are about twice as likely as men to suffer major depression and the highest risk for them is in their mid- to-late 20s. Rumination prolongs depression, but it's too easy to conclude that rumination accounts for the difference between men's and women's depression.

It's okay to feel proud of what you've achieved. It's difficult, partly because depression distorts our thinking. It's odd, but although depressed people doubt themselves in many ways, they tend to be very confident about their depressed interpretation of the world and their setbacks. Forcing yourself to focus on your qualities may be difficult when you are feeling low, but that kind of rethinking is at the heart of cognitive therapy.

Depressive thinking tends to create a cycle and it's essential to break out of it as early as possible. It's not simply a matter of thinking happy thoughts. 'I'm going to be positive today,' does help if you are a little sad, but with depression the benefits don't last. Correcting your thinking errors is likely to be far more effective.

When your partner said you don't do your share around the house, was she really saying, 'Please help me, I'm tired'? Even if it's true that you never help around the house, why should you believe that you can't do anything right? Surely, that's a gross over-reaction?

While you are being sceptical you can also remind yourself that you are great with the kids and you often take them away to the park or on walks to give your partner a break. The scepticism is to help you think more positively and more accurately. It's not about finding excuses or dreaming up ways to show how wrong other people are. If the criticism is fair, you might want to put things right, but most of all, you need to correct the depressive thinking that put you into the depression cycle.

Reframing should include recognising and dismissing the depressive thinking errors. It's not shallow 'positive thinking,' it's simply being sceptical. Is there really any evidence that you don't have the ability or potential? Surely, it's not true that you fail at everything you do? Talk about your setbacks as setbacks (so temporary) not failures.

Does explaining our successes and setbacks in pessimistic ways really cause depression? It's safer to say that pessimistic thinking and depression are strongly associated. As it happens, very strongly associated.

> Explanation for your setback
> Depressed self-talk
> 'It's my fault.' (Internal)
> 'I don't have the ability to be promoted.'
> 'It will always will be like this.' (Stable)
> 'I'll never get promoted now.'
> 'It's the same in everything I do.' (Global)
> 'I never succeed at anything.' 'I'll always be a loser.'

Try some brainstorming and talk to someone you trust about what you can do to improve a situation that leads to depressive thoughts. Depressed people often see only one solution. Even one solution may seem impossible. It's partly because depressed people tend to see their situation in extreme terms. Watch out for these words: loser, never, always, impossible, disaster, failure, ruined, destroyed, useless, hopeless, clueless.

Exercise

We should find ways to raise our energy and give ourselves some pleasant events to look forward to. I recommend uplifting music, letting the sunlight in to help our bodies function better, and changing our routines so that every day has an element of novelty. Depression is a low-arousal state so you should use a workout at the gym or a run in the park to pump your body up to a more normal level. Mental health benefits of regular aerobic exercise. Exercise is effective for mild to moderate depression. It may be effective, but it is difficult to begin if you're depressed. Find ways of exercising that you are more likely to enjoy and ensure that you have some variety.

Be sociable – with care

Being around others, and especially helping out, seems to work well. It helps to stop the ruminating. It also gives us a sense of achievement and helps us to feel appreciated. There is a risk in socialising while depressed. The old saying, 'Misery loves company' checks out. The inclination to find things to make you feel worse, illustrates the challenge of managing depression. It's not easy to snap out of it. You need to be very focused and determined to raise your energy level, find the right people to be around and make healthy comparisons.

Believe it or not

It probably sounds too superficial to be true, but smiling does work. There's research evidence to support it. Try this simple experiment: hold a pen between your teeth lengthways so that you imitate a smile. Okay, it's a silly thing to do so you'll smile anyway, but keep the pen there for say 10 minutes and check how you are feeling at the end. A German study using the pen idea produced encouraging results. The same researchers found that it worked the other way too. Their subjects were less happy after holding their pens end-on with pursed lips.

Robert Zajonc from the University of Michigan, and a leading researcher in the effect of facial muscles on mood, says that as particular facial muscles relax or tighten they raise or lower the temperature of the blood supply to those brain centres that regulate our emotions. Zajonc's explanation is not accepted universally, but many researchers agree that facial expressions don't just reflect moods, they can cause them. The effects are probably relatively minor compared with distressing thoughts or memories, but being willing to smile should be part of our depression-fighting repertoire.

More recent research by Rene Brown has shown that a few minutes of power poses significantly reduces our body's production of the stress hormone cortisol. It's further evidence that the body influences the brain.

Plan your day

You can plan your day to help you break out of the cycle of depression. Making the plan tells you that you're in control. Sticking to the plan underlines the point. Before you go to bed, prepare a list of treats and pleasurable events for the next day. Don't depend on thinking up your treats and events up as you go along or they probably won't happen. Plan to set the alarm for the usual time and get up immediately. Prepare to go to work, do the shopping and walk the dog because doing normal things works against your inclination to withdraw and dwell on the causes of your depression. They also serve as a distraction.

Schedule contact with people who are not depressed. Even contact on the internet seems to produce good results but ideally, create opportunities to have cheerful people around you. If you can help someone out, arrange to do that too. Make sure that your plan includes exercise to raise your energy to a more normal state. Use your list of treats or pleasurable events to provide highlights. Space them out so that you can savour them. Make sure that you include a few easy, but satisfying goals. A sense of accomplishment challenges your inclination to see everything negatively.

And, of course, commit yourself to breaking the cycle of depressive thinking with some healthy scepticism and reframing. Once you've made the plan, stick to it. Apply 'choice therapy'. Giving in to self-talk such as, 'I can't be bothered' and 'I'm too depressed to do anything about it', is a choice.

Manage anger

Anger is a difficult disruptive emotion to manage because it can take over in an instant and escalate quickly. The key is to slow down your response. Give yourself time to examine your beliefs and correct your thinking errors. Breathe deeply. Make sure that you imagine the breath going down to your abdomen. Short breaths to your chest won't help you relax. Repeat a calming word or sentences like a mantra. Try, 'Slow down' or 'Breathe easy. Relax'.

Develop a strategy for handling the situation in a calm and reasoned way. Get to know the symptoms and what sets off your anger. As you feel the symptoms coming on, focus on some healthy scepticism. Am I interpreting what the other person is doing or saying accurately? Is there another way of interpreting the same events or comments? Where's this person coming from? Why is she saying that? (Empathy is particularly difficult when you are angry, but a very effective way to calm down. It's worth the effort.) Ask the, 'So what?' question. So someone used the last of the milk? So what? So someone took my park at the supermarket? So what? What will happen if I lose my cool? What damage will it do to my relationship with this person?

The healthiest way to express anger is to be assertive. Recognize your symptoms as anger. Let's say a colleague has, again, forgotten to pass on an essential message. Try the cooling down process, relax if you can, maybe leave it a while, then say something like, 'When you forget to pass on messages, I get annoyed because it can have serious consequences for my clients, the company or me. Let's work out a system now to make sure that it doesn't happen again.' Many people believe that being assertive is just the same as being aggressive, but it's not. It's a cool-headed way to express your needs and respect others, as well yourself. It also gets results.

Taking time out can be productive, provided you're not using it as a way to avoid an argument. One of my trainees told me he and his wife used to get into big arguments that escalated until they both felt devastated. Now they agree to put the issue on-hold for an hour to break the anger cycle. They have often come back together and wondered what all the fuss was about. Putting a time limit on the cooling down makes it clear that you are willing to talk, but you want to do it in a more productive frame of mind. Relaxation exercises should help you wind down even more.

Women who have a strong fear of rejection are more prone to anger and increased hostility. Men with rejection fears have a higher risk of becoming violent. The fear makes both sexes particularly sensitive and they tend to magnify negative or even ambiguous cues. That misreading and the angry reactions damage the relationship and set them up for more feelings of rejection.

Forget the punchbag

Let's dispel the myth. Punch bags don't relieve anger. They make it worse. The same goes for anything like a punch bag – including shouting, screaming or furious gardening or shopping. You begin with your body highly aroused and the punch bag or the shouting just winds it up even more. Venting, or catharsis, can be quite satisfying and eventually, after you have stopped, your anger will dissipate, but it would have dissipated much faster without all the activity.

Popular belief in the catharsis theory remains strong despite its dismal record in the research findings.

The are some worrying results when they did give people a punch bag. They found that many of those people were not just more aggressive at the end, but were directing that aggression towards other people who had nothing to do with their mood. People often say punching, shouting and the rest is like letting the steam out of the pot. Surely, it would be better to find some way to turn the element off. Venting our anger at other people has another serious disadvantage: It leaves a battlefield of angry, resentful wounded, waiting for their chance to get back at us.

Watching violence on television has no cathartic effect either. One says, the belief that observing violence gets rid of aggressive feelings 'has virtually never been supported by research'.

Self-pity and anger

Venting anger isn't always the issue. People who lock their anger in rather than find healthy, assertive ways of expressing it may be caught in the self-pity trap. Self-pity is a combination of feeling that we are not in control of our lives and envy. They tell themselves, 'Bad things always happen to me' and ask, 'Why not them?' Only aggression, withdrawing from contact with people and giving up rate as less-effective coping strategies. Self-pity is strongly linked with depression. Women are more likely to react to stress with self-pity and it may have to do with the way we raise girls. Certainly, in most cultures, boys have more freedom to express their anger.

Manage anxiety

When does anxiety become unhealthy? When it disrupts your life. It's unhealthy when it's a series of false alarms that activate your sympathetic nervous system, which governs your body's response to danger. Once your brain senses the danger, it signals your adrenal glands to produce adrenalin, your blood pressure rises, blood shifts from your stomach and nervous system to your heart and muscles, your digestion stops and the liver provides reserves of sugar. You are ready for 'flight or fight'. It's useful in times of real danger, but being on a constant state of alert is very debilitating. Prolonged anxiety is a contributing factor to serious depression.

There are good reasons to believe that anxiety is growing in our society. I link anxiety with likely 'environmental' factors – particularly with crime rates, the number of AIDS cases and to a lesser extent the threat of nuclear war. (We can now add the threat of terrorist attack.) Economic conditions seem to be strongly linked to anxiety. The real issues may be social rather than environmental. We can also use measures of 'social connectedness' such as the divorce rates, the number of people living alone and lower ratings of trust to predict changing levels of anxiety.

Beyond a certain point, being on alert doesn't improve our concentration; it makes it worse. A little nervousness when giving a speech helps us focus. Real anxiety makes it difficult to remember what we want to say and it's easy to be distracted by intrusive thoughts. I believe that the intrusive, anxious thoughts reduce our brain's working memory and with it our ability to process information.

Anxiety tends to feed on itself unless you can break the cycle of worry and catastrophic thoughts. Fortunately, anxiety is very treatable because there are so many effective ways to interrupt the cycle, but if your anxiety is seriously disruptive and prolonged, you should talk to a therapist or doctor.

Recognize the symptoms of anxiety and name it. You may have tensed muscles, elevated heart rate, abdominal cramps, light-headedness or chest pains. You may be overwhelmed by panic in response to particular events or you may have 'free-floating anxiety' where you can't find any cause for constant worry. Free-floating anxiety would be difficult to treat yourself. Think about what caused your anxious response and apply some healthy scepticism. Do some 'decatastrophising'. How much evidence do you really have that your job is under threat? Is it reliable evidence? Is it possible that instead of being eliminated your role will simply change?

If the cause of your worry is something you can deal with directly, do it. If it's not, develop realistic action plans to cope if your fears turn out to be justified.

Let's work through an example.

Worst case scenario: I lose my job soon.

Possiblegood outcomes

I find another job with a rival company.

Agency has some work to give me time to find a new job.

I use the severance money to start a business from

home.

I use the severance money while I advance my qualifications.

Action I can take now.

Visit all the rival companies in the city.

Make appointments with all the temporary employment agencies.

Investigate how much I will need to set up business at home and draft a marketing plan.

Investigate the fees and the minimum income we would need while I am studying.

Maybe you'll choose to visit the rival firms and the agencies as your best action plans and keep the options of starting your own business or more study in reserve.

The problem-focused approach improves our confidence and the feeling that we are in control, but sometimes we are so swamped with anxiety that it's very difficult to focus on dealing with the problem. Choose to do it anyway because that it's the most effective strategy of all.

You could also try some physical treatments for anxiety. 'Progressive muscle relaxation' involves tensing then relaxing all the controllable muscles from your head to your toes. Many people find visualising soothing experiences effective too. Focus on the experience, give it a storyline and embellish it with vivid detail. The breathing exercises work for anxiety as well as anger.

If your anxiety is based on a single fear, say of heights, birds or spiders, you could try systematic desensitization. The principle is to replace the fear with relaxation. You must learn how to relax first, then you compile a list of situations that would make you fearful and rank them.

Next, imagine the situations. You start with a very low level of exposure to your fear and work up, using the de-catastrophising process and preferably the relaxation exercises as you go. You might begin by relaxing in a chair then imagining a small spider in a jungle, as you remind yourself of how far away it is and how it has no poison and couldn't possibly harm you.

When you can imagine the spider without your muscles tightening, it's time to move to the next level and imagine, say, a dead spider in a display in your museum as you continue to relax in the comfortable chair.

Maybe next it will be a live and non-poisonous spider in the museum. Take your time and stay focused on the process. Work your way up through experiencing, rather than just imagining, your fearful situations. Therapists have been having success with systematic desensitization for decades.

I also suggest keeping healthy with regular exercise, a balanced diet, not skipping meals and talking to supportive friends and family members about your stress. Finding interesting and absorbing hobbies to give some balance to our lives works too.

Manage stressful situations

Let's put in a good word for stress. Climbing rock faces is stressful, but you'd be struggling to talk some people out of it. It's stressful competing at tennis or chess. Even watching your local soccer team in action can be very stressful. It's good stress, called eustress. Imagine how dull life would be without it. We also need to feel at least slightly stressed when we are in danger – our survival may depend on it.

We can learn to manage stress effectively and people who do are not only less anxious, but less depressed, have lower blood pressure and are much less prone to emotional and personality disorders.

Believe it or not, it's usually not our reactions to crises that make us ill. The evidence suggests that our bodies cope with the big problems well. It's the on-going hassles, frustrations and the daily grind that do the damage. For instance, a study of police officers in a tough part of Pretoria found that they were much more stressed by day-to-day paperwork, irritations with the media and the slow pace of the justice system than the possibility of a shoot-out or intervening in domestic battles night after night.

For the rest of us, the damage to our health comes from equivalent on-going events such as constant conflicts with teenagers, annoying neighbours day-after-day, and 'leave your-brain-at-the-door' jobs. We are especially stressed when we sense that we have no control over a stressful situation.

Attitudes and stress

When you are stressed it's too easy to exaggerate setbacks. Keep reminding yourself that setbacks are opportunities to learn and steps on the way to success. Ask some sceptical questions about the cause of your stress. What's the worst that could happen? Is that likely?

Create a vivid image of yourself calm and in complete control, then play that role of someone calm and in charge of the situation. Eventually, your body will believe it. Perhaps more important, in the meantime, you might have made some progress on finding a solution to your crisis.

If you are a leader, you'll have to pretend anyway as part of your obligation to everyone else. Embellish your pretence. Show off a bit. Use it as a chance to show how cool you can be when things get hot. It's a choice, after all. If you can combine the pretence with a clear plan and a few early successes as you put the plan into action, you'll begin to feel less stressed quite quickly.

Stay cool under pressure

Focus on the problem

Get organised. What do you need to do to attack this problem or diminish its effect?

Focus on healthy emotions

Pretend. Act the part of a super-cool, confident person.

Correct your negative thoughts. Be sceptical about the cause of your stress. Is it really so serious?

Reward your progress with positive feedback.

Focus on stress-reducing activities

Get physical. Keep fit with plenty of walking, swimming or sport. Try relaxation exercises.

Eat well. Have a healthy diet and don't skip meals. Get some balance. Find absorbing, relaxing activities.

Get enough rest. Most adults need 7–8 hours sleep a night.

If you are a perfectionist, put yourself into learning

mode by striving for your current best rather than being perfect. Think of it this way: Striving to be perfect is an imperfect strategy. It will lead you into stress and decrease your performance.

If being less than perfect really worries you, think of perfection as a life-time goal, not something you have to achieve for this particular exam, presentation or game. Do your best today and be content with that. Develop your skills and strive for a new personal best next time.

Control commitment challenge

The three Cs give us a systematic approach to handling stress and disruptive emotions. You can use many of the skills we've discussed so far and it's essential to begin with the supreme liberating choice – to take charge of your own life.

Control means facing reality and striving to take control of the stressful situation. Hardy people know they can choose how they handle situations, and do. They see stressful situations in context, so they make sure they know why the threats are happening and how serious those threats really are. They also have a range of coping skills.

Let's take an example of control in action. Say you develop a life-threatening illness. You decide to reduce your workload and take more exercise (so you are making choices). You know that the survival rate for that illness gives you a good chance of living a normal life (seeing a context for the stress) and whenever you feel stressed you find ways of relaxing and keep reminding yourself of your odds of survival (using your coping skills).

Various studies of people in stressful situations have revealed the power of two particular coping skills that can give us a sense of control: optimism and goal-setting. It's a definition of hope.

People living with cancer, caring for schizophrenics and parents of boys with behaviour disorders who scored highest on a scale of hopefulness were the most resilient. The parents would agree with statements such as, 'I energetically pursue my goals. I can think of many ways to get out of a jam. Even when others get discouraged, I know I can find a way to solve the problem'.

Commitment means being committed to our goals and our belief that we are capable – even when the stress rises to precarious levels. It also means being committed to relationships with family, friends and colleagues. People who make those commitments have a sense of purpose and they know they can call on their relationships in times of stress.

Being committed to relationships may have life-saving benefits. Researchers have found that women with breast cancer who had a supportive husband were 15 per cent more likely to be alive after seven years. A second confidante and a supportive doctor each added one more percentage point to their chance of survival.

Let's say that you are the coach of your sports team and the results for the first few games are so bad that there's talk of you being replaced mid-season. You remain committed to your team's goal of winning the national championships and exude confidence with the players and the supporters (committed to goals and the belief that you are capable). You also make sure that you don't compromise 'family time' (committed to relationships) and draw on the support of your partner, particularly after the team loses another game (calling on relationships).

Challenge means feeling challenged by stressful situations. Stress-hardy people tend to see change as normal and interesting, and an opportunity to learn. It's an attitude we should always be cultivating.

Perhaps your business is under attack from a large rival that has just moved into the market and is beginning to head-hunt your most valuable staff. You decide that you are going to enjoy the battle with your rival (feeling challenged). You remember how the last couple of times competitors threatened the firm, you made some very worthwhile changes and ended up with a much stronger, more efficient organisation (seeing stress as more of an opportunity than a threat).

The everyday of positive emotions

Positive emotions and resilience are closely linked. Positive emotions help people recover from stressful situations more quickly and the research is showing that the effect is cumulative. When we use positive emotions to work our way through stressful situations, the experience makes us more resilient for next time, more optimistic and more tranquil.

Positive feelings, such as gratitude at being alive, increased love for others, humour, optimism and a greater interest in the world around us put our bodies at ease. We become more open to new ways of coping and more resilient next time. People who use positive emotions or feelings in stressful situations create an upward spiral.

Resilience is everyday magic because, using positive emotions seems to be what we are programmed to do. Negative emotions are barriers to a natural human response to adapting to stress.

Even when there is no crisis, we can actively create positive emotions that protect us long-term. It's as simple as counting our blessings, but it's more than homespun wisdom. It checks out.

Protect your immune system

The link between stress and ill-health is well established. Even everyday stressful events can impair our immune system, though normally we recover quickly. People with fewer social ties, so less support and probably more stress, are more susceptible to respiratory viruses. Stressful relationships increase our chances of illness and early death by about the same as smoking, high blood pressure, high cholesterol, obesity and inactivity.

Fit people's bodies don't react to stressful situations so readily. A study showed that breast cancer patients on a fitness programme were less depressed and rated themselves as more positive and more able to manage their lives.

Putting the effort in, to manage our stress and disruptive emotions appears to have a physical payoff. Relaxation, exercises and meditation improves immune systems even for elderly people and people who already have cancer. David Spiegel from the Stanford Brain Research Institute monitored women with advanced breast cancer who attended a therapy group once a week to learn how to handle the fear, anger and depression that you'd expect with a life-threatening disease. They lived twice as long as women who only had medical treatment.

The sexes and disruptive emotions

Generally speaking men and women do handle disruptive emotions in different ways. The conventional wisdom (Okay, mostly men's) might suggest that men are more practical and therefore better at fixing problems as they arise, but the research says the opposite.

Women use more coping strategies than men and are significantly more likely than men to ask for help. It fits what women say about men refusing to ask directions. 'We find no evidence, that men engage in more problem-focused coping.

Women are more likely to seek emotional support, use positive self-talk and reframe. All of them are powerful coping strategies. Women suffer what they call 'chronic strain,' by which they mean they have more pressure from parenting, housework, less social power and feel less appreciated than men. It may be the chronic strain that increases the possibility of depression. Many women find ways of coping with chronic strain by finding support from others or shifting their attention to those parts of their lives they can control.

Reducing stress at work

It's not the managers but the managed, who are most stressed by their work. It's the employees in reception, the warehouse or the factory floor who have least control in a workplace and the least opportunity to develop more healthy conditions.

It would be easy to say that we should give everyone more control over their work, but we can't assume that everyone will benefit from having more control. People who don't have the confidence or skills to make use of the new freedom to control their work and who blame themselves when things go wrong become more stressed. Those self-blamers are healthier when they have less control because, when things go wrong, they are able to tell themselves that they couldn't have done anything about it.

If you lead a business or team, consider whether your team members, individually, have the skills and confidence to handle empowerment. Are they ready for more control? Would they benefit from some training to develop some strategies for coping with the new problems you want them to handle? Consider too, how they explain setbacks. If they blame themselves, consider some retraining and support to help them view setbacks in a more useful way.

If you have team members who have the confidence and skills to handle more control over their work, you may be causing them unnecessary stress and illness by not giving them more autonomy. You are also missing out on the opportunity to develop their skills and motivate them to achieve more.

The Power Of Relationships

Opposites don't attract very often. We find people who seem just like us far more attractive and studies of couples have shown that we are attracted to people who are similar in many ways, including social status, attitudes, nationality, age, intelligence, height and even eye colour. While there's little evidence for opposites attracting, it can happen when the needs are complementary such as when people who need to be the dominant partner meet people who prefer to be relatively more submissive, it's usually the common factors that keep them together.

Here's the not quite-so-good news for most of us: Looks do count in starting relationships, and not just romantic relationships. Perhaps you always thought they did, but in surveys taken many decades apart, most people didn't rank physical attractiveness very high on the list of reasons for liking others. So, people say they don't start relationships based on looks, but the research shows they do.

An interesting experiment with first-year university students suggested that looks were everything – for both men and women. University students were invited to a dance and told them that a computer would match them up with a 'date' with the same interests. During the interview that was supposed to be about their interests, the researchers were actually assessing them for physical attractiveness, intelligence, personality and social skills. Then they paired the dance partners randomly. During a break in the dance they asked the students to fill out an anonymous questionnaire about their date to tell them how well the computer had 'matched' them. I.Q., personality and social skills had nothing to do with their ratings of the date's likeability. In this study, physical attractiveness alone was the best way to predict how satisfied the partners were with their dates.

We don't even need to see people to be influenced by their attractiveness. In a revealing study, men were asked to talk to a woman on the telephone to help them with a study on 'how people become acquainted with each other'. Before the telephone call they showed each caller a photograph, supposedly of the woman they would talk to. All the men spoke to the same woman, but half were given photographs of a very attractive woman and the others a relatively unattractive woman. And as you'll have guessed, those who thought they were speaking to a particularly attractive woman rated her poise, sense of humour and social skills higher than those who thought they were talking to someone who looked more ordinary.

It seems that being good-looking is an advantage that starts early. Undergraduate women students were asked to consider the cases of five and six year olds who were said to have misbehaved. A small photograph accompanied the outline of the children's misdeeds. The researchers reported that the women were much more likely to rate the less attractive children as more dishonest and unpleasant. They also tended to believe that what the good-looking kids had done wasn't really too serious and when asked to predict their future decided that the attractive ones were more likely to have happy marriages and be more successful in their professional lives.

Psychologists say there's some evidence that physically attractive people also have more attractive personalities. It's hardly surprising. If they are treated better than everyone else, it's natural that they should assume that the world is full of friendly, encouraging people. It may not be just, but it's bound to help.

Basic instincts

If starting relationships on good looks seems shallow, it gets worse. An analysis of many studies, large and small, and across cultures, suggests the women are most interested in a man's resources or potential to earn. One study showed that physically attractive women tended to weaken men's commitment to their current partners. Physically attractive men didn't shake the women's confidence in their relationships, but men of high status and wealth did.

So what should humans do to attract a mate? If they follow David Schmitt's findings published in the British Journal of Social Psychology, women should make themselves as physically attractive as possible and not bother criticizing their competitors, because that's ineffective. Men should display their intelligence, status and wealth, or at least their earning potential. They should disparage their competitors because, apparently for men, it works.

Researchers have added a useful qualification: that we need to make a distinction between the necessities of attractiveness and earning power, and luxuries. Compare the necessities to water and oxygen. If we didn't have them, we would want them – we'd really want them. But most of us have plenty of both, so we're more focused on other things. We only need so much attractiveness or earning power in a potential mate and that still leaves us with plenty of choice, so we start looking for relative luxuries. The same study found that intelligence and kindness rated as necessities.(Feeling better about being human now?) Luxuries included creativity and liveliness, but could be anything else that we value in a potential mate.

Strategies for starting relationships

The research shows that being similar in even trivial ways makes us more likable and finding common points of interest, shared experiences and shared opinions builds a bond. In the beginnings of a relationship, give information away as you gently probe for more about the other person's interests.

Starting conversations

Let's imagine that you're the new employee. You're now in the staff cafeteria and amongst the blur of heads, you notice vacant seats at a table in the corner. The one person already sitting there is facing the window as you arrive, a closed book in front of him. How do you get to know him? Try giving information away, using open questions, finding things you have in common and picking up on what the other person is saying. Maybe something like this...

You: 'Hi. I'm new here. Is it always this difficult to find

a seat? (Greeting, giving information away and reference to something you have in common.)

Colleague: 'Yes. Usually. It's not so bad if you can get here before 12.30'.

You: 'That might be difficult. (Nodding at a book on raising children.) I haven't read that one; what do you think of it? (Giving information way, picking up on visual cue, open question.)

Colleague: 'Quite helpful. Some useful ideas. We've got two. The younger one's at Kindergarten.' (Giving information away)

You: 'Our son's just turned three. He could go to Kindergarten soon. What are your impressions of it?' (Giving information away. Picking up on a shared interest in children. Open question.)

When the person you are meeting is giving information away, you have a cue to continue. Follow up with an open question. If you don't get that cue, or the body language suggests the person is unwilling to talk, ease back.

Giving information away without being asked is a valuable way to open up a relationship, but follow-up with an open question so that you don't end up dominating the conversation. Disclosing information gives you both an opportunity to pick up on points of common interest.

If you are asked a closed question, give more than it asks, then end with a question. For instance:

Your colleague: 'Do you have extended family living near you?' (Closed question)

You: 'Yes. We have both families within about 30 minutes of home and it's been a great help. Our parents have all been really supportive...What's it like having two preschoolers?

Psychologists call the sharing of information about ourselves, reciprocal self-disclosure. The reciprocal part is essential, especially in a new relationship. If you give away so much that the disclosure gets out of balance, you'll probably find that your partner discloses less, not more.

Empathy seems to be a useful tool to encourage self-disclosure. Focusing intently on the other person's words and the subtle emotional content – provides a way to practise our empathy skills.

In intimate relationships share intimate information about yourselves in an equal way. Intimacy and trust will develop as you reveal more and you are able to discover that your partner is accepting and just as open about feelings, fears, hopes and past events.

Men and women have different ways of encouraging other people to open up, at least when talking to the opposite sex. Women are most successful when they express sympathy, exhibit social skills, speak fluently and appear relaxed and comfortable. Men who get women talking tend to interview the other person and show their interest. Incidentally the least successful women were ill-at-ease, talked at the other person, used sarcasm, criticism or expressed self-pity. The least successful male conversationalists compared themselves to the other person, talked too much and expressed interest in fantasy or day-dreams.

As we've noted, having similar attitudes does help in building new relationships, but different attitudes may be even more significant in the selection process. Our potential companions and partners are likely to use those differences to screen us out at an early stage. It's best to wait until the relationship has gathered some momentum before mentioning that we support a rival sports team or hate her favourite country music singer.

Compliments work and, if you can stand it, ingratiation, including flattery. We're much more impressed by flatterers and less suspicious of their motives, when they're flattering us than other people.

We tend to think the flatterers are wrong when we have low self-esteem and remarkably perceptive when our self-esteem is peaking, but in either state we find them likeable.

Being seen with the right people helps too. It works both ways, if you and I are seen together, your popularity (That's a bit of flattery) makes it more likely that the next people I meet will regard me positively, even after you have gone home.

The most remarkable thing is how far that reputation spreads, because having picked up kudos from being seen with you, I can then give some to other people seen with me.

Once we have gained or lost by being with the right or wrong people, other people take a long time to lose their initial impression of us. An emotionally intelligent person has the self-awareness and self-management skills not to be swayed by such a purely emotional and prejudicial process, but it's largely unconscious. Of course you have to know about it to resist it. Now you do.

Feeling blirtatious?

How would you describe your conversational style? Do you speak as soon as a thought occurs to you, or wait, consider the effects and maybe mention it later? Blirters not only respond more quickly, but speak more rapidly and more often than most people do. They are blirters in the sense that they score high on the Brief Loquaciousness and Interpersonal Responsiveness Test.

Quick and frequent responses make us seem attentive, interested, on top of things and competent. People are also more likely to think we are intelligent, likable and someone they want as a friend.

Blirting is a high-risk strategy. It amplifies our qualities – good or bad. Whether we are truly interested and competent, or we are ill-informed, aggressive, surly or insensitive, other people will find out faster. Blirting pays when we are well informed, genuinely interested and feeling agreeable, otherwise it's better to hold back, talk a little more slowly and maybe not respond at every opportunity. You could use the same strategy if you are trying to establish your credibility in a meeting with people you don't know.

People who score low on the BLIRT scale are 'brooders'. Brooders can hide a disagreeable mood or scanty knowledge for longer, but being too restrained has disadvantages too. If your colleague or your partner says something that upsets you and you brood on it for a couple of days, raising your objection so late would do nothing for your relationship or your credibility. They might say, 'If it was so important, why didn't you say so right away? Are you sure you're not just in a bad mood today?'

Love and romance

Do we need to define liking and loving? Don't we just know when it happens? Perhaps so, but some researchers have gone to the trouble of analyzing the difference. And this is love – what could be more important than that?

Kinds of loving

It's homespun wisdom that to love others you must love yourself first. But researchers are showing that the relationship between self-love and loving others is not as simple as it seems. What they have found reveals some significant information about our most intimate relationships.

If by self-love we mean our self-esteem, then it's a useful addition to a relationship, but no guarantee the relationship will be healthy. People with high self-esteem are more likely to reply to threats with anger and hostility and more likely to behave in a destructive way in a conflict. The angry reaction is particularly likely if the self-esteem is something the person has to strive to maintain, rather than an enduring trait.

There is a second kind of self-love and it has very little going for it. Psychologists talk about the 'narcissistic personality'. It's based on the mythical Greek youth, Narcissus, who fell in love with his own reflection.

Narcissists have a grandiose sense of self-importance. They also crave admiration and fantasize about fame, power or love and associating with high status people.

Narcissists are not just self-confident dreamers. They are game-players – manipulating, exploitative, lacking empathy and focused on themselves. Their goals are status, power and sex, and they use their self-confidence and superficial charm to achieve them. They want everyone's attention and admiration and react to criticism with rage or a feeling of humiliation.

Narcissists have a strong sense of entitlement, but it only applies to them. They give you the impression that the world revolves around them. A manager once told me about a young staff member she had assigned to a project. The deadline was approaching so the manager checked on her progress. The young woman informed her that she hadn't started because she had decided that the project wouldn't help her in her career.

Narcissists want relationships, but not too close in case they lose control. They like to keep their romantic partners guessing about their commitment and enjoy 'the game of love'. Their partners report discovering that the narcissistic one has lied, played 'head games' and controlled them. The narcissist's deceptive charm and confidence makes people with low self-esteem easy prey.

In its more extreme form, narcissism amounts to the narcissistic personality disorder. Personality psychologists see narcissistic behaviour on a continuum, so it is possible to be a little bit narcissistic.

Romance and time

It's perhaps the most exciting time in our lives. The new romance takes the emotions on a roller coaster of anxiety and relief. There's the loss of appetite, light-headedness, the sudden loss of interest in anything else. (Okay, it affects some people more than others.) Before long, we relax into the relationship and it moves on to be based on attachment, caring and trust. There's still room for bursts of passion, but before long it's less demanding on the mind and body than in the first few weeks. We expect it. It's the natural progression of things.

One study compared married couples, who had married for love, with couples in arranged marriages and found the early differences in passionate love and sexual interest soon dissipated. After 10 years, couples from both who were still together rated the love in their relationships about the same – and it was the companionate love we associate with long-term relationships.

Marriage and health

Men and women in happy marriages live healthier lives. Women from satisfying marriages have stronger immune systems than women who were unhappy in their marriages or were divorced or separated. One study in the 1970s revealed a significant difference in health with just one question about the quality of the relationship. The researchers asked 10,000 men, 'Does your wife show you her love?' The men who answered no were twice as likely to develop angina as those who answered yes.

What makes successful long-term relationships?

There's a reasonable consensus about successful relationships. Researchers have looked at long-lasting and happy marriages and say that the key characteristics are goodwill, good communication and emotional warmth. Those results and many of their other observations seem to fit relationships with our children, friends and close colleagues just as well.

It's common knowledge that people with compatible personalities have the best hope of successful long-term relationships, but more than sixty years of research has produced only modest support for the notion that any kind of compatibility is essential. One research team analysed 115 long-term studies that looked at the links between personality and the stability and quality of marriages. Their meta-analysis involved 45,000 marriages and the correlations ranged from nil to just .(A correlation of +1.00 would indicate a perfect association.) While like attracts like, in the longer-term, having matching personalities or backgrounds, education or religious orientation doesn't seem to be important. Robert Sternberg of Yale studied couples who had been together for up to 36 years and found that as the relationship continued, the partners found it increasingly important to try to understand each other's wants and needs, to support each other and to have values they shared.

Researchers interviewed 66 volunteer couples, married for up to five years, to explore which needs the most successful partners were meeting. They concluded that 'emotional warmth' was the strongest predictor of successful relationships.

The successful couples created their emotional warmth by being sympathetic, comforting, welcoming requests for help and readily doing favours. They also enjoyed the company of family and friends.

The least successful partners became angry easily and were critical of each other. They were independent to the point of making decisions without consultation and believing that the relationship should not restrict their freedom.

The analogy of 'the emotional bank account' which describes the amount of trust that's built up in a relationship through 'courtesy, kindness, honesty and honouring commitments'. When you support your partner through a rough patch or help a colleague with a report, that's a deposit in the emotional bank account you have with each of them.

You can make withdrawals from the emotional bank account too. If you tell a client you'll deliver in time to meet her deadline, then forget, that's a withdrawal from the account you have with her.

We need to keep topping up the emotional bank accounts simply to stop them getting into deficit. The closer the relationship, the more we need to invest. If you live together, the expectations for closeness, for unconditional acceptance, for courtesies and practical support will be greater. You can't meet every expectation every time and you need 'funds' in the account to cover the inevitable withdrawals.

Raising children, especially teenagers, creates opportunities for rapid withdrawals. You have your responsibilities as a parent and they have their need to rebel and learn from poor judgements. It's easy to go for days when everything about your relationship is negative. The safest top-ups are the ones that don't look like a bribe or suggest that the behaviour you were unhappy with yesterday is now okay. Usually, they'll have nothing to do with any dispute you may be having at the time.

Couples who contribute to the emotional bank account without much thought about what they'll receive in return, tend to have the most successful relationships. One may be happy to do most of the housework for months while the other is studying, or give emotional support even when the other is grumpy. Couples who need to see the contributions balanced either immediately or very soon, often relate according to the rule: 'I'll be considerate or pleasant, if you are'. Generally, their relationships don't last as long.

Self-respect can make a useful focus for partners who want to develop their relationships. Successful partners develop their self-respect by acting honourably when their partner or their relationship was under stress. If say our partner or colleague is upset and takes it out on us, we might choose to resist the impulse to respond with anger. Maybe we will choose to express our concern for the other person instead.

Principled behaviour should have some limits so that we don't become doormats, but giving some latitude and developing a pride in being someone who does the honourable thing has payoffs for the individual partners and the relationship. More than that, it creates a virtuous cycle. Partners who built their self-respect are better adjusted emotionally, in better physical health and more satisfied with their lives, than people who 'wing it'.

Successful intimate relationships

A reservoir of good-will.

It's generated through love, intimacy, kindness, thoughtfulness, being sympathetic, comforting, welcoming requests for help and readily doing favours.

Handling negative emotions constructively
Each partner looks for a positive outcome in the interests of the relationship.

Negotiating to achieve win/win solutions

Includes a genuine interest in understanding the other person's wants and needs.

Acting honourably

Each partner chooses to act in ways that build self-respect.

Accepting and valuing differences

It includes not wanting to change the other person to be like ourselves.

Respecting boundaries

It includes accepting that we can not expect other people to meet all our needs. Also accepting that people must be free to make their own decisions.

Let's get specific about intimacy

It's natural to assume that intimacy is inevitable in loving relationships, but a research team has taken a more detailed look at intimacy and it provides some useful insights and a focus for improving the relationships we value most.

Kathleen White and her colleagues interviewed partners separately about their relationships and graded their responses on a three-point scale. Level 1 was for responses that suggested the partners were focused on their own needs. Level 2 was for responses that suggested that a partner saw the other primarily as a person in a traditional role – responses such as, 'He's a good dad'. Level 3 was for the most 'mature' level of intimacy, where the person valued the partner's special qualities.

Most partners in the study were level 2, which suggested that their relationships were not as intimate, or rewarding, as they could be. Asked about caring or affection, a level 2 partner might say, 'I support her when I can'. A partner with a mature level of intimacy would express concern in a way that focused on emotional support and could supply evidence such as, 'When he was struggling with his new job I thought it was really important to listen and tell him how much I believe in him.'

As they expected, the researchers found that men with high 'intimacy' scores were in more rewarding, better-adjusted relationships.

They also found something very significant: The women's scores told them nothing about the quality of the relationship. For example, women could be capable of mature intimacy, but be either satisfied or dissatisfied with the relationship. The real issue was the men's contribution to the relationship.

Men and women's perspectives on intimacy differ too. Men tend to find doing things together sufficient for intimacy. Women tend to prefer to talk things over and especially to talk about the relationship. The difference is greatest in traditional marriages. It's a big issue and men's particular focus on doing things together, suggests they are uneasy about the kind of intimacy most women need. The more comfortable a man is with intimacy, the more satisfied with the marriage the wife will be.

The five dimensions of intimacy

Being focused on the relationship

Being committed to the relationship

Caring and being concerned for our partner

Communicating well with our partner

Sexual intimacy

The emotional sex

It's women, right? It depends on how you look at it. It's certainly true that both men and women believe that women are more emotional in the sense of being more emotionally intense and more willing to express emotions. Researchers have a different view of how emotional men and women are. They have shown that men and women are equally intense, open and sensitive to feelings of anxiety, sadness and happiness – when those feelings were measured from moment-to-moment. One study revealed that changes in couples' heart rates matched exactly as they discussed emotional issues.

If we are talking about being more knowledgeable – the nuances of emotions and words that describe emotions – women lead the way. The women whose heart rates matched their partners' rates were able to describe how other people would feel in particular situations in more complex and detailed ways. That emotional literacy is a key to empathy.

Empathy and communication

Empathy is the ability to understand another person's emotions, needs and concerns and develops from the time we are a year or two old. (Researchers heard one toddler say, 'You sad Mommy. What Daddy do?)

Empathy is a very useful skill in communication and for building relationships throughout life. It's not surprising that women should be more skilled than men in cultures that encourage girls to be more aware of other's feelings and talk about them openly. But the research reveals that the difference may be more to do with motivation than innate ability. Men seem to be less motivated to be empathetic. Perhaps it doesn't fit the macho image.

Empathy is a particularly important part of successful intimate relationships. Men who believe that learning to read other people's emotions would be a threat to their masculinity are missing a valuable opportunity to improve their closest relationships.

We can improve our empathy skills by active listening and focusing not just on the facts, but the feelings. We can give the feelings names: angry, upset, apprehensive, frustrated, delighted, excited, annoyed, disappointed or sad. We can check that we have understood. We can listen for 'us' rather than just ourselves and train ourselves to listen all the way through, rather than hearing just the beginning, then waiting for a chance to respond.

A chief executive once told me that he found it very difficult to listen to less experienced colleagues because over the years he had heard the same issues aired many times. He was bored with listening and would move the conversation on to something more productive, especially solutions. His poor listening skills were being mentioned in his performance reviews. His colleagues were annoyed with his impatience and frustrated that they were not being heard.

After some discussion, the chief executive chose a range of solutions. The first was to declare to his colleagues that he intended to change. In some meetings he even put a stuffed toy with big ears in front of him to remind himself and them of his commitment, then invited his colleagues to let him know whenever he was not living up to his good intentions.

In more formal meetings he asked one supportive colleague to give him a pre-arranged, silent, signal if he was off course. He used questions more and built empathy by summarising the facts and feelings. How did he cope with the boredom? He found a new interest, not in the same old issues, but the challenge of developing empathy with a vital professional skill – active listening.

Worrying signs

Researchers who followed couples from the newlywed stage through the next 13 years have revealed that the most accurate predictor of divorce is not the inability to handle conflict or communicate, but disillusionment.

The study is particularly useful because there are some risks in simply asking couples to look back over the years they have been together. It's very easy for them to think of behaviour that made them unhappy, but not so easy to know whether the behaviour was the cause of the unhappiness or the result of it.

The researchers saw the signs of disillusionment or 'future delight' within the first two years. Their study provides support for the notion of 'emotional warmth' being the key to success. After 13 years the disillusioned partners saw the other as unresponsive, ambivalent and lacking affection. The happy couples had a strong sense of belonging and closeness. They also had compatible and high scores for 'responsiveness' – which in a relationship setting includes being pleasant, friendly, forgiving, sincere and generous.

Some of the 156 couples in that longitudinal study were still together after 13 years partly because they had very low expectations of the relationship. The research team described one type of relationship as 'passive and congenial' – in which the partners treated the relationship as a background to their lives and put their energy into other things. The other unrewarding but enduring relationship was dominated by conflict, but the partners saw conflict as inevitable and some seemed to enjoy their sparring.

Sex and work

An interesting study at the University of Wisconsin questions the belief that when both partners have careers, their sex life inevitably suffers. The belief certainly appears to make sense. We only have so much time and energy, but the Wisconsin researchers found that it's more complicated than that and their work reveals useful information about our relationships generally.

The Wisconsin researchers interviewed more than 500 couples on three occasions from pregnancy through to their child's first birthday. They reasoned that it's a demanding time for parents anyway so any additional stresses from being dual earners should show up then. They found no link between both partners being employed full-time and either the number of times they made love or how satisfying each partner reported their sex life to be.

They did find a link between the work the women were doing and the couples' sex lives and presumably their intimacy. Couples reported the greatest satisfaction with their sex lives when both had satisfying jobs – whether they worked full-time or part-time. The least satisfied couples were not those where both had unsatisfying jobs, but where the woman had a satisfying the job and the man didn't.

The researchers also reported a strong link between fatigue and decreased libido, but found that women who were full-time homemakers could be just as fatigued as women in employment.

Having a range of roles appears to provide people with more resources to help them reduce stress. Their stress and dissatisfaction in one role can be balanced by satisfaction in another and they may also benefit from being exposed to a wide range of viewpoints. Many women in satisfying work have a feeling of increased power, which reduces depression and their contribution to the family income reduces tensions about their finances.

Handling the rough patches

Differences in the ways that couples handle negative emotions such as anger, sadness, depression, or anxiety have a major effect on their relationships. People who score high on tests of negative emotions such as depression, anxiety and anger tend to be more defensive, more inclined to stonewall or to be more critical of their partners, even contemptuous. All those behaviours are particularly damaging for intimate relationships.

We can use the re-framing skills that help us to handle disruptive emotions and create alternative ways of handling tense moments in all kinds of relationships. In processing disruptive emotions we can look at situations from a different perspective so that we can come up with a considered response, rather than just react.

Playing the 'sceptical supportive friend' can help us to question whether a colleague's sudden aloofness is really evidence that he and maybe the rest of the team have turned against us. Perhaps he has a family problem or is preoccupied with a looming deadline.

Is our partner's cool response really evidence that we've said or done something to offend her or is she tired or reacting to something that happened at work? It does, of course, make sense to ask, but the re-framing helps to stop us matching the other person's anger with anger or withdrawal. It can help us to avoid taking the other person's behaviour personally.

Optimism and tension

Re-framing also helps us to see the current state of our relationships in more optimistic ways.

Pessimistic people are more likely to see behaviour they don't like as what usually happens and a reflection of their partners' personality. They may believe that the conflict is permanent and think, 'He'll always be selfish' or 'I'm too old to change'. The most pessimistic partners also believe the problems in their relationships will affect everything else in their lives – 'I can't be happy or successful because my marriage is such a disaster.

Couples in successful relationships tend to describe their partners' good and bad points in ways that are similar to the optimistic self-talk.

They see the good points as enduring and a part of their personality, so they'll think, 'She's a loving person' or 'He's a great supporter'. It's similar to the belief we create in ourselves with the assumption: 'I'm on my way to being a first-class leader, parent or public speaker'. We can see lapses in our partner's behaviour as temporary and caused by something that will pass or can be dealt with – not evidence that the relationship is collapsing. Of course, it's possible that our partner, or colleague, has changed from the reasonable, generous, admirable person we knew yesterday and will remain irritable, angry or withdrawn for the rest of her life, but surely that is less likely.

How typical is your relationship?
These observations are taken from a survey conducted in 22 countries and numerous studies of couples between 17 and 86 years and in their relationships for up to 36 years.

His side

Perceived internationally as being more aggressive, ambitious and courageous. Relatively positive view of the relationship, including listening to each other, tolerance, sex and finances. Listening style: Irregular eye contact, nods infrequently, more likely to interrupt, uses questions to analyze the other person's contribution. Speaking style: few pauses, more use of I and me yet self-disclosure rare, may change topics abruptly, speaks louder than his partner, humour expressed as separate jokes or stories.

Her side

Perceived (in the same international survey) as being more emotional and affectionate. Less rosy. Even in happy marriages reports less agreement on finances, affection, friends, sex etc. Listening style: More eye contact, nods frequently, uses questions to find out more of the other person's perspective. Speaking style: frequent pauses, makes connections with what other person has said, more use of us and we yet more self-disclosure, matches the volume of the other person, weaves humour into the conversation. Says he needs a partner who is not aggressive, anxious, critical or highly reactive to stress. Believes the relationship is in trouble if they have to keep talking about problems.Presents a flattering image of the relationship to friends.Inclined to withdraw to avoid confrontation.Sees withdrawal as constructive. Even in happy relationships, not as skilled at finding a conciliatory end to an argument. Says she needs the same but also a partner who is able to express positive emotions and can control impulsive responses. Believes that being able to talk through problems is a sign that the relationship is working well. More comfortable sharing a realistic picture of the relationship with friends. Wants to resolve the tension so that she can be closer to him. Sees withdrawal as aloof or smug. In happy relationships, much more able to find a conciliatory outcome.

Reframing so that we think more optimistically and generously about our partner's or colleagues' lapses is far more likely to create a pleasant atmosphere in which to resolve problems. Optimism is a choice. We can choose to call on the supportive, sceptical friend to examine our pessimistic interpretations at any time.

Arguments

Researchers have found couples they couldn't provoke into an argument no matter what they tried and the couples appeared to have a strong bond and to be able to sort through differences of opinion very effectively.

Whether we argue or not is irrelevant. It's how we argue that counts. It takes determination and emotional skill to avoid being swamped by negative feelings, trying to win at all costs or withdrawing. John Gottman and his colleagues have studied thousands of relationships over the last 30 years and found that couples in successful relationships handle disagreement very differently. They tend to come in three types: those who listen effectively and compromise, those who argue passionately and often, but are more affectionate and romantic than most couples and those who avoid or minimize their problems and focus on the positive qualities of their relationships. In happy relationships, at least, women are generally more comfortable with arguments. They want to settle issues and they are more skilled at finding a way to end disputes in a conciliatory way.

Most of us have come across men who don't mind confrontation as long as they are winning and who shout and bully till they do, but generally, men tend to avoid confrontation. They don't want things to escalate and the typical male withdraws, either to let things cool off a bit, or to avoid facing the conflict. Withdrawing is a risky manoeuvre when your partner wants to resolve the problem. Women find it aloof or smug and researchers have found that women will retaliate by raising the tension, which encourages the men to withdraw even more. In intimate or close working relationships, if one of you has a problem, you both have a problem. That's true, even if you don't agree that it should be a problem. If your partner or colleague says he has a problem with something you are doing, that's at least a relationship problem and it will grow if you refuse to hear about it.

Arguing well and coming up with a satisfying solution can be a bonding experience, but you have to cooperate on the rules of engagement. You and your partner or colleague must be prepared to commit yourselves to understanding the other's point of view and to looking for a positive outcome. The rules of engagement include showing goodwill, even when you are feeling hurt or angry.

Choose a time when you can talk without distractions and make sure that you are in a fit emotional state. When our bodies are in a high state of alert we can't concentrate on another person's perspective. It's better to agree to take the time we need to cool down.

Set the tone of your discussion carefully. Beginning with criticism or a contemptuous remark would set up confrontation. Try something constructive and low-key. Perhaps, 'I'd like to discuss something important with you'. Some counsellors suggest giving each other up to 15 minutes of virtually uninterrupted time to explain your perspective, followed by a general discussion. If you do that, make sure that you listen attentively with regular eye contact and nods or encouragement to continue. It can be useful to interrupt just long enough to concede a valid point, but don't give in to any temptation you might feel to deny, correct or explain.

'I statements' can be a useful way to get into the issue from your perspective. An I statement takes the focus off the other person. Begin with an I statement about what you know. You might say to your son or daughter: 'I've noticed that the pets were not fed till late all this week...'. Mention what effect that behaviour is having and what you want changed. 'When that happens it's unfair on the pets and I want you to make sure that they are fed before seven every night.' If you begin your sentence with 'you' you will create an accusation: 'You are trying to claim all the credit for the project' or to your teenager, 'You slam the door when you come home late.' Use neutral language, aim at a solution, and avoid blame. It can sound artificial without some practice, but even if you are a bit clumsy at first, you'll be making it clear that you are trying to be constructive.

Sometimes it's useful to add questions so that the other person has a chance to explain.

You: 'I noticed that when you came in last night the door closed very loudly. Did you intend that to happen?'
Teenager: 'I was in a bit of a mood and I had some cans in my hands – and it just sort of slammed.'

You: " When the door is slammed late at night it's very disturbing. Could you ensure that you close it quietly?'

Feelings not just facts

Men, generally speaking, find it difficult to accept that in resolving conflicts, the feelings are just as important as the facts. Most women need to express their feelings, not just state the problem, and they find it very irritating when a man just listens for the facts and the moment he thinks he has them, comes up with a solution. In men's defence, I should say that they may be doing it with the best intentions. It can be a man's way of saying, 'I want to take away the thing that's hurting you'. Many women find that attitude patronising rather than supportive. They don't feel listened to until the man has heard their feelings about the problem. Many women have told me that they're often less interested in a solution than having the opportunity to tell their partners how they feel. They'll come up with their own solution when they are ready.

Make sure that you focus on one problem at a time. Dragging up faults of the past comes across as attack or retaliation and it's very difficult to keep a sense of goodwill. You'll lose focus too as the argument changes to 'everything that's wrong with our relationship'. Many counsellors suggest that you stay out of touching range because physical contact can easily be misinterpreted as condescending, manipulative or prematurely intimate. Some suggest that you keep reminding yourself of the strengths of your relationship. Think of blame as unhelpful. If one of you forgot to put oil in the car, it has happened. Now that the motor has seized and the repair bill has come in, your partner will be well aware of the mistake without regular reminders. If the children were not collected from your mother's till late, does it matter who didn't make the arrangement clear or who wasn't listening? Just agree on a better system next time.

The no-blame principle works with relationships between colleagues too. In my company we certainly expect people to learn from their mistakes and correct them, but it's not part of the culture for people to say, 'That was your fault,' or look for scapegoats. Not blaming is no soft touch – just more productive. We're happy to admit mistakes, even before anyone else knows about them. We have often discovered that our colleagues' mistakes were based on incorrect information so we've been able to make some useful changes to our systems to make sure they do have the information they need. Of course, even conscientious people make errors of judgement too, that's being human. It's the putting right and learning that count.

Blame is most damaging to relationships and morale when it's dredged up repeatedly – especially, of course, publicly. The most successful couples are those who, even as newlyweds, refused to accept hurtful behaviour from one another. The lower the level of tolerance for bad behaviour in the beginning of the relationship the happier the couple is down the road. Most counsellors include attacking, point-scoring, exaggerating, shouting and attempting to humiliate in their bad behaviour list. If you notice bad behaviour, name it right away and remind your partner or colleague of the aims of the discussion:

'That's point-scoring. It's going to be very difficult to talk this through constructively if we do that. I feel intimidated when you shout like that and we both need a chance to explain our point of view. It's very difficult to continue bad behaviour once it's been named. Naming it, remaining calm and reminding your partner or colleague of the purpose of your discussion, is an effective combination. We know from research with couples and from the experience of counsellors, that fighting fair as it's often called, is a feature of successful long-term relationships. It's part of maintaining the emotional bank account and emotional warmth. If it all seems a bit 'nice' and you'd rather let it all out, ask yourself whether you would both have an equal opportunity to do that and what that has done for your relationships in the past.

These suggestions for resolving disputes come from a range of research and counselling sources. You could apply them to all close relationships, at home and at work. Choose to be comfortable with a difference of opinion. See it as perfectly normal and an opportunity to make things better.

Choose the time.

Make sure you can both hear each other's point of view without being distracted by other people or deadlines.

Listen actively.

Define the problem together as objectively as you can. Make sure that both of you have a chance to explain your perspective and your feelings. Check your understanding.

Watch the body language.

Keep your arms uncrossed and try to relax your hands. Avoid pursed lips or sharp intakes of breath. Try sitting back with your arms as relaxed as possible beside you.

Choose your words.

Use 'I' statements. 'When that happens I feel humiliated/hurt/angry/frustrated and I...' Use calming words such as, 'sometimes, I feel, I think, perhaps, one possibility would be to..., what if?'

Focus on one problem at a time.

If something new comes up. Park it.

Brainstorm some possible solutions.

Consider both separate and joint brainstorming. Look for several solutions to your point of conflict. As you are brainstorming trying to think of solutions your partner or colleague is likely to accept. If it's a big or complex issue, try coming up with solutions independently, then together.

Find a solution you can both agree on.

Genuinely looking for win/win together is a very powerful way to build the bond between you.

Agree how to make the solution work.

If one loses, you both lose

If win/win isn't possible, compromise or concede. Whether the context is intimate, collegial or commercial, the relationship is probably more important than the issue that's dividing you.

Put these strategies on your banned list

Bullying, blaming, personal criticism, contempt

Bringing up an issue in front of friends or family in the hope of shaming The silent treatment or stonewalling

Inflaming, including: 'You always, you never, you can't, you don't' and name-calling

Defensiveness

Exaggerating

Cross-complaining – answering a complaint with one of your own Storing grudges and bringing them out when there's a new conflict. Giving in, but seething inside and thinking, 'Wait till next time!' Walking out and slamming the door

Learn The Art Of Negotiation

Could we get through life without negotiating? It's very unlikely. Perhaps, if we were dictators or domestic bullies, or we were content to live and work alone it would be possible, but we would miss many of life's great opportunities. The issue may be as simple as who will cook dinner tonight, as significant as which city to live in, as heart-rending as custody of the children, as pleasurable as which island resort to choose, or as intense as a wage negotiation with a union. We have the opportunity to negotiate, well or badly, most days.

Negotiation is a valuable skill and certainly not just an intellectual exercise. To be effective negotiators, we need a range of emotional skills, such as self-awareness and empathy. We need the ability to regulate disruptive emotions, particularly anger and frustration. We also need to value healthy relationships. In this chapter you'll see a method that's used in some of the most complex negotiations and some of the simplest. Top negotiators use the same method to negotiate deals in commerce and international peace-keeping. You could use the method at work and at home.

We'll talk about negotiations with one person, but the same method will help you negotiate with several parties at once. It's common for negotiators to say they are looking for a win/win outcome. It sounds admirable and fair, but is it really an effective way to negotiate? The anecdotal evidence says it is and the research confirms that negotiators who use cooperative strategies such as exchanging information and concessions and building relationships do achieve better results than those who compete.

A method in action

Imagine this: Ester and her co-workers are being relocated to a new floor. They won't be having separate offices any more because the new chief executive likes cubicles. The boss is even moving into a cubicle herself. Ester hears that she will be sharing a cubicle with Victor. He's not the cubicle mate she had hoped for, but she has nothing against him. They inspect the new space together and discover that there is only one window and it's narrow and near the corner of their cubicle. They've been allocated one whiteboard, permanently fixed to a section of cubicle wall near the window. Ester wants the window. She needs a sense of space and hates the thought of being enclosed for up to eight hours at a time. Henry wants the window too. Unfortunately, Ester also wants the whiteboard. It's essential for the kind of thinking she does.

Victor: 'I need to have my desk near the window.'

Ester: 'So do I. And there's only room for one.'

Victor: 'But I need to be next to the window. I need regular sunlight – for medical reasons.'

Ester: 'And I need it for my sanity. I made it very clear that I wasn't moving unless I had a window.'

Victor: 'You'll have a window. It's just that you won't be right next to it.'

You can see where it's going. It's positional bargaining. Positional bargaining assumes that only one party can win. Ester has a fixed position and Victor has his and they'll keep bargaining until one of them wins, they reach some compromise neither is happy with, or the process breaks down with shouts, sulks, a walkout or appeals to higher authority. It's hardly flattering and does nothing for their relationship. Usually, both (or everyone) can win, and not in some weak compromise. Think of real negotiating as problem-solving. You look at the problem from both perspectives and brainstorm together until you find the solution that best meets each other's needs. It takes goodwill and emotional skills. It's easier if the relationship is already strong, but it works in the most difficult of situations.

Looking for win/win

Ester and Victor could certainly use the problem-solving process. First, they would draw up a list of their individual needs – together. It pays to think what your needs are before you begin the process, but listing them together without defensiveness or criticism sets the scene for a cooperative approach to negotiation. It would be easy to say that they both need to put their desk by the window, but that's a solution. Set possible solutions aside until you have a full list of needs. Perhaps Victor and Ester will note that Victor does need regular sunlight for medical reasons. His doctor has told him that he has 'seasonal affective disorder' (S.A.D.) which explains why he is depressed and grumpy in the winter. They'll note that Ester needs a sense of space so that she doesn't feel as if she is in a cell.

Ester has her eye on the whiteboard because she had one in her old office and needs somewhere to write her thoughts and reflect on them. Victor doesn't. The whiteboard is near the window, which is another reason for Ester to have her desk there, but that would be a solution, so they just note her need to have something on the wall to write on. Both of them need somewhere to store files and the only filing cabinet is Victor's and it's stuffed with files. Both would also like to have the new chair that's been supplied.

Ester has another need that might have led to an accusation if they were not cooperating. Windows have become a source of status and she is resentful that the men have grabbed or been given windows in the other cubicles. She feels that her pride is at stake. When she explains her need Victor admits that he, too, feels that that the window has status and that's one of his needs.

Let's sum up their progress.

They examine the possible solutions carefully for the best one or best combination. For both of them, trying to find another colleague who doesn't care about a window or whiteboard may be the best option if they can't negotiate a solution. That backup solution is the standard they can use to measure any new solution that comes up in a negotiation. They can ask, 'Would I be better off accepting this solution or taking my backup solution?'

A strong backup solution can put you in a powerful position to negotiate. You will know that if you can't reach agreement, you'll choose your backup solution and the other person misses out on what she could gain through negotiation. Ester and Victor probably realise that their backup solutions are the same and not particularly attractive. It's not likely that they will find someone to complement their interests exactly and it won't look good if they can't work out an agreement together.

Fortunately they don't need their backup solutions. They have a reasonably easy task finding some solutions to meet their needs. Perhaps you have spotted them yourself. They move desks every six months (which shares the status of a window seat).

Victor has the desk near the window in colder months (which gives Victor sunlight at the time he needs it most).

Ester has a large poster of a city or rural scene for at least the autumn and winter (which gives her a sense of space, even if it is artificial). They move the cubicle partition with the whiteboard attached to wherever Ester is sitting (which ensures that she has easy access to the whiteboard all year).

Whoever isn't by the window has the new chair (which helps to share the status). Henry sorts out his files to create some space in one drawer.

They haven't used all their possible solutions. Victor taking a walk in the sun is not part of their agreement. They can still point out to anyone who comments that they both agreed on the arrangement, but they decide that status not such a sensitive issue that they need to discuss it again. They've come up with a combination of solutions that meet their needs. They've also shown that they can work together well, so their relationship is off to a good start.

In that simple example our negotiators have succeeded by taking a win/win approach, listing their needs without defensiveness or criticism, brainstorming some possible solutions without judgement, then looking for the solution or solutions that best meet each party's needs. They've used their backup solution to help them decide whether it's worth accepting any solution, or combination of solutions. Notice that the method works when people cooperate but at the same time are assertive about their own needs and selfworth.

What if the needs don't match?

You might say that Victor and Ester were just lucky. Their needs were a good match and maybe the world isn't arranged that way. Sometimes there do seem to be only two solutions – the other person's and ours, but some goodwill and creativity can bring surprising results. Often a compromise, just something in the middle of your bargaining positions, is a sign of failure. What happens if you want your boss to raise your salary five percent and the boss says two percent sounds better to him? You might reach a compromise of, say, 3.5% but neither you nor the boss would be happy with the outcome and will try to drive a harder bargain next time.

Perhaps you can do better than your backup solution or a compromise. You and the boss could brainstorm and come up with non-monetary benefits that might reward you as much or more than three percent more in salary. Maybe you'd rather have the two percent plus five extra days as holiday to be taken in off-peak times, or maybe one day a week working from home. You might be happy to settle for two percent plus another three percent if you reach an agreed performance target. A friend of mine accepted an afternoon a week to play golf because the company wouldn't let his boss pay him more.

Sometimes the possible solutions are not complementary, but both of you may still have options that could allow your negotiations to succeed. If you are buying a car, you may have your price and the dealer his. You could say, 'This is my offer. Take it or leave it,' but you might be able to do better by suggesting some other possibilities. Perhaps you won't trade-in your current vehicle. Instead, you'll sell it privately or at an auction for what you hope will be a better price. Perhaps the dealer will let you know when another car of the same model comes in with your ideal colour and better extras, and sell it to you at something close to his price for the one you're looking at.

What do you do if the solutions really don't match the needs, after all your attempts to brainstorm? Consider your backup solution. How does the best alternative (including doing nothing) compare with the other party's offer? Take whichever gives you the best outcome.

Start so well they'll want to play

What if the other person doesn't know about negotiating for win/win, or doesn't want to play the game? Sell the idea of cooperation. Begin by describing the negotiation in a neutral way. Maybe, 'We are here to see if we can find a solution to our disagreement over the roosters'. It's more likely to encourage cooperation than, 'We are here to discuss whether you should be allowed to keep roosters in a suburban street'. Make sure the other person can answer the question, 'What's in it for me?' You can say, 'If we work together on this we might be able to find some ways you can get what you need and I can get what I need – without even having to compromise.' You can also suggest goals you could both achieve. Sit next to the other person rather than opposite and use your own cooperative behaviour to sell the idea that it's a 'side-by-side' process. You could also point out that you are not likely to make much progress unless you can find ways of satisfying both of you.

There will be other incentives to cooperate that you might not discuss. It's clearly less expensive to negotiate than let the lawyers fight it out in court and the fact that you may have to work together in future makes cooperating now more attractive.

With respect your honour...

We imagine two judges working together to decide a case on the evidence they have in front of them. I don't know about you, but I would be disappointed if judges didn't treat each with at least professional courtesy and examine the evidence with a cool detachment as they worked towards a decision that satisfied them both. To build cooperation use questions to uncover the other party's needs and check your understanding regularly. You need to show that there may be more on offer through a win/win approach than taking a fixed position, but you do that through exploring needs thoroughly rather than being pushed into suggesting solutions too early.

Add some polish to your technique

Prepare

To be effective when the issues are complex, you'll need to think about your goals, the other person's perspective and the problems you're about to negotiate.

Consider your priorities. Make a list of your needs and how important each really is. What would happen if each need were not met? Now think about your backup solution. Be creative, but keep in mind the 'Do nothing' option.

What needs would the backup solution satisfy? What can you do now to ensure that your backup solution is real and available to you if the negotiations don't go well? Developing an attractive and practical backup solution is the most effective thing you can do to prepare when the other person appears to be in a stronger position.

Think carefully about the other person's perspective. Are you aware of her backup solution? What are her likely needs? You'll be using the negotiation process to ask her about her needs, then explore them and perhaps expand the list, but it pays to go with some understanding of what the needs might be. Think about what the other person has said about the problem before. Do those statements suggest values that might have a bearing on the negotiations? Do the statements suggest assumptions or incorrect information that you could examine in your discussions? What assumptions might you have made that you will need to test once you begin?

Develop your active listening skills

Active listening will help you ensure that you really understand each other's position. Avoid using the listening time to plan your reply. Make sure you listen for both the facts, and the feelings behind them.

Let's say you are a sales manager negotiating with the leader of your company's dispatch team. The dispatch team's slow performance is increasing the risk that your team will appear to be letting its customers down.

First, set the agenda.

You: I'm hoping that we'll be able to come up with some solutions that both our teams are happy with. First, let's do some listening to see where we're both coming from.

Dispatch leader: I suppose so.

You: We should really take some notes so that we have a clear picture of what's important to each of us. Do you want me to do that?

Dispatch leader: Okay.

Now ask your questions

You: As you know, we would like to find a way of getting products in transit to our customers faster, but I realise that it may not be as easy as it sounds. I want to get an idea of what concerns or difficulties that raises for you.

Dispatch leader: It's not easy at all. We're understaffed and we're under increasing pressure from the management team to keep costs down – on staff and everything else.

You: What effect is that pressure having on your team?

Despatch leader: Well, it's making matters much worse. We had one day with half the team on sick leave – I put it down to stress. And your team was sending us demanding emails. Ed and Christine rang us as well – as if we were just sitting around drinking coffee! I tore strips off Ed and it's kept both of them quiet since then.

You: Mmm. We're clearly adding to your stress. What else do we need to take into account?

Dispatch leader: Definitely the quality of the information we're getting.

You: From us?

Dispatch leader: And the rest, but Ed and Paul are the worst. They insist on missing essential information out – just don't bother to put it in!

You: Mmm. That would be frustrating. What other problems do we need to take into account?

Dispatch leader: Mistakes. That's another big one. Emma took half an hour to track down one of your people the other day to correct the information he'd sent through and then he had the cheek to say he hoped she wouldn't take too long processing it.

You: Okay that's helpful. If I've understood you correctly, your team is under pressure from management to cut costs, even though you are understaffed. We're adding stress and frustration with unnecessary phone calls and by leaving essential information out and giving you incorrect information. You'd like us to be more understanding of the pressure your team is under too.

You are revealing both needs and concerns – or interests. You are also reflecting your colleague's feelings which helps to show her that you really are listening. You might wonder about the wisdom of taking so much care to show that we fully understand the other person's perspective. Don't we risk giving unreasonable ideas legitimacy? Maintain the distinction between understanding and agreement. Even if you disagree with much of the other person's perspective, it is still real because that's what she believes. If you have shown that you have fully understood the facts and feelings so well that you can sum up the other person's case even better than she did, you will have established some credibility. That credibility will be particularly useful if you then begin to present a very different perspective. It will be difficult for the other person to assume that you are saying what you are simply because you don't understand her point of view.

Be specific

The negotiation can't be successful unless you are both open and specific about your interests. It's essential that you convince the other person that your interests are important enough for the other person to want to find a solution. Describe your interests in detail. In your negotiation with the leader of the dispatch team, you'd list your interests alongside hers. Perhaps by the time you've finished your notes would look like this.

Your interests

More harmonious relationship with dispatch team Honour all commitments to customers Documents returned in order of priority

Accurate forecasts of when a product can be dispatched

Processing team's interests

Reduce stress

Cope with inadequate number of staff More accurate information from sales team Complete information from sales team.

More understanding from sales team when under pressure

Better explanation and justification of priorities so that time is spent more efficiently

Control your responses

It may be tempting to respond when the other person

lists her needs, but comments like, 'That's not important surely', 'That's not true', 'That's ridiculous' only get in the way. Be unfailingly calm, confident, diplomatic and curious about the other party's needs and ideas for possible solutions.

There are benefits for you too in your calm, professional approach. You are more likely to hear the real needs. The other party might offer some creative solutions that appeal to you. You'll create an obligation to hear you out when it's your turn. You can insist on it, if you've set a good example.

Negotiation can easily be taken over by point scoring and 'clarifications' about things that happened in the past. It quickly becomes a charade – not negotiation, but a cover for war. It is relevant to look at what has happened, but only as a source of interests so that you can both concentrate on making things better in future. Respect the other person, be courteous and understanding, but don't let diplomacy stop you being firm and absolutely clear about your interests. It's a trap to allow sympathy to get in the way of resolving the problem and your commitment to listing and explaining your interests is a key to the process. Welcome the other person doing the same. Resist the temptation to jump in with solutions whenever someone mentions an interest or need. You should both hold back. Just list the interests, all the interests, then look at possible solutions. If you suggest solutions too early, you will invite objections and stall the process.

Build the cooperation

Your active listening and your interest in hearing the other person's possible solutions will encourage cooperation. You can build on that cooperation by going for the easiest source of agreement first. Perhaps you can find a detail you agree on, or simply a perspective you share. Maybe you'll find it in the big picture. Leigh Steinberg, agent to 100 top sports people negotiates multimillion dollar deals and suggests trying to reach agreement on a general framework that's still sketchy, then working out the rest of the deal, 'Because at that point, conflict has been replaced by partnership, and both sides have dropped their defenses'.

If you stop making progress, review what you've agreed so far. Go back to the needs and ask some questions to try to open up some more interests or more possible solutions, 'Tell me more about that. Why is that important? What would happen if we were not able to address that? Is there anything else we need to take into account?'

Think creatively

Brainstorm as many solutions as you can. Try to include some that would help the other person so that it's clear that you are looking for a fair solution, but most of all, try to keep the ideas coming as fast as possible without censorship. Make sure that the other person understands that you are only exploring possibilities and that adding an idea to the list doesn't suggest that either of you is recommending it. Later you can see whether any ideas on the list prompt you to think of others. You'll also think of possible combinations of ideas.

Preserve self-esteem

Preserving the other party's self-esteem makes negotiation more productive. Your cooperative approach and active listening will help the other person to feel heard and respected and less tempted to take an aggressive stance. Whatever the outcome, try to ensure that the other person ends the negotiations with some success. It's particularly important if he is representing a group and will have to report back to it. Help the other person to concede a point. You may be able to show that agreeing makes sense now that he knows more about the background or because the circumstances have changed. You're also helping him explain his new position to himself and anyone he represents.

Don't react

Experienced negotiators talk about responding rather than reacting and even let insults, threats and ultimatums wash over them. It's difficult, particularly when the stakes are high or you're under pressure and tired, but controlling your emotions can be vital.

Impatience or any other surge of emotion, can ruin a

negotiation. A few moments of uncontrolled emotion can encourage you to concede something you'll later regret or damage a carefully-developed relationship at a sensitive stage.

If you sense an emotional moment coming on, try focusing on being curious about the other person's needs or suggested solutions. Take deep (silent) breaths. If the tension is rising or you reach an impasse, go to the list of possible solutions you've created so far and review them together. Refocus for a while on your common ground. Talk about how you might both benefit if you can work your way through to a solution you are both happy with. It's important to keep your focus on achieving win/win, even if the other person is unreasonable. Setting an example often calms the other person down, but if unfair behaviour continues, you can name it and ask him to stop. 'When you shout like that it makes it difficult for us to work towards a solution,' or name the behaviour and ask about his motive. 'I've noticed that you've adopted quite an aggressive tone since we started talking about possible solutions. Why are you doing that?'

Make it easy for the other person to back down and save face when you name unfair behaviour, 'Negotiating gets really tense sometimes doesn't it?' or 'I'm feeling tense too, but I'm sure we can find something that's fair for both of us'. If necessary, take a break. When you come back, try changing chairs.

Make your agreement last

We have to find a way to make the deal appeal to both parties. We'll have a legal agreement with 'easy out' clauses that allow us the freedom to abandon the arrangement if it doesn't work, so the success of our agreement will depend on being fair to each other and negotiating for the long-term. Listening and attempting to match the other's needs, will give you a more satisfying outcome and also builds up a fund of goodwill that makes the agreement more durable. Even so, keep it businesslike and build in transparency and some objective measures to ensure that both sides know that they are keeping to the agreement.

The method in a more challenging scenario

Let's imagine that your grandfather is in a rest home. He's been happy there, but over the last two years one of his close friends has died and, though he puts a brave face on it when you arrive, he has become increasingly depressed and inactive. He admits to being bored and you've noticed that the staff organize everything for the residents – even the entertainment is passive. Granddad resents the staff taking over things he could easily do himself. He confides that his resentment recently led to an angry exchange with a nurse who was treating him like a sick child. He doesn't want to make a fuss, but agrees to you approaching the owner to negotiate some changes, in the interests of all the residents. As you leave he shouts through the door that you won't get anywhere because the owner is a control freak who's just in it for the money.

The word spreads and in the next week other residents and relatives contact you at work to say they would like you to represent them too because they share Granddad's views. Almost all have suggestions for hobbies, outings and other activities and several say they want to have pets.

You call the owner, from your office. You tell her that you are representing your grandfather and several other residents and would appreciate an opportunity to discuss some changes to their care. She says she always welcomes comments from residents and relatives, but questions you closely about the numbers you represent and the way you were appointed. You are relaxed and tell her that your appointment was informal, but the residents and relatives did take the trouble to track down your number and discuss the issues.

You explain the need for negotiation in a non-threatening way.

Mrs Jakes: What changes are they talking about?

You: They'd like to have more independence and more to do – a wider range of activities.

Mrs Jakes: What activities? We're busy enough already, providing activities. Can you tell me what else they want?

You: Well, they have some suggestions, but it would be a matter of finding things they like and that are practical for you and the staff. That's something I'd like to explore with you. You think about the negotiation ahead. You consider the needs and issues the residents have told you about personally, or through their relatives and define your goal: 'To achieve more choice and a wider range of activities to improve their health and morale'. You rank the residents' needs according to how relevant each is to your goal.

They need more independence, specifically, the freedom to make more choices about what they do and when.

They need more activities they can organise themselves and which are more challenging than being an audience for other people.

They need to keep fit.

They need interests outside their own, such as doing things for other residents or looking after pets. You decide that your backup solution is to complain to the authority responsible for the standard of care in rest homes or go to the media. You develop your first solution by ringing the authority's call centre to check that it's the kind of issue the authority would be willing to investigate. You also think about Mrs Jakes's possible needs. You rank them on the limited information you have so far and by imagining yourself in her place. You remember her tone on the telephone. Mrs Jakes seemed to be anxious, perhaps threatened, by your call, but making an effort to be professional.

She seemed to think activities were important, but that they were already a source of stress. You remember her words: 'What activities? We're busy enough already, providing activities. Can you tell me what else they want?' Perhaps her needs will be to:

Avoid additional stress for her staff

Keep costs down

Keep control of the activities programme

Save face.

You decide that her backup solution is to agree to a few minor requests and hope that the residents will be satisfied that she listened and did what she could. Your research reveals that elderly people who have opportunities to make choices about their lives, have regular exercise and keep pets, live longer and more healthy lives. You decide that a satisfactory outcome for you would be to build a cooperative relationship with Mrs Jakes and for residents to be allowed to choose their entertainment and activities. Ideally you would like the cooperative relationship to lead to regular reviews to ensure that the benefits continue.

Next Wednesday afternoon, Mrs Jakes welcomes you without warmth, but retains her professional demeanour. You tell her you appreciate having the opportunity to talk over the residents' and relatives' concerns and that you would like to find some solutions that work for everyone.

You summarize what led you to ask for a meeting. You recall changes in your grandfather's morale since his friend died and refer to the comments from the elderly residents and their families about the passive nature of their existence.

Your tone and language are neutral to suggest that although it is a serious issue, it is something you expect to be able to work through. You suggest that you take notes so that you can go through them together later. You mention that many of the residents have said they want the freedom to make more choices of their own.

Mrs Jakes: What choices?

You: Routine things. Those things that are practical for them to do. We would need to discuss what's practical, but how do you feel about the principle of giving them some choices? (You've given her a sense of perspective, but avoided proposing solutions.) Mrs Jakes: It's fine in principle, but I don't think it's practical. This is an institution and, for better or worse, we have to do things in an institutional way, simply because of the numbers. Most of the people are here because they didn't manage out in the community.

You ask the other person to raise her issues first.

Mrs Jakes says that she was disappointed to find that the residents were dissatisfied with the activities. It becomes clear that she is very experienced in arranging entertainment for elderly people and the current programme is based on one that she says worked well in a previous rest home she managed. She is worried about the cost of increasing the number of outings.

You go into active listening mode.

You: And from what you were saying on the telephone, I guess you'd also be worried about the workload for the staff?

Mrs Jakes: That's right. We're fully stretched. I don't have the budget or the people to provide different conditions for everyone. We'd have some residents exploiting the situation too. Some are quite demanding already. They'd expect us to provide a five star hotel service. I'm sorry, but it's just not practical to give them any more.

You: We might be able to find a way to give the residents at least some of what they need without stretching the budget or stressing the staff, but what else would we have to take into account?

Mrs Jakes: There's the risk factor. I can't have people doing things that might cause them injury and for some of them it could be as simple as taking a walk on their own.

You: Anything else?

Mrs Jakes: It's all I can think of at the moment.

You: Let's make a note of your concerns and the residents' concerns, then we can see if we can find some solutions.

You list the needs and concerns in neutral language, taking care not to discuss positions or introduce solutions at this stage. As you make your notes, you continue to develop a better understanding of each other's needs and perspectives. At the end of this part of your discussion, your page looks like this...

Residents' issues

More activities they can organise themselves.

More independence, specifically, the freedom to make more choices about what they do and when.

To keep fit.

Have interests outside their own.

Rest home's issues

Avoid increased costs
Avoid additions to staff workload

Ensure the residents' safety

Ensure that residents' expectations do not exceed what the rest home can provide.

Keep control of the rest home.

Have satisfied residents and relatives.

You identify some possible solutions.

You: 'I find that it's more productive to just list as many solutions as possible without judging them. We can decide later which solutions or combination of solutions would be best to meet everyone's needs'.

You identify your possible solutions together and the list ends up like this...

Allow the more able-bodied residents to choose activities after consulting the others.

Form a committee of residents and staff to choose activities.

Allow residents to choose pot plants from a list of hardy plants prepared by the staff.
Allow residents to keep caged birds if they are able to feed them unaided.

Allow residents to keep a cat if they are able to look after it by themselves.

Provide one cat for the whole rest home.

Mrs Jakes to allow her own dog to visit residents who agree.

Ask staff to encourage residents to make choices about anything that does not add to the staff workload or to cost and would not endanger the residents. Encourage residents to help other residents with a buddy system.

Introduce a 'keep fit' class for those able to walk to it unaided.

Ask if any residents or relatives would be willing to take a 'keep fit' class – unpaid.

Involve residents and relatives in taking hobby classes chosen by the residents.

Now you consider the value of the solutions and the possibility that a combination of solutions might give you the best outcome. Perhaps you'll eliminate the idea of a cat for anyone who can look after one because you don't want the rest home overrun by cats. Mrs Jakes says that, on reflection, her dog wouldn't be suitable without supervision, but you both like the idea of one cat that's free to roam. You might decide that asking the staff to encourage residents to make choices is too ill-defined. Maybe you both like the buddy system to help residents who are less independent and can think of some, including your grandfather, who would benefit from being active buddies. Eventually, you decide on the best combination of solutions. The staff will encourage the residents to form a committee with a clear brief that their role is to advise on the wishes of all the residents.

Mrs Jakes will make the final decision whether activities and entertainments are practical, but she agrees to welcome any suggestions that don't involve significant extra cost or stress for the staff. She will assign a senior staff member to organise a trial of the buddy system with a few volunteers. The rest home will collect a cat from the animal home by the end of the week and set up a basket for it in the laundry. Both of you will ask if any relatives are prepared to volunteer their time to take fitness or hobby groups. The rest home will offer a limited choice of meals, hardy pot plants and anything else that doesn't involve significant extra work, expense or risk of injury.

You make commitments to implement the agreement.

A formal contract seems out of place, but you read out your notes on the key points of the agreement and offer to email Mrs Jakes with a full version so that she can add any corrections or comments.

You undertake to report the agreements that you've reached to the residents who approached you. You'll report that Mrs Johnson is cooperative, but has some significant constraints.

Mrs Jakes commits to all the changes you have agreed to and proposes that she invite the residents to form their committee. You decide to meet in six weeks to review how well the agreement is working out.

You would almost certainly have achieved more with the problem-solving approach than you could have by bargaining from fixed positions. You've built the cooperative relationship with Mrs Jakes you wanted and the residents will get most of what they need. It's not a compromise because you haven't given up anything significant and Mrs Jakes hasn't had to commit to spending money, increasing the workload for her staff or allowing activities or choices she would consider risky. Together you've identified the needs and met as many as possible.

When they're not interested in win/win

'What do you do when they just want to make demands?' It's one of the questions we are asked most often in training people in negotiation. The bargainer with plenty of power, an attractive backup solution, an aggressive manner and not the slightest interest in win/win, is a formidable challenge. Even so, there are ways to bring him around.

Sell the benefits of finding a win/win outcome. In what ways would your positional bargainer gain from having the issue resolved? Present those benefits in as constructive and balanced a way as you can – not so that it could be interpreted as a threat. Keep away from specific solutions. Maybe something like this: 'I'd like to see if we can find a way to get what we both need – so that we can at least reduce the tension between our two teams'.

It's also important to treat the other party's position as simply a possible option. Then look at what is behind that option. Choose to assume that the other person is playing the game. It won't be true at first, but there's a reasonable chance that it will become true. Continue to treat every demand as just another option behind which there will be interests to explore.

Your prefrontal cortex may be very busy helping you ignore the aggressive tone, the demeaning comments and the apparent intransigence, but keep probing. Keep telling yourself that your diplomacy under duress and your determination to find a win/win solution makes you the emotionally intelligent one, because it's true.

The Secrets Of Being persuasive

The ability to persuade is more than a useful skill. It's an outstanding characteristic of top achievers. The most successful persuaders don't rely entirely on facts or logic. They don't see persuasion as a one-off event. Nor do they use pressure. They use a wider range of strategies than most other people, but manage to remain genuine and altruistic so that the effect is persuasion, not manipulation. Logical arguments can be influential, but persuasion is not a simple, logical process and hard-sell just creates objections.

Why isn't logic enough?

What we say is simply part of the mix. We talk about being persuasive, but we don't actually persuade directly. We influence people and they persuade themselves. Even if our logic is impeccable, our attempts to persuade may encourage them to move even further away from agreeing with us.

Most of us tend to hold on to an opinion even if when we can't remember the arguments we heard at the time we formed it. Sometimes there was never any judgement or reasoning involved. Just feeling good about a speaker, or even an advertisement, can be enough to convince us to accept the argument or buy the product. So our opinion may have no more logic behind it than, 'He was a nice person', 'She sounded as if she knew what she was talking about'. Even when we can't remember those irrelevant justifications, we're unlikely to question our decision, because it just seems right. Even urging people to be open-minded doesn't work because most people believe they have an unbiased view anyway. Even the most ardent racists are convinced they have the facts and everyone else is out of touch with what's really going on in the world. When we ask people to be objective, most will continue to consider new information with their usual biases. They may read or listen to contrary information objectively, then ignore it when they make a decision. They may also use faulty reasoning, such as seeing events that are associated, and assume that one causes the other. It's as logical as: 'People I've seen shaving wear trousers, therefore wearing trousers causes hair to grow on your face'. Fortunately, there are some effective ways to overcome the obstacles of bias and faulty reasoning.

How to prepare to persuade

Effective persuasion is a 'learning and negotiating process' and that the most effective persuaders consider their arguments from every angle, before they even start to present their case. Effective persuaders establish their credibility first. It's essential for persuasive people to have both credible expertise and relationship credibility with their audience. Audiences may resist our arguments simply because we have no relationship with them or because we need to put some work into the one we have. It helps to be liked, but just finding common interests, experiences or values that draw you together helps to make you more persuasive. Genuine consultation will help build your relationship credibility. Ask how other people see the current situation. What problems or opportunities do they have? Resist the temptation to suggest any solutions until you have asked about the size or significance of the problems or opportunities, 'How much of a problem is that for you? What effect is that having? How often does that happen? What would happen if we did nothing about it?'

Next, you could use consultation to explore some options, but you need to phrase the options to make it clear that you don't yet have a fixed view. You might say, 'One possibility would be to dispose of most of the existing computers and issue everyone with a tablet' or, 'I'm looking at various possibilities. We could paint the clubhouse roof, or use our funds to re-carpet the changing rooms. I'm also looking at the possibility of suggesting to the committee that we leave things as they are until we've raised enough money to renovate the whole building. Do you have a feeling about any of those ideas?'

When you present your proposal, enhance your relationship credibility by recalling what the people you consulted told you and emphasising what you have in common – perhaps shared experiences of working for the same company, shared pride in what your team does for customers or shared worries about the current economic trough. You can also acknowledge their doubts, caution and scepticism about your plans. Invite them to express their scepticism and choose to welcome it when they do. Perhaps you are sure that you must reduce staff numbers, or close a division of your company, but you could leave open some of the issues, such as how you think it should be done and when. Your consultation and openness will have developed your credibility with your audience and an understanding of their perspectives. It's now time to answer the question, 'What's in it for me?'

'If you tidy up quickly, there'll be time for a story.'

'This process will save us manufacturing costs and improve our bottom line by the end of the financial year.'

'If we buy our new car now, we can save money on the run-out model.'

If you are proposing that your company move offices from the centre of town to an industrial park, you might have heard in your consultations that some people would be concerned about the cost of transport. You could focus on the benefits of cheaper and more convenient parking. You could show how they could use the road for a quicker trip to the new location. If you don't know how your audience might benefit, or you want to encourage them to think about the benefits of a solution, you can ask. 'If we did do it that way, what would be the advantages for you?' or 'If we did choose that option would it be enough to overcome the problems we've talked about?' If you are preparing to persuade a large audience, you could ask the same questions of a few people who are typical of the group. Their answers should help you present your proposal in a way that highlights the real benefits – the ones your audience thinks are important.

Often it's sufficient to appeal to your audience's core values. You can make safe assumptions that most people want to do good work, to treat customers well and make high quality products. We can also sell the benefits of making a sacrifice for the good of others such as asking people to give up their time or money for a worthy cause, or to help others in the team. Sometimes there is no common ground in your proposal – you can't come up with any significant benefits for your audience. You may have to consider whether the proposal is saleable. An alternative could be to use the salami method – persuade them a slice at a time because your audience is not going to swallow the whole salami in one serving.

Engage the emotions

Emotions are an essential part of the decision-making process. Humans find it extraordinarily difficult to make decisions without knowing how they feel about the options and the facts and data that support them. Most facts or data are emotionally neutral. We might have an instant emotional reaction to the figure of our new salary or a major plunge in stock market prices, but usually, facts need some help to do their work. We can provide a context – particularly what they mean for our audience or for other humans.

You can often introduce emotions or feelings by putting things in perspective. You might for instance offer reassurance that goes beyond simple facts or data. A chief executive once told me that his fertilizer firm often takes calls from reporters who say, 'We've heard that your fertiliser has cadmium (a naturally occurring, but toxic heavy metal).' He says, 'Yes, that's true. It's present in many rock-based fertiliser. 'And,' say the reporters, 'The people at the works are condemning the kidneys of cattle raised on those pastures.' It's an emotional issue and the chief executive knows he must put the contamination in perspective.

The chief executive could offer figures in parts per million, but he needs to be more reassuring than that. He always has the figures handy, but he says, 'Yes that's true too, but even if you ate one of those kidneys every day for the rest of your life, it's very unlikely that the cadmium level in your body would exceed the World Health Organisation's guideline.' Kidneys for dinner every night for the rest of your life? How do you feel about the risk now? (His claim is consistent with the international research.)We can engage our audience's emotions by painting pictures with words. Orators have shown that they make key ideas memorable. Winston Churchill's iron curtain analogy became a media cliché. Martin Luther King's I have a dream speech in 1963 was full of memorable images and made a powerful case for the Civil Rights Bill. Word pictures get audiences interested and encourage them to think more carefully about the arguments. There is one important qualification: The word pictures must match the listeners' feelings, preferences and interests. Ask your audience to imagine how different things could be. Give them detail. Make sure you put people in your pictures. If you want to persuade your management team to buy new software, give them the facts showing how obsolete the current programmes are, but tell them too about the irritation it's caused for the people who're using them. Tell them stories about people. Give them details and name names.

Here's an engineer persuading by painting pictures about people...

'The last time we developed a prototype using that method, it wasn't just slow, it was frustrating because the circuit board was riddled with problems. I came in one Saturday night to find John, Sue and Damien here working away in the half-dark, trying to get the project back on track. It turned out that it was their third six-day week. They're pretty laid back people as you know, but they were mighty tense that night – and there were more long weeks to come – all because we'd decided to take shortcuts to save a little money on the development.' Feeling words like frustrating and tense give your dry facts a human dimension. You might also find opportunities to use others such as, annoyed, proud, delighted, upset, satisfied, angry, thrilled, exhilarated or anxious.

Use names and feeling words well and you'll be showing what your argument means in human terms. That's not padding: It's showing its relevance to your audience. But think it through carefully because if you use feeling words that overstate your case, you're into propaganda. You risk losing your audience's trust and your relationship credibility.

If you have any remaining doubts about the power of

emotions consider the apocryphal story copywriters tell about one of them walking through a park and coming across a blind man with his hat out and a sign reading, 'I am blind.' The copywriter approaches him and says, 'I think I can improve your donations.' He changes the sign to, 'I am blind – and it is spring.'

What to do about objections

Most salespeople are taught to handle objections, which usually means having an answer ready for them. I once shared a suite of offices with an insurance agent who had the answer to every objection he could remember hearing in his long career displayed on his office wall. He would sit back in his chair as he spoke to his prospective customers and look across to the appropriate answers. Salespeople have been taught for decades that an objection is a sign of interest and the more objections, the greater the prospective buyer's interest and the chances of a sale. No doubt it helps to lift their spirits to believe it, but it's not true.

The Huthwaite Research Group observed 10 thousand salespeople and found that the most successful didn't handle objections – the objections didn't arise. They were destroyed early in the sales process as the sellers listened carefully to what their potential clients needed and sought to find a solution to match. The Huthwaite researchers found that an objection is not a sign of interest and the more objections you get, the less likely the prospect will buy your product or idea. Handling objections or hoping they won't come up is far less effective than 'preventing' them early in the sales process.

Set out to remove the objections early. I like the term pre-empting objections, because it suggests a preemptive strike. It might sound aggressive, but it's a very honourable and open process that also focuses our attention on any weaknesses in our argument so that we can think of ways to overcome them before the audience raises them. The alternative to pre-empting objections is to hope that your audience won't mention them. But the objections will be lurking there, ready to destroy or damage your argument. If someone does raise them, you will be forced into a
defensive position. You may find yourself filling silences as you desperately search for an adequate reply. Your audience may think it suspicious that you didn't mention the other side of the argument yourself.

The process

Here's how you prepare to preempt objections.
Summarise your proposal at the top of a blank page and create two columns below it.

Think of any objections the audience might have to your proposal and write them in the left column. I always write their objections in the form of quotes and I like to assume that the people I'm about to persuade have a bit of attitude so often the quotes will qualify for an exclamation mark. It helps me to think of their objections in a more focused way.

Think how you might answer each of those objections. You have three options:

to answer the objection in a way that destroys it

to concede that it's a fair objection, but minor, considering the value of the proposal overall

to amend the proposal because the objection would be so strong that your audience would reject the proposal if you don't.

Let's see the pre-empting objections method in action.

Years ago, the was a campaign to persuade people 65 and older to get vaccinated against influenza. It was a serious issue, because influenza can lead to fatal complications. It was serious for the hospitals too because elderly patients were exhausting their resources during the winter. The previous year patients had been waiting in corridors for beds. It was easy to discover the objections because doctors heard them regularly.

We used the objections to create a modest leaflet headed, 'Influenza. Mistakes many people make.' We quoted all the main objections and answered them.

Proposal: if you are 65 or older, get your influenza vaccine well before winter sets in.

Their objections
Our answers to the objections
'It's too expensive!'
If you are 65 or older, it's free.
'It's just a bit of 'flu'. Hardly worth worrying about.'
Influenza is not just a bad cold. It's a serious disease and it can lead to serious complications. You might die.
'I may be 65, but I'm very fit, so I never get sick.'
If you are 65 or older, your immune system is not as strong as it was. You could catch influenza no matter how fit you are.
'I had one last year.'
Influenza vaccines wear off in less than a year. You need another now.
'I'm too busy now. I'll do it later!'
You need to do it now so that the vaccine has time to work before the expected epidemic arrives.

Within a few weeks the inoculation rate for the region had gone from average, to the highest in the country.

One-sided or two-sided arguments?

If your audience already agrees with you, make your presentation one-sided – give them only the arguments that support your case. It's what politicians do at their party rallies and it's the right choice in that context. The research confirms that presenting an alternative point of view would only rehearse the partisan audience in counter-arguments they might not have considered before. If your audience may disagree with you, a two-sided argument works much better and you can use your skills in pre-empting objections to help you prepare. With a two-sided argument you'll raise the objection and show how wrong it is.

Let's imagine that you want to persuade members of your neighbourhood support group to join you in leaving their cars at home and taking public transport to work. If you spend the next 20 minutes telling them that they will be helping to reduce pollution and the traffic at rush hour and they would save money on transport, your one-sided approach will encourage them to put up barriers. They'll probably have their counter-arguments ready and even if they don't, research has shown that just knowing that there is another side to the story would make them more resistant. They'll also see your one-sided presentation as bias.

When you include arguments against your case you break down that resistance. Acknowledge that they would have the inconvenience of walking to the bus or train and that public transport doesn't have quite the same comfort or status as a car. You can then argue that the inconvenience of the walk is outweighed by having to park the car, the difference in comfort minor and that they would be making a useful contribution to the lives of their fellow citizens. Having conceded the other side of the argument, you can claim that when we take everything into account, catching the bus or train makes more sense.

Two-sided arguments come with a long-term benefit when the audience is likely to disagree with you. If you present both sides and someone else comes along to argue against you, the audience is less likely to be swayed. The more open approach will have given them the opportunity to consider points on both sides and build a fund of counter-arguments against the newcomer.

Positive or negative?

It's an old debate. Should you 'accentuate the positive, eliminate the negative' or give them a reality check by telling them how serious things could be if they don't accept your argument? It depends on their starting point.

Philip Broemer of the University of Tubingen in Germany believes that the key issue is ambivalence. If your audience is likely to have conflicting feelings about your cause, choose the negative argument. Broemer tested negative messages in a study that promoted exercise and a low fat diet to reduce the risk of heart disease. Most people are ambivalent about exercise and diet and the study suggested that emphasising the dangers of not changing our lifestyle is more effective than telling us how we will benefit. Broemer found that people who were ambivalent about using condoms to prevent HIV were much more often persuaded by messages about the dangers of unprotected sex than assurances that they would feel much safer if they used them.

Addictions offer a special challenge. Most smokers want to give up, but they also believe that smoking relieves stress and they find it pleasurable. According to Philip Broemer's research, we should keep telling them how dangerous it is. The strategy has helped, but millions of people around the world read messages as strong as 'Smoking kills' and 'Smoking causes fatal diseases' and still light up. Earlier research suggests that our perception of risk is a significant issue too and it's clearly a factor in our ambivalence. Positive messages, telling us how we'll benefit, work best if we think the risk is low or non-existent. There's no great risk, for most of us anyway, in walking to work, so use a positive message – say, 'Walk to work and you'll keep fit and healthy and save a fortune in transport. It should be more effective than the negative, 'Walk to work or you'll lose your fitness, get sick more often and lose a fortune in transport'. Most people rate medical checkups as risky and researchers recommend negative messages to spur us into action: 'If you leave a tumour to grow, it may be too late to treat it. See your doctor for a check-up.' The research is confirming that negative information or messages about checkups tend to be more effective than similarly positive messages. Don't overdo the negativity. If you raise strong fears, you run the risk of your audience repressing the message because it's too difficult to face.

Effective persuaders can't assume that the natural human motivation to protect ourselves from harm is enough to change our behaviour. We need to show people that there is a real danger and that they are personally vulnerable. We also need to convince them that the action we are suggesting will help them avoid danger and that it's practical for them to take that action. We may need a series of messages targeted at those four issues.

Let's say you want to persuade new employees to use ear protection every time they are using machinery – not just when you are around. You might explain how prolonged exposure to noise damages the inner ear and that it's a gradual process. ('There is a real danger.') Perhaps you could arrange for them to meet, or hear about, someone who operated the same machines and became deaf. ('You are personally vulnerable.') You could provide information about the effectiveness of hearing protection and ask them to put on the industrial ear protectors you want them to wear while you start up your noisiest machine. ('The action will help you to avoid danger.') You might explain that their ear protectors will be stored within easy reach of the machines. ('The action is practical.')

With risky behaviour it's particularly important to focus on the consequences of the behaviour rather than harp on about the solution. People who, for instance, speed, drink excessive amounts of caffeine, smoke or are consistently late for work, may process your messages defensively – 'It won't happen to me. The risks are exaggerated. I heard that you can smoke till you are in your thirties then stop and it doesn't do you any harm.' Work on those rationalisations. Show them repeatedly that their beliefs are false.

Inoculating against other arguments

Once you've persuaded people, you can help them to resist counter-arguments by encouraging them to rehearse their defences. The researchers call it inoculation and it does work in much the same way as a measles injection. A little of the other side's argument is like a weak form of the virus. It stimulates the defences.

Inoculation works best if you use three steps. Tell your audience that the other side is likely to attack soon. Offer some weak arguments that the other side might come up with. Encourage your audience to think about what they might say when they hear from the other side. If it sounds manipulative, let's take an honourable use of it. Imagine that you've persuaded your teenager that smoking is a very unhealthy thing to do, but you suspect that the peer pressure to smoke will begin soon. Both of you could think of ways to respond to the pressure and jibes. You would alert your teenager to the possibility that her friends might offer her cigarettes soon and tell her she is chicken if she refuses. You could then brainstorm some replies – for instance, 'I'd have to be chicken to smoke just to impress you.'

A high school took on the pressure to smoke in just that way. The teachers also encouraged the children to respond to advertisements that implied that women who smoked were liberated. They suggested replies such as, 'She's not really liberated if she's hooked on tobacco.' They were prompting defensive responses, rather than hoping the children would develop them. The programme was twice as successful as more conventional anti-smoking programmes for the same age group. Ideally, you should leave people to come up with their own defences. They'll be more committed to them if you do.

Techniques the advertisers use

Infomercials, direct mail and advertising provide some useful examples of researched techniques in action. If you are repulsed by the idea, try to keep an open mind. It's easy to use some of the techniques at work in ways that won't seem commercial or manipulative.

Focus on the audience

Effective marketers never lose their focus on the audience. It's the golden rule of all communication and essential to persuasion. In your preparation ask yourself, what's important to my audience, how might they react to this idea, how would they benefit, what objections might they have? Speak and write to them as individuals, using the word you, and inclusive words such as us and we. As you present your case, monitor their reactions constantly. Pick up on body language that suggests doubt or resistance. Do they need more information? Should you give more reassurance? Do you need to acknowledge their doubts or scepticism before going on to talk about the benefits? Try to make it two-way communication, rather than simply a presentation.

Everybody else is doing it!

Evidence that other people approve or are doing something can be powerfully persuasive in marketing too. It's such a standard technique of advertising that we rarely question the objectivity or motives of those who give their support to a persuasive message. In one series of infomercials the producers asked people in the street to view the world through a brand of sunglasses. People all over the country would look around them and gush such lines as: 'That's incredible!' and 'If I had not seen that with my own eyes, I would not have believed it!' In television commercials include taciturn farmers praising, with low-key rural credibility, the virtues of brands of fence-posts and sheep drenches. You can even see people in the street praising the quality of prunes.

The need to compare ourselves with others is so strong that it's easily exploited, but checking what others think or have decided can provide us with useful information. If your consumer organisation reports that 96 per cent of its members found that Brand A smartphone is reliable, it's surely only sensible to take that into account. If your friends enjoyed a book, maybe you will too. It's only sensible to draw on our networks of relationships and particularly those people whose opinions we trust.

It makes sense to add a list of testimonials from satisfied clients to our proposals. It makes sense to mention that other branches of our organisation or other teams in our sport are already doing successfully what we are advocating. We are answering the natural questions, 'Has anyone else done this before?' and 'What happened?'

Referring to what others are doing or thinking also adds human interest to facts. It can be a legitimate way of appealing to the emotions. If for instance you were shooting a commercial for your town, you'd want your audience to see plenty of people enjoying themselves. Your message would be far more effective if you could show that it's already a place other people like to visit. But how about this? Imagine that you are preparing an anti-litter commercial for television. To highlight just how widespread littering is, you're thinking of showing some particularly disgusting shots in what would otherwise be beautiful locations. Would that be effective? The research suggests it wouldn't. You'd be mixing two messages: 'Stop littering' and 'Lots of people are littering.' Lots of people are littering suggests that we might as well join in.

It's easy to confuse our messages when we ad lib and we find ourselves saying, 'Everyone's been leaving dirty dishes in the staff room so let's make sure it doesn't happen again,' or 'Hardly anyone is sending their reports to me on time and I want to see an improvement.' Instead, thank those who are already stacking their own dishes in the dishwasher and sending their reports to you on time.

Use endorsements

Producers of commercials and infomercials love endorsements from celebrities and authority figures. Why not use them too? There are some significant ethical issues, but endorsements can be very persuasive. You may need an endorsement from an authority figure to support your 'expertise credibility'. It can help your audience as much as it helps you. An expert, especially one who is genuinely objective, helps us cut through all the available evidence. The expert need not appear in person – maybe a relevant quote will be enough. Experts help us reach the decisions we might have made ourselves if only we had specialised in such things as the intricacies of international exchange rates, the most effective way to exercise, or the hazards of particular chemicals. People with credible expertise have power. A single story on national television in South Africa quoting an expert has been shown to shift public opinion nationwide by 4 per cent. Endorsements from likable or glamorous people are persuasive too because we use people we like or admire as a reference when we are uncertain.

Glamour rubs off on the product or idea and creates an image.

Use the need to be consistent

Our need to seem consistent, not just publicly, but to ourselves, is a powerful influence on our behaviour. Once we take a position on an issue we can be influenced by that action weeks later. A study from the 1960s showed how far-reaching the need to be consistent can be. Jonathan Freedman and Scott Fraser, from Stanford University sent research assistants into the suburbs of Palo Alto California to ask homeowners to agree to a simple request. They invited residents to sign a petition to 'Keep California beautiful'. As you might expect, not many people turned them down.

Two weeks later other members of the research team arrived at their door, pretended to be from a fictitious organisation, didn't mention the petition and asked the homeowners to agree to erecting a billboard reading, 'Drive Carefully' on their lawns. Each research assistant had a photograph to show how the billboard would look – very large and with unprofessional lettering, obscuring much of an attractive house. Twenty per cent of a control group said yes to the billboard, but fifty five per cent of those who had previously agreed to sign the petition agreed. The researchers reasoned that signing the petition helped the homeowners to see themselves as public-spirited citizens. Two weeks later they were still seeing themselves as public-spirited – the kind of people who would help to save lives on the road. The pressure to be consistent was their own. They had no reason to believe that the second researcher knew anything about the petition.

You could use the consistency principle to persuade yourself. Writing your goals creates a commitment to them, but public commitments are the most powerful. I remember a young teacher who enjoyed her work, but felt that she should see something of the world. She worried about giving up the security of her job. She procrastinated for a while, but at her farewell to her family and friends she mentioned that telling everyone that she would be travelling overseas soon gave her the motivation to make definite plans and begin saving. She's lived overseas ever since.

If you want to give up smoking, tell your friends. Tell them when you will be stopping. If they ever see a cigarette in your hands, you're being inconsistent.

If a colleague says she's unhappy with the way clients' enquiries are handled, invite her to research and recommend ways of improving your customer service. You are asking her to be consistent with her expressed concern. If you want your colleagues to deliver their projects on time, consider asking them to commit to their deadlines in a meeting with the whole team. You can use the human need to be consistent constructively when your children express healthy values or ambitions and you create opportunities for them to put those values into action. If your teenager says he would like to be fitter, you can point out that the new computer game he wants might distract him from his goal. The research shows that it would work better if you avoided pressure and your teenager felt free to decide whether to buy the game.

MAXIMIZE YOUR POTENTIAL

Chapter 5

Once upon a time there were two incredibly intelligent and capable boys. Their wonderful talents were obvious from an early age, and they easily outdid everyone around. They had always known they were special, and they harboured inside them a desire that, in the future, everyone would come to admit how exceptional they were. Each of them developed in a different way. The first used all his talent and intelligence to have a successful career and show everyone his superiority. He took part in all kinds of competitions, visited all the most important people and places, and was great at making friends in high places. Even when still very young, no one doubted that some day he would be the wisest and most important person in the land. The second boy, equally aware of his own capabilities, never stopped feeling a heavy responsibility. He would do almost any task better than those around him, and he would feel obliged to help them. This didn't leave him enough time to follow his own dreams of greatness. He was always busy looking for ways to more effectively help others. As a result, he was a much-loved and well-known person, but only in his own small circle.

Destiny was such that a great disaster struck that land, spreading problems and misery far and wide. The first of those brilliant young men had never come across anything like this, but his brilliant ideas worked successfully throughout the land, and they managed to slightly improve the situation. But the second young man was so used to solving all kinds of problems, and had such useful know-how in certain subjects, that the disaster hardly affected the people in his region at all. His admirable methods were then adopted across the land, and the fame of this good and wise man spread even more than had that of the first young man. Indeed, he was soon elected governor of the whole nation. The first young man then understood that the greatest fame and wisdom is that which is born from the very things we do in life, from the impact they have on others, and from the need to improve ourselves every day. He never again took part in competitions or vain shows, and from then on, whenever he travelled, he took his books along with him, so he would be ready always to offer a helping hand to all.

Man regularly moves toward becoming what he trusts himself to be. If I continue saying to myself that I can't complete a specific thing, it is conceivable that I may end by extremely getting to be unequipped for doing it. Actually, if I have the conviction that I can do it, I will clearly obtain the ability to do it regardless of whether I might not have it toward the start.

We each possess skills and abilities that nobody else possesses quite like we do. We are each gifted with unique strengths and talents, whether this is a talent for display on the world stage, or on a small stage as someone who makes a difference to just a few other people. So how do we make the most of our personal capability? By creating the right mindset. Here are the key features of the expand capability mindset.

Identity- development

There are two pulls in the human condition: to stay where we are and consolidate what we have or to discover what is still possible, what we could achieve, how far we could go. The result of these two opposing pulls is that some of us - perhaps the majority - choose the path of safety and security while wondering what we might have missed. Others take risks, go on adventures, seek to expand what they possess, even at the expense of a quiet life. Managing the discovery of potential at minimum risk is the skill of self-development.

Contentment and Purpose

Contentment is linked to the attainment of purpose. That is why we find so much satisfaction when we fulfill our purpose and contentment in the effort that takes us there. For many people however, life is without contentment and unfulfilled. 80% of people wished they were in a different career than the one they were in, more than one in four people are unhappy with what they do in there daily lives.

Our Rare Gift

It is the mix of gifts and other factors, which produces potential. Potential can be regarded as the sum of gift, personality, will power, self-belief, drive and ambition, circumstances, opportunities and positive thinking.

If a man has a gift and cannot use it he has failed, If he has a gift and uses only half of it he has partly failed. If he has a gift and learns somehow to use the whole of it, he has gloriously succeeded and won a satisfaction and triumph few men ever know.

Every single one of us possesses a gift in some form or another. Our gifts do not depend on background, upbringing, social class, job, ability or disability; hence the belief that they are divinely gifted. None of us possesses a greater or lesser gift than any other person. It is their use and application, which distinguishes the so-called "gifted" from the so-called "less-gift".

Particular Intelligence

The word "intelligence" means innate gift.

More popularly, the name "intelligence" is given to people who have displayed outstanding human achievements, endurance or accomplishments. But these people are no different from us. Their physiques, brain sizes, human strengths and qualities were essentially no different from any other. What was possible for them is also possible for us.

The Character of Intelligence

So just what are the characteristics of those who we regard as "intelligent"? Intelligent people are those displaying the following qualities:

1. Dream: the ability to see yourself succeeding in your goal
2. Wish: the passion or desire to accomplish the goal
3. Confidence: the belief that you will succeed
4. Dedication: the willingness to act on the vision
5. Preparation: the definition of how to realize the goal
6. Perseverance: the persistent determination to reach the goal
7. Focus on Information: a thirst to know about your subject
8. Intellectual literacy: an understanding of the brain's power
9. Optimistic mind-set: a belief that things will work out
10. Perception: the ability to sense that something will work
11. Team player: a team of others who support you master
12. Mentors: a mental image of supporters
13. Reality: an awareness of what is true and real
14. Bravery: the ability to face fear and go on.

Self efficiency

Super-nations and super-organisations with cradle-to-grave care and dependency cultures, it is easy to adopt the view that it is up to others to manage our own self-development. After all, maximising your potential results in self-motivated individuals; people who achieve more; people who learn more and can apply more: The conclusion is that self-development is a do-it-yourself skill and a do-it-yourself activity.

Condition of Survival

All of us in our lives find ourselves predominantly in one of three states: survival, maintenance or development. Survival means just getting by, a state that is like a shipwrecked sailor afloat on a life raft in a hostile sea struggling to cling to any passing wreckage. Maintenance means reaching a safe balance between ourselves and our environments where with luck we'll come out alright. Development is the only state that we control and determine. If survival is like a swimmer in a hostile sea and maintenance is like a plumber on a leaky boat, development is like a man with a course, a plan and a destination.

Make Your Future

Our lives are in our own hands and the extent to which they are pre-ordained. Some believe we are who we are because of our inherited characteristics. Others believe we are the product of birth and upbringing. But all of us can set ourselves on the path we want by simply making our minds up to do it. Even in the most limiting society, we still have the free will to try. And that is the first step to creating our own destiny.

The Decision of Transformation

So, if you are stuck in one of the survival or maintenance modes of development, ie just keeping your head above water, or just getting by, what are the options to take you to the state of development? There are usually 4 options:

- Getting nothing done. This may work but it also leaves you open to what others may do. It also may extend the unhappy situation that you don't like.

- transform the circumstances. It is not always within our power to change the situation.

- Disappear. This may not be possible either.

- change yourself through personal development. This is always possible.

The Maximum Rewards

All of us have two distinct choices to make about what we will accomplish with our lives. The first choice is to be less than we can be. To earn less, have less, do less, and think less. These are the choices that lead to an empty life, a life of constant apprehension, instead of a life of wondrous anticipation. Our second choice is to strive, produce and accomplish as much as we possibly can. Just as a mighty oak reaches up towards the sky, we have the worthy challenge to stretch to the full measure of our capabilities.

Our ultimate life objective should be to create as much as our gifting, ability and desire will allow us to create. The greatest rewards are reserved for those who bring the greatest value to themselves and those around them as a result of who they are and who they have become.

Input Position

1. Potential is the possibilities we each have inside us to perform to our maximum capability.

2. We each have unique talents not possessed by anyone else.

3. It is the way that talents are developed and used that distinguishes the so-called "talented" from other people.

4. What we can achieve in life is a blend of talents, drive, circumstances, skill and positive self-belief.

5. Self-development is a do-it-yourself skill and a do-it-yourself activity.

Character-Enlargement

Everyone has it in them to develop themselves to their fullest potential, whether in work, relationships, family, endeavours, sport, whatever. It requires a mix of qualities, mindsets, and behaviours. Here are the most important of these qualities.

Mindset

Mindset is the start and end point of all self development . Without the right positive attitude and confidence, you will not achieve anything of importance in your life. With it, everything is possible. I am convinced that life is 10% what occurs to me and 90% how I respond to it.

There are three key mental attitudes you require:

- security based on your past experiences and an awareness of who you see yourself to be;

- faith based on a belief in your gifts, your opportunities and your abilities;

- anticipation based on a certainty that you can advance towards your goals.

Capability

You'll have a tough time achieving your full potential in life if you try to do something you have no gift for. It is much easier to take time to find out your own unique gifts and develop these. It's no good running a chicken farm badly for thirty years while saying, Really I was meant to be a Singer. By that time, chickens will have become your fashion.

Confidence

The one thing that distinguishes those who realize their full potential and those that don't is confidence. In fact, the strength of your confidence is the one thing that determines whether you conquer mountains or conquer foothills. But confidence, or faith, is not easy. It means a belief in something that you can't prove or be certain of. It means believing in life's supernatural. Confidence is like a bird that feels dawn breaking while it is still dark. There are many inspiring stories of people in everyday situations who refuse to give in to received wisdom and limit their dreams.

Hard work

There is a common fallacy that self-development is purely a mental undertaking. Much of it is, perhaps most of it. But when the mental side is right, you still need to take action and work your socks off to achieve the goals you want for yourself. Hard work is the heart of production and the foundation of success.

Bravery

It is easy to start the process of self-development; much harder to keep it going, particularly when the score seems to be going against us. That's when we need bravery. Lots of it Sometimes we need a bold David versus Goliath kind of courage. At other times, we need a quieter bravery. Bravery doesn't always shout. Sometimes bravery is the quiet voice at the end of the day saying: "I will make an effort again tomorrow. It is not the wall we triumph over, but our fears.

Opportunity

The combination of all the factors of genuine self-development, such as ability, faith, confidence, and awareness, are the factors that produce what we call "chance." Everything that happens to us is a result of our mental confidence and our physical action. In fact, we always get what we expect to get, no more, no less. Opportunity is the stage name God brings into play when he doesn't desire to signal his name.

Determination

All self- developers know the feeling of working hard to what they imagine is the finishing line only to find that the line has moved further on when they get there. In truth, when we have big goals and many goals, there is no finishing line. But we still need to persevere. All efforts identify with the skill to march the final journey, form the ultimate preparation, and persist the remaining time sweat. In the struggle to the end, courage is the one quality we must occupy if we are to be potential winners. All human being advancement follows a similar bend, which has its own drive and takes its own moment. We can recognize phases on the road to attaining a goal:

1. the original malfunction on the growth turn is the original enthusiasm of new goals. Our inspiration is elevated.

2. disappointment sets in soon after the initial malfunction when we realize things aren't going to be as easy as we thought.

3. failures outshine successes and we begin to wonder if we did the right thing. This is the time for a strong faith.

4. the barren plateau at the bottom of the drain is when we stabilise things. This is the time to invest in the future.

5. steadfast persistence accompanied by learning sends the curve upwards.

6. the point of breakthrough occurs when we find the formula that works for us.

7. we move comfortably to the goals we set and are able to think about setting new ones.

In the final analysis, it doesn't much matter whether you become a champion on the world stage or a champion in your own little neck of the woods. The feeling you will have will be exactly the same: one of satisfaction, achievement, and triumph.

Key Points

1. No matter how bad things seem, every situation in life has strengths which can be exploited.

2. The limitations on what we can do in our lives are largely self-imposed.

3. Sound values and character-building principles are the foundations of personal growth.

4. When we use the principles of self-management, our growth towards a goal is teleological, like a missile.

5. Just as individuals can develop themselves, given the right principles, so can organisations and teams.

6. Organisations cannot develop the potential of their people unless they change their styles of managing from disempowering to empowering ones.

Know Yourself

Self-knowledge is the starting point on the journey of self-development. Self-knowledge gives us a window onto our potential. It indicates where our strengths lie, what things we are naturally good at and how we might combine our natural gifts with the opportunities around us. Here are some of the main ways to find out just where your potential lies.

Self-Research

The starting point for your journey of self-development is you, the person in the mirror. Looking at yourself, your strengths, likes and dislikes, preferences, and skills is an essential first step in your self-development plan. Here are some of the ways you can carry out your own self-research.

- look in the mirror and notice what you see

- journalise and diarise. Diaries are useful for recording events and your reactions to events.

- write down a dialogue with parts of yourself. If you have a fear, call it "Steve" and have a chat with him. He might give you insights into what really makes him happy and what makes him afraid.

- get feedback on your work and behaviour from colleagues and friends. For a balanced view ask your critics' views as well.

- study your relationships and how they make you feel

- draw your life history to date and project it forward.

Strengths

five ways we can discover our strengths.

1. Listen for yearnings. Yearnings are often triggered when we see someone doing something we'd like to do or feel we could do better.

2. Watch for satisfactions. When we get a glow of satisfaction from doing a work, even though we don't know why, it's likely to be a strength.

3. Watch for rapid learning. A strength is characterised by initial rapid learning that continues for a lifetime.

4. Be aware of moments of excellence.

5. Watch for total performance of excellence. Total performance of excellence is a flow of behaviour when there are no conscious steps in evidence or in the mind of the performer.

Easy to Learn and Easy to Do

You can divide the things in your life into 4 categories according to the degree of difficulty in learning them and the degree of difficulty in doing them.

1. things that are hard to learn and hard to do. These are likely to be your weak areas. No matter how much you try and how often you come back to them, they are things you are never going to enjoy or do with ease. Make them a small part of your life, done out of necessity not choice.

2. things that are hard to learn and easy to do. These are likely to be everyday skills that take time to learn but, once mastered, are never forgotten, like riding a bike and tying your shoes.

3. things that are easy to learn but hard to do. These are likely to be activities that, although you know how to do them, always present a challenge. They include physical ac-

tivities like chopping wood and changing a car wheel.

4. things that are easy to learn and easy to do. These are where your natural talents lie because you engage in these activities with carefree, natural and unrestrained ease and joy.

Your True Passion

The secret to finding your strengths is to do what you love. And the only way to do great work is to love what you do. If you haven't found it yet, keep looking. Don't settle. As with all matters of the heart, you'll know when you find it. And, like any great relationship, it just gets better and better as the years roll on. So keep looking until you find it. Don't settle.

Your time is limited, so don't waste it living someone else's life. Don't be trapped by dogma - which is living with the results of other people's thinking. Don't let the noise of others' opinions drown out your own inner voice. And most important, have the courage to follow your heart and intuition. They somehow already know what you truly want to become. Everything else is secondary.

Your Personality

Your personality is the set of characteristics that don't change during your life but can develop in healthy and positive directions. Your personality characteristics also indicate what things you will find come naturally to you. There are many different kinds of personality typologies and assessments, these personality models can offer clues to the things you prefer to do in your life, which are invariably the things you are good at and where your natural strengths lie.

Values and Life Centre's

In growing up, we develop a set of values that become important to us. These values become the source of our sense of self-worth, our security, wisdom, and power. Our set of values are like the bedrock to our life and work. They are the things that create our own personal circles of influence and centre. Some of the common centres are focused on the following: our spouse, our family, ourselves, pleasure, money, work, possessions, friends, enemies, and institutions such as church or organisation.

Some people are lucky enough to perceive their talents at an early age, perhaps at school or in the family. Others come to them slowly after a process of wrong turns and failings. Others may not come to self-knowledge until late in life when they suddenly see with blinding clarity where their lives have been taking them. The important point to remember is that, at whatever point it comes, it is always possible to turn self-knowledge into self-realisation.

Key Points

1. By getting to know ourselves better, we can discover our own strengths and potential.

2. We can research ourselves by noticing how we perform in different life situations.

3. When we see someone doing something that we feel we could do better, it is likely to be a strength.

4. Insight into the way we tend to behave normally or in certain circumstances.

5. We invariably describe who we are by reference to what we do.

6. We each tend to prefer to work with one of the following: people, things, data, ideas, or knowledge.

Goals and Goal-Setting

Goal-setting is the one activity that sets apart self-developers from those who survive or just get by. Goal-setting enables us to create the future we want to happen rather than live the future that others want to happen. In goal-setting, we take charge. Here are 7 ways to set reachable goals.

Start With Your Strengths

Although you can base your goals on anything you

want, your chances of success are greater if, first, you base them on your strengths and second, on the current opportunities in your field. To find out your strengths, do some self-research, such as a personal SWOT: your strengths, weaknesses, opportunities and threats.

- strengths are the things you are good at and enjoy doing. Strengths-based goals provide their own motivation.

- weaknesses are the things that you have to do, but either dislike doing or make slow progress in.

- opportunities are the external circumstances you expect to arise or can create which will aid you in moving towards your goals.

- threats are those external circumstances that are unlikely to help you and may set you back.

While we must keep an eye on weaknesses and threats, our goals should be built around strengths and opportunities.

Written goals have a way of transforming wishes into wants, can'ts into cans, dreams into plans and plans into reality. The act of writing clarifies your goals and provides you with a way to check your progress. You can even add reasons to give you more motivation. So don't just think it - ink it!

Dream Big

One of the factors that restricts the realisation of our full potential is the belief that we shouldn't go for big goals. Yet all the evidence of those who realize big goals is that we can always achieve far more than we think. Big goals attract big resources like a magnet.

There is nothing wrong in thinking big when you set your goals. But you need to remember that a goal and a dream are not always the same thing.

Pitch Each Goal

Once you have set your ultimate goal, you then need to set the intermediate goals that will get you where you want. Don't pitch these too easily or too ambitiously or they will drop into the Drop Zone. Aim to make them challenging: out of reach, but not out of sight.

Imagine Yourself Succeeding

When your will, your rational left-brained self, comes into conflict with your imagination, your creative right-brained self, your imagination wins every time.

Express Them Right

It's important to express your goals in the right way.

- never express your goal in terms of what you don't want; always in terms of what you do want

- express your goals in performance terms not reward terms

- express your goals in terms of how others benefit

- express your goals according to the principles which matter.

Whilst focusing on goals is a sure way to move towards them focusing on some goals at the cost of neglecting others is a way to achieve hollow victories. It is like the man who worked so hard to provide for his family that he neglected them in the process and ended up losing them from his life in separation and divorce. Some of the other areas that need to be considered when you set goals in, say, your work life are the effects on home, marriage, health, social life, leisure activities, spiritual life. When we manage to harmonize or align goals in one area with those in another, we find that motivating forces in one area actually help those in other areas at the same time.

Set Goals In Terms of Behaviour

When we set goals for ourselves, they should be expressed in behavioural terms, rather than in terms of status, rewards or position. That's because behaviour is something within our power, while status, rewards and position are not. Formulating goals in behavioural terms also means we present a strong positive image of ourselves to our brains. The brain, not knowing the difference between a real or imagined experience, then seeks to act in accordance with the presented image.

Pursue Your Goals with Passion

The driving force behind your goal-achievement is Desire. You must desire your goals constantly, vividly and with a burning passion, knowing that you have already achieved them and now only need to realise them. If you do, you cannot fail to achieve them.

Goal-setting is central to maximising our potential because it enables us to create something unique and new in our lives. Goal-setting allows us to feed our goal-oriented brain and puts us in control of our futures.

Key Points

1. Goal-setting is the one activity that distinguishes self-developers from those who just get by.

2. Write your goals down, so that you have a way to measure your progress.

3. Build your goals around your strengths.

4. Set your goals as big as you can.

5. Pitch your goals so that you can just reach them.

6. Express your goals in terms of the actions within your power, not the rewards outside your power.

Programming Your Goals

Programming is a computer term that aptly describes what happens when we feed a goal into the network of our minds. We give it the goal and then programme it to achieve it. It then works like a locked-on missile seeking out its target. The following are proven programming techniques that will ensure you land right on target.

Affirm What You Want

Affirming what you want means stating your goal in the present tense as if you'd already achieved it. The brain takes whatever action needed to comply with the affirmation. Affirmations should be positive, realistic and expressed in emotive words such as "I love..." and "I enjoy...". All of life's outstanding achievers use affirmations. World champion boxer Muhammed Ali said, "I am the greatest". Composer Ludwig van Beethoven said, "I know that I am an artist". Affirmations can also be made for teams or even whole organisations:

"We are proud of what we do."

"We enjoy maintaining and improving our high standards of what we do."

Visualise It

Visualisation means seeing yourself in your mind's eye having achieved your goal. The secret of visualisation is to do it in such rich detail, and with all your senses, that you are fully there. There are many examples of how mental visualisation can aid actual performance, especially in the sports world.

Motivation

The likelihood that we will reach our goals depends on our level of motivation. The word "motivation" comes from the Latin verb "movere", to move. Motivation is a drive that causes movement or a reason to move. We are in a static state but going nowhere. When we present a new goal to our subconscious brain, we move out of the static state into a state of positive discontent. This state provides us with the motivation to move towards the goal.

When our goals depend on others, there are two main motivation techniques, push and pull. These are a matched pair. While pushing is shooting with a high-velocity rifle, pulling is fishing with a tempting bait. With pushing you create repulsion and fear often based on the loss of something desired; with pulling you create desire and attraction, often with the promise of something desired. Pushing is more difficult than pulling and may be far less effective. When you push, you're like a sheepdog telling a flock of sheep where to go but sometimes they can scatter in all directions. When you pull, you're like a shepherd calling the flock towards you; they know there's only one place to go. The best motivation is a mix of push and pull. You push to break people away from their current stupor; and you pull to see them come home to the goal.

Practise Your Shots

The more you practise your shots, the more likely you are to score well when the need to act arises. It's what cricketers do in the nets. Or teams that rehearse fire drills each week. Or entrepreneurs who visit their dream home each day as if they already owned it. The brain cannot tell the difference between actual reality and imagined reality and so will simply believe you have already achieved your goals.

Positive Self-Talk

Just as a computer programme occasionally gets infected with viruses and bugs, so your own goal-setting programming can get infected with setbacks, doubts, and feelings of failure. That's when you need an antivirus mental programme to get rid of the bugs. One such programming is Positive Suggestion which is activated whenever you have thoughts of fear, panic or doom. Simply replace your negative thoughts with positive ones and remind yourself of your progress: Every day in every way I am getting nearer and nearer my goals.

Leave It Alone

Once we feed our goals into our subconscious brains, it's very important that we let our brains get on with the job without interference. The conscious brain is like the machine operator while the sub-conscious is the machine itself. This means that you have to let go and resist the temptation to analyse or check how it's doing. It is like the penalty shooter who starts worrying about how he should hit the ball, which way the goalkeeper might move, what the crowd might think if he misses. Inevitably, his worry makes him take his eye off the goal and he misses the target.

Pray With Heartfelt Gratitude

Prayers are a form of programming that people have practised for centuries. But with one important difference from other kinds of programming. As well as verbalizing or internalizing something you want, you give thanks as if you already possessed it. Such gratitude connects you to a mightier power than you possess and unleashes great forces that work on your behalf.

When you practise these programming techniques to achieve your goals, you will achieve with scientific certainty whatever you desire.

Key Points

1. Programming is a way to create a mental focus for our goals.

2. The brain works best when it is left alone to find its way to a programmed goal.

3. Affirmations should confirm your self-image as an individual or team.

4. Visualising yourself having reached your goal sends powerful images for your brain to work on.

5. The best kind of motivation is an internal one driven

by a desire to achieve a goal we want.

6. We can motivate ourselves if we associate achieving our goals with thoughts of pleasure, and missing our goals with thoughts of pain.

Super-Energy

The biggest threat to self-developers is lacking the energy to reach their goals. This can happen in three main ways: through physical tiredness; mental exhaustion; or emotional and spiritual fatigue. These three energy drains can be restored with three kinds of energy source, what we can call "super-energy".

Physical Energy

A programme of regular exercise and aerobic fitness creates the physical energy necessary to see us through to our goals. Aerobic exercise is any exercise which is done "with air". It includes walking, ski-ing, running, jogging, rowing, and physical lovemaking. The benefit of aerobic exercise is that it sends messages to the brain that we need more blood. The body responds by increasing the amount of blood in circulation, ups the level of red blood cells, haemoglobin and plasma and creates masses of additional blood capillaries. The result is more energy and vitality to do what we want.

Aerobic Exercise

Aerobic exercise can have beneficial effects on all parts of the body:

- on the lungs. Aerobic exercise draws replenishing oxygen into the capillaries of the lungs and helps to eliminate waste

- on the heart. A healthy heart beats less per minute than an unhealthy heart. This means that it has less work to do and so is more efficient.

- on the brain. 40% of our blood supply goes to the brain and feeds it oxygen. The more blood we produce as a result of aerobic fitness, the more productive are our brains.

- on the muscles. The muscles become leaner, finer and longer. When they are strong, they also act as mini-pumps for the heart.

- other effects. Other effects of aerobic fitness are that the digestive system is massaged and cleansed; we sleep better; and we feel psychologically better.

Deep Breathing

Deep breathing is essential in creating a healthy bloodstream, the foundation of all good health. As well as filling you with fresh air, deep abdominal breathing relaxes the solar plexus, the source of much of our tension, and internally massages the stomach muscles. It also activates the lymph system to oxygenate each cell of your body and remove waste.

Breathing is life. When we think of life, we think of animation and the Latin root for animation, "anima", means both "breath" and "soul". Breathing is the soul of life. Yet many people do not breath properly. They breath in shallow bursts, erratically and only with the lungs. The result is that they do not attain a state of relaxation or full energy.

There are two keys to deep breathing:

1. exhale all the air from your body before you breath in

2. inhale using your abdominal muscles. As you fill your abdomen with air, your lungs also expand and gradually you fill with air up to your throat.

As well as filling you with fresh air, abdominal breathing relaxes the solar plexus, the source of much of our tension, and internally massages the stomach muscles.

Diet

The quality, quantity and type of food you eat makes a significant difference to your health and fitness and so to your energy levels. Put simply, you are what you eat. A number of dietary principles have been established for years as being the basis of good health. These include...

- eating fresh food

- eating a varied diet

- eating plenty of water-rich foods

- eating less

- listening to what your body needs.

The brain needs to be well-nourished to provide all the energy it is capable of. Foods that are good for the brain include: oils from fish such as mackerel and salmon; carrots which contain vitamin A, good for scavenging up free radicals that can attack the brain; vitamin B1, found in wholemeal bread, vegetables and cereals, which helps burn up the carbohydrates which provide the brain with its energy; iron in liver, eggs and leafy vegetables which assists in bringing oxygen to the brain; and linoleic acid, part of the make-up of brain membranes, which is found in polyunsaturated fats.

Mental Chains

To be mentally fit, we need to be free of some of the chains that shackle us to erroneous and unhelpful beliefs. These include the "not...enough" beliefs such as, "I'm not clever enough" or "I'm not pretty enough" or "I'm not brave enough". Other mentally limiting chains include believing what others tell us we can and can't do, accepting that things won't change, and believing that change requires impossibly difficult demands on us. When you free yourself of the mental chains that come from others, you break out of the mental limitations that stunt your growth.

We often stop growing by accepting the chains of our past. If we wind up in spaces too small, it's because we make the decision not to grow any more. We poke ourselves into a small space. However, just as we have the power to limit our growth, we also have the power to break through the limitations and become all we can be.

Setbacks

When you set yourself up to achieve big goals, it is inevitable that you will meet setbacks at some point through rejections, early failures and frustration at what appears to be a hopeless task. But it is how you deal with setbacks that determines how long it will be before you are back on course. Don't be discouraged. Learn something from every setback. Find some smaller successes instead. Recognise that adversity builds mental muscles.

Worry

Worry arises when we start to let doubts creep in about what could happen to us if things go wrong and is a close friend of fear. To free yourself of mental worries, turn worry inside out by thinking about the best that could happen not the worst. Take things one step at a time by living in day-tight compartments. And, whenever you have fears, remember that FEAR is a mnemonic for False Evidence Appearing Real.

The Energy from Others

Self-developers achieve most when they work with others, rather than against them or in isolation from them.

Self-developers listen more than they talk.

Self-developers develop the likeability personality.

Self-developers don't see people as superior or inferior

to them; just as people.

Self-developers take advice from others.

Self-developers welcome criticism non-defensively.

Self-developers don't use comparisons with others to put themselves or others down.

1. learn to remember people's names

2. be an "old-shoe person" - someone who is easy to get along with

3. acquire an easy-going nature, so things don't ruffle you

4. guard against the impression that you know it all

5. cultivate the quality of being interesting

6. study to get the "scratchy" features out of your personality

7. drain off your grievances; heal your misunderstandings

8. practise liking people until you genuinely do

9. never miss a chance to praise people

10. give spiritual strength to people and they'll give genuine affection back.

Give Spiritual Strength

When someone has this quality in a group, they are like the sun coming out on a cloudy day. Such people have the following features:

1. they never see the dark side of things

2. they are energetically proactive

3. they don't seek the limelight

4. they bubble with ideas

5. they infect others with their upbeat nature

6. they respect everyone they meet

7. there is a sparkle in their eyes

8. they live in the moment.

Like the sun, such people have a great attraction about them. By demonstrating super-energy, they are natural leaders.

Synchronicity

Various writers have alluded to a curious phenomenon that happens when you tune in to other people. Without exchanging words you can have the same thoughts. Others might call it coincidence or a synergistic response. What has been found is that when you tune in to others, you are able to tap into a collective consciousness as if all resources and knowledge came from a higher existence. Scientists have discovered it when they produce similar work at the same time but with no contact. It has also been discovered in the natural world when animals in different parts of the globe adopt similar behaviours at the same time. And in a mundane way, it is what happens when you and a colleague have the same thoughts, hum the same tune and do the same thing at the same time.

Super-energy is a mix of physical, mental, emotional and spiritual energy. Physical energy is ours for the taking if we learn to stay fit and look after our bodies. Mental energy is available if we learn how to turn negative into positive thinking. Emotional and spiritual energy is available if we connect with others in ways in which we can get along.

Key Points

1. Exercise is a reminder that we can act and not just be acted upon.

2. To increase your energy, practise eating healthily

and eating less.

3. We deplete our mental energy when we allow doubts, excuses and limiting beliefs to creep into our thinking.

4. It is how we deal with setbacks that determines whether we will win in the end.

5. Put effort into getting to like others and removing those "scratchy" features of your own make-up.

6. Tap into the combined energies of others who are working in the same fields as you.

Action and Progress

Although goal-setting, programming and energy sources are the fuel for achieving our potential, nothing happens until we take action. Action is the one thing that distinguishes high-achievers from dreamers and hopers. Here are the important features of the Action stage of goal achievement.

Preparation

Time spent on preparation is an important prelude to effective action. Some of the best preparation techniques are those used by professional sports people. There are 5 techniques they often use to get themselves ready for a competition.

1. preparation: of equipment, materials, and themselves

2. attunement: switching on to time, place and mood

3. warming-up: practising some simple preliminary moves

4. awareness: pinpointing outcomes for the task

5. relaxed concentration: believing that your best work is done when you are relaxed and focused at zero-point arousal.

Focusing

The word "focus" comes directly from the Latin word "focus" meaning a hearth or fire. In ancient times, the fire was in the centre of the house. There are 2 types of focus. Hard focus is when we concentrate on our goal with all our attention. We have tunnel vision. Nothing else matters. Soft focus is the opposite of hard focus and allows us to open up our awareness to include the whole environment connected with our goal. We are aware of all opportunities in a quiet way. We are even aware of being aware.

When we direct our thinking on what we do to the exclusion of all distractions and diversions, we gradually find ourselves in a state of single-minded immersion. We can get to this point only by letting go of thoughts of the past and worries about the future.

Commitment

If faith is a mental belief that we will achieve our goals, no matter what the evidence suggests, commitment is the physical act that confirms our faith. Many people get to faith - a belief they could do it - but hesitate when it comes to commitment. They prefer to keep a way out in case it all goes wrong. When you truly commit yourself - possibly in money, materials, time, energy, and certainly yourself - you take a leap in the dark. It is only when you fully commit that you create powerful forces to help you.

Patience

For many people who have set themselves a goal that they passionately desire, accepting that "everything takes its own proper time" is a hard lesson to learn. They want to speed things up, hurry them along, get there quickly and move on. Patience teaches us that, to do things effortlessly, we must work with the pace rather than force it.

Persistence: the Law of the Seed

Patience, perseverance, and persistence are woven into the way that Nature works. Take an apple tree. Before it sheds its leaves and fruit in autumn, the tree may produce as many as 100 apples, each with 10 seeds. That's the tree producing 1000 more seeds of itself. Nature is saying, "Most seeds never grow. So, if you really want something to happen, you have to plan for failure. That way, you'll be certain to succeed." It's the same with us. You might need to go to 20 job interviews to get one job. You might need to interview 40 people to find one good employee. You might need to talk to 50 people to get one sale. It's all about numbers and persistence.

Practice

Practice may not make us perfect but it gets us to our goals. Psychologist Michael Howe of Exeter University has spent years studying the lives of great men and women. He rejects the theory that geniuses are somehow different from the rest of us but believes that so-called geniuses become high achievers because they practise their art with patience. For example, Howe found that 73 of the 76 leading composers in the world were all well advanced in their careers before their major works were written. They achieve the most because they practise the most.

Breakthrough

Somewhere on the route to your goals, after the initial blip of excitement, the disappointments of failure and the arid plateau of learning, comes breakthrough. The breakthrough point comes when more things are going right for you than wrong. You still might face obstacles and setbacks but now they don't bother you. You know how to deal with them. You no longer worry about whether you'll make it. You know for sure you will.

A time comes (on the path to your goal) when you reach a breakthrough point; when enough things are going right in your world. You are delighted to be doing your work, yet like everyone else you still face obstacles; but whereas before you tried to avoid them now they no longer oppress you. They are part of the grist for the mill of your life and you no longer need to fight them. They are simply situations to be dealt with...no more and no less. You have used the strategies that seemed appropriate... perhaps you have suffered...and perhaps you have tasted success. From now on, your satisfaction is not measured in terms of favourable or unfavourable circumstances: what you do has become a natural part of being alive.

Key Points

1. The best work is done when you are in a relaxed state at zero-point arousal.

2. Worries about the future or fears from the past get in the way of concentrating on the present.

3. When we fully commit ourselves to a course of action, unexpected avenues open up to us.

4. In moving towards our goals, we should work with the pace of things rather than force them.

5. Research shows that high achievers are not quicker than the rest of us; they practise their art with patience.

6. When you reach a point of breakthrough in your work, the obstacles no longer become a burden but simply situations to deal with.

Positivity

Our positive spirit is the Adventurer in us. It is the part of us that glimpses what we are capable of. Through learning how to think positively about our goals, and to act positively in our daily habits, we attract to ourselves all the means which make our goals achievable. Here are the main ways you can become more positive.

Create a Positive SelfImage

Your self-image is the person you think you are. You are your own creation. When your self-image is low, you attract into your life all the experiences and conditions that tell you how poor you are. Conversely, when your self-image is high, you attract experiences telling you how great you are. The easiest way to create the self-image you want is through your self-talk. Simply control the chatter in your head. Boost your morale regularly, morning, noon, and night with what you tell yourself.

"What I am giving you is gold.

Mothers, fathers, managers, bosses, superintendants, company presidents, everybody, heed this: raise your own self-esteem to where it belongs and good things will happen, both for you and others. How do you do that? You do it through your self-talk. You must think well of yourself. You must know you're good. Start by controlling your own self-talk. From here forward, it is out of place in your life or your business to be devaluative, belittling, or sarcastic. Such junk has no place in a high-performance organisation just as it has no place in a high-performance individual.

What you will do is start looking for ways to boost your morale with your self-talk. You are going to do it regularly. You are going to do it every day: morning, noon and night.

Talk in Terms of Positive Goals

Our brains need images of positive goals to work towards. They become confused if we feed them negative goals. So, if it is your aim to give up smoking, don't say: "I want to stop smoking". Instead, say "I want to enjoy a pleasant evening out with a couple of refreshing drinks, breathing in fresh, revitalizing, clean, pure, uncontaminated, healthy air."

Have Positive Expectations

Numerous experiments confirm the truth that when you expect the best, you usually get the best, and when you expect the worst, you usually get that too. This is known as the self-prophesying principle. So, at the start of any new venture or at the start of each new day, look forward with expectations of the very best.

Turn Negatives into Positives

Like the man who had too many lemons and turned them into lemonade, or the man who bought snake-infested land and learnt how to turn their skins into shoe-leather, every seeming setback can be turned around and made into a triumph.

Always Review Positively

If we are positive at the start of an venture, we should be equally positive at the end when we review. Many people become discouraged when things don't go to plan and they beat themselves up for missing out on the one thing that didn't work. But there are always gems of real worth in every situation, even apparent disasters, if we only look hard enough. So, an obstacle is not a "barrier" but a "challenge"; a setback is not a "disaster" but a "chance to learn"; and a tough problem is not a "failure", but "a nut we're going to crack".

Mix With Positive People

One of the biggest drains on our enthusiasms is to be surrounded by people who are negative. They may be well-meaning with their warnings but they are misguided. You have two choices if you want to survive as a positive person: avoid them or train them. One clever way to train negative people is to simply ignore them when they use discouraging conversation. Simply blank them. Then when they return to positive expressions, re-connect. Very soon, they will learn that you are a person who has a sunny disposition and they will simply drop their previously gloomy attitude with you.

Use Positivity for Good Health

Study of old age also found that a positive attitude was one of the key ingredients of long living. More recent studies have shown that brain cells actually shrivel up and die under the effect of negative thinking while positive thinking actually changes the composition of body cells for the better. Which all goes to show that positivity is better than any medicine you could buy from the chemist store.

Get the Positivity Habit

Good habits are as easy to make as bad ones. It's simply a matter of choice and repetition. So, if you want the positivity habit in your life, do these things every day:

- dress the best you can

- smile more

- try to genuinely like others

- give people positive strokes of recognition

- give people the most precious gift you have: more of your time

- when you meet a stranger, be the first to shake hands

- be interested in the world around you

- be thankful for everything you get.

Positivity is not a view of things which ignores reality, but a choice we make about thinking, acting, and speaking which creates reality. As such, it has the power of change.

Key Points

1. Positive ways of thinking do not distort reality but rather make choices in how we see and interpret reality.

2. All lasting change about ourselves starts with the way we think and then moves to the outside.

3. It is the imagined self-image that determines how we feel about ourselves not the actual way we are.

4. High-performance individuals and teams never devalue themselves in their self-talk.

5. The brain cannot work towards achieving a negative goal.

6. When you expect the best, you usually get the best; when you expect the worst, you usually get that too.

From Mastery to Mystery

There comes a time on the journey of self-development when we reach a level of working that is different from all the previous levels. It is likely that the new experiences are no less challenging than before; it's just that we see them in a different way, accomplish them with more ease and flow; and put them into new contexts and meanings. We have few words to describe this new state: "mastery" is one of them.

Up Your Game by Just 2%

The difference between mediocrity and superior performance can be attributed to as little as 1 or 2% more in terms of more planning, more study, more application, more interest, more attention, more positivity, more effort, and more determination.

Love What You Do

Love for one's work is the simplest recipe for mastering one's goals. It also makes the process of self-development one of joy.

- love is self-acceptance and recognition, rather than the need for acceptance and recognition by others.

- love has no boundaries as action has. In the words of Mother Teresa: "We cannot do great things on this earth. We can only do small things with great love."

- love is emotional intelligence, which along with technical intelligence and intelligent action is the route to mastery.

- love is doing difficult things simply.

Become an Artist

When we grow and develop, we do not simply acquire new and improved skills. We gain a depth of understanding that changes who we are and how we see life: we reach artistry.

The apprentice knows the rules. The craftsman knows the rules and performs the skills. The master knows the rules, performs the skills, and sees the point. The artist knows the rules, performs the skills, sees the point and understands the deeper meaning.

Pursue Excellence Not Perfection

The difference between perfection and excellence is that perfection is a prize in the gift of others and nearly always impossible to achieve while excellence is a standard which we can work towards each day.

Perfection: completion, arriving, ending, reaching the peak, receiving the ultimate prize.

Excellence: a process, a journey, a quality standard, a way of life, relationships, attitudes, personal well-being, strategies for living, giving.

The Gratitude Attitude

The dictionary tells us that gratitude is "the expression of gratefulness and thanks" but this doesn't begin to convey its real effect. Here are an alternative set of definitions.

Gratitude stops you taking your life for granted and helps you realize how many good things you have in your life.

Gratitude makes others feel better

Gratitude makes you feel better. In the words of an Arabian proverb, "The hand that gives the roses always keeps some of the scent."

Gratitude raises your awareness of things around you. Gratitude is easy, quick, and simple.

Gratitude is an instant blues-breaker and stress-reliever. Gratitude changes your view of so-called "bad" things. Gratitude frees you from petty annoyances.

Gratitude inspires you

Gratitude puts your thoughts and feelings on a high vibration level that in turn attracts back to you more things to be grateful for.

Gratitude nourishes the soul.

Gratitude is like compound interest on money in the bank: the more you put in, the more you get out.

Gratitude is a spiritual act because it acknowledges that the origin of all good things is a source outside ourselves.

Identify Yourself with what you do

The ultimate awareness is when what you do is no longer apart from you but a part of you. The features of mastery as the ultimate awareness are that...

- we feel whole; everything falls into place; layers of meaning make sense

- what we do is simple if not always easy

- what we do is like a love affair

- we are fully in the experience of what we do, body, mind and soul, the way children often are

- there is no more tension or effort

- doing is all that matters, not the rewards

- we are what we do.

Peak Experiences

The ultimate stage of personal development of our skills is often glimpsed as a peak experience. This is when we do our work with a different feeling: confident and humble, invincible and connected, calm and at the highest level of awareness.

Celebrate and Give Thanks

Celebration at achieving our goals is right and proper. For hundreds of years, men and women have worked for six days and then stopped on the seventh to give thanks and celebrate.

- celebration marks important milestones on the journey to our goals.

- celebration marks life transitions, such as birth and beginning, endings and change.

- celebration is a sacred rite and ritual.

- celebration is a way of sharing goal achievement with those who have made it possible.

- celebration is where work meets fun.

Key Points

1. Love for one's work is the simplest recipe for mastering one's goals.

2. We tithe when we give something back to help others.

3. No matter who we are and what we do, we are all capable of turning our work into artistry.

4. Feeling at one with your work is a feature of the ultimate awareness.

5. When you master your work, you feel a connectedness with others.

6. There is a deeper meaning to your work when you

move beyond performing the skills to a state of new awareness.

ABOUT THE AUTHOR

Harold Mawela is an inspirational speaker, coach, writer, teacher, providing effective, practical, down-to-earth advice based on his own leadership experience and the application of relevant leadership thinking.

As a trainer and coach, Harold's focus is simply to help people maximize their potential better by helping them develop their self-confidence and equipping them with the necessary skills and behaviors to up their game.

The advice that Harold is able to share with his clients is based on his own leadership and management experience, he is able to offer insights into best practice and to draw on the experiences of others as to what works and what doesn't.

www.ingramcontent.com/pod-product-compliance
Lightning Source LLC
Chambersburg PA
CBHW030605220526
45463CB00004B/1173